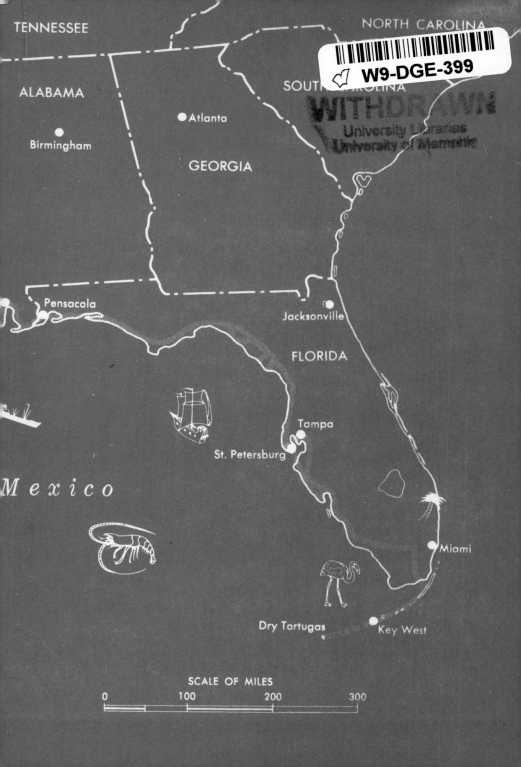

TENNESSEE

NORTH CAROLINA

ALABAMA

SOUTH CAROLINA

●Atlanta

Birmingham

GEORGIA

Pensacola

Jacksonville

FLORIDA

Tampa

St. Petersburg

Mexico

Miami

Dry Tortugas

Key West

SCALE OF MILES

0   100   200   300

THE CURVING SHORE

THE
CURVING SHORE

The Gulf Coast from
Brownsville to Key West

By LEONARD ORMEROD

HARPER & BROTHERS · PUBLISHERS · NEW YORK

Library of Congress catalog card number: 56–11081

To Joy

The years and the miles have been long
But her affection has never faltered.

CONTENTS

LIST OF ILLUSTRATIONS

ACKNOWLEDGMENTS

Traveling more than eight thousand miles up and down the Gulf Coast in the preparation of this work the author drew on the knowledge and experience of hundreds of persons. Many of them deserve mention on this page, but the list is so long that a blanket expression of appreciation must serve. Therefore I hereby acknowledge my debt and my gratitude to the managing editors, motel operators, chamber of commerce personnel, filling station attendants, Audubon wardens, waiters and waitresses, librarians and policemen who furnished me the mountain of information from which I have attempted to screen these nuggets of interesting fact. Particularly am I grateful to the agricultural agents and their secretaries who, I found, were always well informed about the past as well as the present of their several communities.

It is not to be expected that the full story of the Gulf Coast could be contained in one volume. Often the problem was not what to include but what to omit, so I have tried to put in not only what is most essential but also what is most interesting. Many historians and many volumes have covered the exciting past of different sections of the curving shore. Where there was some dispute as to the facts I have placed reliance on an authority whose word cannot be lightly challenged.

Sometimes it is necessary to read a book in order to write one or two intelligent paragraphs. No bibliography was kept of the many volumes consulted, but I am happy to acknowledge my special obligation to three authors: to Stanley Clisby Arthur, of New Orleans, and his exciting biography, *Jean Laffite, Gentlemen Rover* (Harmanson, 333 Royal Street, New Orleans); to Karl A. Bickel, of

Sarasota, author of the very readable volume *The Mangrove Coast* (Coward-McCann, Inc., New York); and to my valued friend, Marjory Stoneman Douglas, of Coconut Grove, whose book, *Everglades: River of Grass* (Rinehart & Co., Inc., New York), is in my opinion the best thing that has ever been written about the southern portion of our most southern state.

The majority of the photographs in this book were taken by the author, but inclement weather, bad light or the time of day or year sometimes prevented him from personally taking all the pictures he wanted. To those people and organizations who responded so kindly to his requests for additional pictures the author is extremely grateful. Space does not permit listing all the individuals, but he does wish to single out the following: the Houston *Chronicle;* New Iberia Chamber of Commerce; Bureau of New Orleans *News;* National Park Service; Mobile Chamber of Commerce; Naval Air Station, Pensacola; Florida State News Bureau; City Publicity Bureau of St. Petersburg; Tampa News Bureau; Miami *Daily News.*

LEONARD ORMEROD

North Miami Beach, Florida

THE CURVING SHORE

I. *The Curving Shore*

THE curving shore of the Gulf of Mexico, even that part within the confines of the United States, is not all of one piece. Geologically it represents several methods by which the land areas of the globe have been built up. Historically its culture, now under a single flag, is underlaid with a mosaic of varied influences—Spanish, English, French, Early American—each of which left its fingerprints on this cup that holds the warm waters of a Southern sea.

Of our three major coastlines, the Gulf Coast ranks second only to the Atlantic in total length. According to figures supplied by the U.S. Coast and Geodetic Survey, under the heading "tidal shoreline, general," the total coastline between the mouth of the Rio Grande and Key West is 4,097 miles. The airline distance between them is 987 miles.

The Texas coast, 1,100 miles, from the mouth of the Rio Grande to the Sabine, is guarded by long, narrow islands and peninsulas of almost pure sand thrown up on the shallow bottoms by violent seas that for uncounted centuries swept up from the south, often driven by the resistless power of a hurricane. Behind these shifting ramparts are narrow, shallow bodies of water such as Laguna Madre, part of Matagorda Bay, and East and West Galveston bays, with a few extensive indentations cutting into the mainland and furnishing natural harbors. A number of comparatively small rivers, the Brazos, Colorado, Nueces, Aransas, Trinity and Guadalupe, pour their waters into the Gulf along this stretch and all but the first two have their headwaters in Texas.

Although the breeze that blows in from the Gulf is laden with moisture the coast frequently suffers from drought. The annual rainfall at Brownsville and Corpus Christi is seldom more than twenty-six inches, and at Galveston and Port Arthur it averages but forty-six inches. There are no mountains or forests along the flat coastal plains to cool the clouds and make them precipitate their waters, so their moisture is carried through the air to the North where it falls to flow back to the sea in rivers.

East of the Sabine River the Louisiana coast, 985 miles, has an entirely different character. Here are whole counties that are little more than salt marsh broken by lakes, bays and sluggish bayous. It is the land of "trembling prairies" where even a heavy footstep will shake the uncertain sod. There is a firm beach of sand for a short distance in the southwestern corner of the state but this is covered to a depth of several inches with a thin black mud. This country is still subject to the great geologic forces—a foot or two higher and it will be rich riceland, a little lower and it will be part of the sea.

Most of the Louisiana coast is the child of the "Father of Waters," that magnificent stream which with its tributaries carries down the rich topsoil of the central valley of the continent from as far away as the Canadian border. This great delta of the Mississippi was building up for uncounted millenniums before it was seen by man, and it is the most prominent irregularity in the sweeping curve of the Gulf Coast between the Yucatan Peninsula and the tip of Florida. The river has not always followed its present course but in times of flood spread out over hundreds of miles of lowlands. Centuries ago its principal channel was the present Atchafalaya River, and when high waters come part of its stream is still diverted into that river from a point 125 miles above New Orleans. Restless in the confinement of its levees the Mississippi still threatens to break out and wander through the sugar cane fields that flourish on the rich soil it carried down from the North when the continent was young.

Due to the fortunes of war and the vagaries of national and international politics the states of Mississippi and Alabama each extend a small "panhandle" to the Gulf, so narrow that they can be crossed in half a day's drive. The coastline of Mississippi is only 155 miles, that of Alabama 199. Yet these outlets are important factors in the economy of the two states, for Mississippi has the busy ports of Gulfport and Biloxi, and Mobile is the second city in size in Alabama. There are several offshore islands along this coast but for the most part they are forested and do not hug the shoreline where the solid land comes right down to tidewater.

Florida has a total coastline greater than any other state, and its Gulf coastline, including that along the inner side of the Keys, is 1,658 miles. The outline of Florida is like a pistol pointed toward the west, the long peninsula forming the handle and the western portion a short barrel. The illusion is heightened by a bulge of land suggestive of a trigger, at the point of which is the sizable town of Apalachicola. Here again are several long sandy islands that break the force of storm-bred waves before they reach the mainland. There is a similarity along the coastline from the Louisiana marshes to the St. Marks River at the top of the Florida peninsula, but somewhere along there geology turns a new page. It is apparent even on a highway map. West from New Orleans an improved road hugs the beaches but along the west Florida coast the highway is from fifteen to twenty miles inland and only a few side roads lead down to small villages at tidewater.

The Florida peninsula is the newest piece of land in continental United States although it was the first to be explored and mapped. It was the floor of a warm sea long after the continents had been outlined. Then as though Mother Earth were taking a deep breath the land began to rise slowly out of the sea, a little higher at first on the eastern side, and the water drained from the shells and sponges and corals on what had been the bottom of the ocean. This is what geologists call the "Florida plateau" and when the rising stopped the land area was much wider than it is now. But the level of the sea did not remain constant. As the great glaciers melted and released their waters, and then froze and recaptured them, the peninsula narrowed and widened and narrowed again—how often is a story for the geologists to tell. Today the Florida plateau extends more than a hundred miles out into the Gulf and a lesser distance into the Atlantic. Fully half of it is submerged at a depth of less than fifty fathoms. Beyond it the bottom drops sharply to three hundred fathoms.

Along the Gulf Coast of Florida the cold war between the sea and the shore still goes on. With mangrove roots and salt marsh grass the land strives to creep seaward, and with hurricanes and the wash of the tide the waters counterattack. Meanwhile mankind builds sea walls and jetties and causeways which do not always withstand the onslaught of natural forces.

The first white men to reach the New World found various Indian tribes living along the Gulf Coast, but archaeologists have discovered traces of still older cultures that disappeared before Columbus sailed on his first voyage. Such finds have been made along the Rio Grande and the Neches River in Texas, and in Okaloosa and Collier counties in Florida. That there was some pre-Columbian contact, probably for trade, between the Indians of the Florida peninsula, the Carribbean Islands and Central America has been fairly well established.

Cabeza de Vaca left a detailed description of the Indians he found along the Texas coast. They were the Karankawas, a semi-nomadic people with a very primitive culture. Their principal food was shellfish and this diet was augmented in late summer and fall by *tunas,* the dried fruit of the prickly pear cactus. Occasionally cannibalistic, they were nevertheless most .hospitable to the shipwrecked De Vaca and his companions. There probably were not more than thirty thousand Indians in all of what is now Texas at the beginning of the sixteenth century and the settlements along the coast were very scattered.

It was a different story in the Florida peninsula where the coast from Tampa Bay south was occupied by the warlike Calusas, the Mayaimis and the Tekestas. These were augmented later by infiltrations from the Creek nation in north Florida, Georgia and Alabama. The docile Arawaks of the Caribbean Islands and even the more hardy Caribs had fallen like wheat before the sickle as the Spaniards tried to enslave them, so by the time the conquistadores reached the Florida mainland they met determined resistance. There were truces and temporary friendships, and treachery on both sides, but the names of those early tribes now live only in old history books. The word "Seminole" is not more than two hundred years old and is variously described as meaning "distant people," "renegade" or "runaway." The Seminoles of today are of mixed Indian parentage but stem principally from the Creek nation. They are divided into two groups, the Mikasukis, or Hitchiti-speakers, and the Cow Creeks, or Muskogee-speakers. Until the present generation the tribal chiefs would not allow the two groups to intermarry.

Just when the first European looked on the low islands, the shell beaches and the mangrove thickets that rim the waters of the Gulf of Mexico is a matter on which historians are not agreed. There is even some dispute as to who he was. It may have been Amerigo Vespucci, that little-known Italian who gave his name to two continents. Amerigo, who claimed to have sailed from Cádiz in May, 1497, and to have voyaged along the coast of the New World for more than nine hundred leagues, has been a controversial figure for 450 years. Some historians have expressed doubt that he ever made such a voyage but his latest biographer, German Arciniegas, insists he skirted the new continent from Yucatan to Cape Hatteras. There are other aspirants to the honor of being first. In old Fort Morgan at the entrance to Mobile Bay is a tablet "In memory of Alonso Alvarez de Pineda who landed here in 1519, being 101 years before the Pilgrims landed at New Plymouth."

However, it is beyond dispute that the first century of the white man in what is now the United States had most of its setting along the shallow waters of the Gulf Coast. In 1513, ninety-six years before Henry Hudson sailed his *Half Moon* up the river that bears his name, Juan Ponce de León was careening his ship on the Gulf Coast of Florida to scrape the sea growth from its bottom. Seventy-nine years before the first English settlement was made at Jamestown, Virginia, Pánfilo de Narváez landed near Tampa Bay with three hundred men to search for treasure along the western coast of the peninsula. In June, 1559, Don Tristan de Luna, acting under orders of King Philip II of Spain, sailed from Vera Cruz with five hundred soldiers, and accompanied by priests, women, children and servants, to establish a colony on Pensacola Bay. More than sixty years would pass before the *Mayflower* landed its immortals at Plymouth Rock.

De Luna failed to include any farmers among his fifteen hundred colonists, and hurricanes and hostile Indians eventually wrecked the venture. Ponce de León returned eight years after his first visit only to be mortally wounded by an Indian's arrow. Of De Narváez' army that started out so bravely in April, 1528, only four ever saw civilization again. One of these, Captain Alvar Nuñez Cabeza de Vaca, wrote a detailed account of his experiences, one of the most remarkable documents to be found in the annals of adventure. It was published in Spain in 1542 and, among other things, contained the first description of the American bison (buffalo) to reach Europe.

De Vaca, first European to see the entire Gulf Coast east of the

Rio Grande, was treasurer of the De Narváez expedition which started up the west coast of Florida and planned to rendezvous with their ships farther north. The plans miscarried and eventually the explorers found themselves at the mouth of St. Marks River, just south of Tallahassee, harassed by Indians and insects, wracked by fevers and threatened with starvation. In desperation they constructed five barges in which they hoped to reach the coast of Mexico, believing it to be within a few days' sail. But adverse winds drove them westward along the coast and strewed it with their wreckage.

The barge that De Vaca commanded was washed up on what has been identified as Galveston Island and most of the occupants were drowned in an effort to refloat it. For six years the Spanish captain was a prisoner of the Indians, who did not confine him but would not permit him to leave. Eventually with two other captains and the Moorish slave of one he escaped and traveled westward with varying fortunes as far as the Gulf of California, the first Europeans to cross the continent of North America. Turning back they reached Mexico City, and De Vaca returned to Spain. Although his story was one of hardship and tragedy, with little about gold and treasure, it inspired new adventurers there, many believing the captain had deliberately refrained from telling of the wealth of the New World.

Fired at least in part by De Vaca's recital, Don Hernando de Soto started northward from Tampa Bay in 1539 with a force of more than six hundred foot and horse to look for gold and glory. De Soto was not inexperienced in adventure, having fought under Pizzaro in Peru and explored Guatemala and Yucatan, After three years and four thousand miles of fruitless wanderings he reached the Mississippi River. There he died and his followers buried him beneath its muddy waters near the present Louisiana-Arkansas line.

In the half-century that followed Ponce de León's first voyage a dozen or more adventurers dropped anchor along the eastern and northern shores of the Gulf, but no permanent settlement resulted. The jungle was too inhospitable and the Indians, knowing what had

happened to the natives in the Caribbean Islands at the hands of
the Spaniards, were generally hostile. In the meantime St. Augustine
had been established on the eastern coast of Florida (1565), the
French and English had begun to contend with Spain for footholds
on the Atlantic Coast, and Spain was willing to leave the Indians
and alligators on the Gulf Coast in comparative peace.

Eventually the first permanent settlement in that region was made
in 1696 right on Pensacola Bay where De Luna had made his try
131 years before. But no longer was the banner of Spain to wave
in undisputed sovereignty over the lands along the curving shore.
In 1682 Sieur de La Salle had floated down the Mississippi River
from Illinois to its mouth and claimed its basin for France, naming
it "Louisiana" in honor of Louis XIV. England, too, was looking for
a place in this southern sun and soon another chapter would be
added to the long and sordid chronicle of national ambitions. One
thing, however, was certain: whoever won, the Indians would lose.

The first European to reach these shores came with dreams of
treasure and visions of a paradise in the tropics. Some found their
treasure, though it did not come easily, and some learned to love
the tropics as one may learn to love a cruel mistress. For others
there was nothing but disappointment and tragedy.

Those early adventurers set the tempo that still characterizes the
curving shore after more than four hundred years. It is the eternal
land of promise—for the poor who would be rich and the rich who
would be richer. Some of them succeed, some fail, and some just
manage to break even. The successful ones here as elsewhere are
usually those who stick it out and are not easily discouraged. Of
high adventure there has been aplenty and of blasted hopes too
many. There have been booms based on land, on cattle, oranges,
pears, sugar cane, rice, sponges, shrimp, tung nuts, figs and oil—
oil, the greatest gamble of them all. Fortunes large and small have
been made and are still being made along the wave-washed shore,
while the lush semitropic vegetation quickly covers the abandoned
roadways, the crumbling walls and the forgotten furrows where lie

the hopes of yesterday. The call of the sunlit South still finds a response in country, town and city to the north. As the French proverb has it: "The more it changes, the more it remains the same."

The doldrums that are remembered in history as "the Panic of 1893" had their beginnings several years before that date, due to causes still debated by economists and historians. At the beginning of the century's last decade farm mortgages were being foreclosed up and down the Mississippi Valley, unemployment was increasing, and a silver dollar, the common currency throughout the Middle West, "looked as big as a wagon wheel." The last free land of the government fertile enough to provide a living for a farmer had disappeared when "the Cherokee Strip," 1,888,000 acres in what is now Oklahoma, was opened in April, 1889, to twenty thousand settlers who rushed in at the crack of a cavalry officer's starting gun to grab what they could, and the devil take the hindmost. It was a time of distress and unrest and there were no government programs of WPA, CCC, or "made work" of any sort to take up the slack. Nor was any such relief expected, for the popular mood was one of individual independence and all the average citizen wanted was "a chance."

Against this background a syndicate of businessmen bought up a few thousand acres of flat, monotonous country lying astride the Gulf, Colorado & Santa Fe Railway thirty-six miles from Houston and half that distance from Galveston. In 1890 they promoted the Alta Loma Investment & Improvement Company, putting on a campaign in the Northern states to attract buyers to this marvelous new country where a little scratching of the soil would make anyone rich. The bait was pears—not the "pears" of Florida where the word means avocados or "alligator pears," but the luscious fruit with which the North is familiar. In later years the catchword of similar booms was to be figs, and farther east it would be oranges or tung nuts, but there was a peculiar reason for the Galveston County venture's being based on pears.

Three miles south of the little railroad station at Alta Loma lies the much older hamlet of Hitchcock. Situated along one of the innumerable bayous that flow sluggishly into the Gulf its soil is much richer than that of the raw prairie. There sometime in the late 1870's a man named Stringfellow had put out fifteen acres of pear trees and under his tender care, aided by plenty of fertilizer, they had flourished exceedingly.

Railroad excursions at special rates brought in the Alta Loma prospects, who were taken first to the grove in Hitchcock where Stringfellow told them in an eloquent and well-rehearsed speech how easy it was to grow pears. Then they were driven a few miles north to where the little depot crouched beside the railroad tracks and a single road, made by four horses drawing a scraper, stretched from infinity on the east to infinity on the west. The only trees visible, other than a little cluster around Hitchcock, made a line of green along Hall's Bayou, six miles to the northwest. Through the shimmering haze that danced above the steel rails could be seen a few buildings that made up Arcadia, another boom town three miles to the north. Somewhere on the great unfenced expanse one could usually see a scattered herd of lean, mosquito-bitten, tick-infested longhorn cattle, the property of an aged Frenchman who originally owned most of that part of the county.

But the hopeful prospect from the North was asked to picture the scene as it would be in a few years with pear orchards dotting the vast area and the happy owners living in white and green houses shaded by chinaberry trees. Many believed and bought, and wrote home to the wife to pack up the furniture, collect the children, and come to paradise. The beauty of it was it did not take a large acreage to be a successful pear grower. Stringfellow had told them that fifteen acres was more than enough, so the standard plot was ten acres, though several bought forty acres or more.

Up in Saline County, Missouri, lived two brothers, Leverett and Abiel Leonard, cousins of my father. They came, they saw, and were conquered. But no ten-acre plots for them. They bought four hundred acres a mile west of the railroad and prepared to put it all in pears. The year before my father, a cattle breeder, had gone busted importing black cattle from Scotland and paying 10 per cent interest on borrowed money. So it was arranged that the Ormerod family should go to Alta Loma and supervise the planting of the four-hundred-acre pear orchard.

That was in 1892. I was not quite ten years old and my two sisters were aged six and two. The only building on the place was a barn with accommodations for six mules below and four rooms, separated by seven-foot partitions above. There was an outside stairway and the water supply was caught off the roof and stored in a large wooden cistern aboveground. The stock was watered from a shallow well filled with surface water. It was not considered fit for human consumption but I doubt that it was worse than the stale, tepid cistern water that was always full of wiggletails (mosquito larvae).

We put a three-strand wire fence around the buildings but beyond that the prairie was free of obstructions. "Downtown" a mile away was a grocery, a blacksmith shop, and a two-story twelve-room hotel put up by the town company. Later a doctor moved in, and a drug store, a barbershop and a lumberyard made us feel quite metropolitan. There was no school and no church until we had lived there two years. The planting of the pear trees proceeded apace, not only on the four-hundred-acre project but also on big and little plots on the surrounding prairie. Most of the houses were built on "stilts" three to six feet above the ground because the flat land had such poor drainage. Sweet potatoes grew the year 'round and that was our principal food much of the time. Other vegetables did well when fertilized but there was no market for them. As a boy I helped load a carload of fine watermelons for which the growers received but $2.75 net, freight and commission charges having absorbed all the rest.

After two or three years it became apparent that the future of the pear business was not very bright. It dawned on the community

that a fruit orchard is a headache and an expense for six or eight
years before it brings in a dollar. Nor was the raw land suited to
growing pears. Some turned to other types of farming but with
poor success. Clothes began to look shabby and money was very
scarce. The Leonard brothers repented of their venture after father
had put out 120 acres in pears for them. By shrewd bargaining they
persuaded the town company to take the land back and return the
purchase price, but the brothers lost all the considerable amount
they had spent for improvements.

Within a period of four years there were no less than a thousand
acres of pear trees set out in that vicinity, from which not one bushel
of pears was ever harvested. Twenty-five years later most of the
pioneers who had first turned the new soil had left the country. Here
and there the skeleton of a small pear tree, bare of leaves or bark,
leaned like a pale ghost above the coarse grass to show where some
early settler had tried and failed.

The future looked dark and unpromising for the community in
1895 when a totally unexpected stroke of fortune put new life in
the town. It became the source of Galveston's city water supply.
The only potable water in that region, other than rain water, came
from artesian wells. There being no rocks in the soil it was not
difficult to sink a pipe seven or eight hundred feet, whereupon a
stream of sweet, soft water rose to the surface and flowed continuously. The town company drilled such a well near the depot and
it was used by many residents of the village. The city of Galveston
had sunk a well on the island but although they went to a depth of
two thousand feet and the water flowed readily it was too salty to
drink. "Water trains," consisting of a string of flatcars, each with
two wooden tanks mounted on it, came up almost daily to Hitchcock where they were filled from a railroad tank supplied by a
flowing well. The train then carried the precious stuff back to Galveston where it was sold for ten cents a barrel. This and the rain
water caught in aboveground cisterns was the only fresh water the
city had ever seen. But in the early nineties a bequest to the city

to which was added public funds gave Galveston one of the finest water supply systems in the country.

Thirty-two artesian wells, each eight hundred feet deep, were sunk just south of Alta Loma in a row that stretched east and west of the Santa Fe tracks. A forty-eight-inch main was run south to Galveston, two miles of it lying on the bottom of the bay. At first the wells themselves furnished the pressure necessary to maintain the flow, but later deeper wells were sunk and a pumping station installed.

It was a sunny Sunday morning when Will Skirvin, manager of the town company and its local representative, came out to "the barn" to tell us of the new development and to persuade us to move into town and take over the operation of the hotel. The water project was certain to bring in a corps of engineers and supervisors, and Skirvin, who had eaten Mother's biscuits, was sure that her cooking would keep the hotel clientele happy. The pear orchard boom was pretty well bust by that time, so we moved into the hotel. Every morning, seven days a week, I and the older of my two sisters made up twelve beds, swept twelve rooms, carried out the contents of twelve slop jars and chamber pots, and carried up water to fill twelve pitchers.

Today power-driven machines would dig the trenches for those water mains within a week, but back in the nineties it was all done by mule power and manpower, mostly the latter. Mule-drawn plows and scrapers took a little off the top but after that it was spadework, from the bottom of the ditch to a platform halfway up, and by spade from the platform to the surface. That was a lean decade all over the country and word went out by the grapevine that work was to be had in Alta Loma. So the hungry came from the North to the South—as they still do—and when they found the payrolls were full they came to the little hotel for something to eat. Mother turned away none unfed, and over the period of a year she fed 127. There were no handouts. She sat them down to a table and gave them whatever the pantry afforded. If they asked for work she told them they might split some wood after they had eaten, and only one ever left without taking a turn with the ax. Frequently she felt impelled to tell them they had worked long enough to pay for their food. There were some touching incidents. One man seemed hesitant about starting to eat so Mother left the room and watched him through the crack of the door. He bowed his head and asked God to bless the food he had begged, and Mother stood behind the door and cried into her apron.

The Skirvin family, father, mother and two daughters, lived in the largest house in the village, a two-story structure of resinous southern pine. It caught fire one afternoon and in fifteen minutes was only a smoking ruin. The family moved into the hotel until another house was built, and the older girl, Pearl, went to school with me and my sisters. Later she was to be internationally famous as a Washington hostess and minister to Luxembourg, Mrs. Perle Mesta. When the waterworks were completed the community once more began to fade out. The Skirvins moved to Oklahoma City, where Will Skirvin put up the Skirvin Hotel and the Skirvin Towers, two of the finest hotels in the state, and his daughter began her exciting career.

Most of the other residents of Alta Loma who could raise the money for a railroad ticket got out of town, the Ormerods going back to Missouri and renting part of the old farm. Then in September, 1900, the supreme disaster occurred—the hurricane known as the Galveston Storm. The waters of the Gulf were blown far inland and while they did not reach Alta Loma, buildings were shattered, many persons were injured, and the morale of the community reached a new low.

But the "boom and bust" cycle of the Gulf Coast was still potent. Hardly had the debris of the hurricane been picked up when oil was struck at Beaumont, less than one hundred miles away. A number of the erstwhile pear growers hurried over there and got in on the ground floor, and several became comfortably rich. Eventually the land in the region was bought up by a syndicate and today it is rice-growing country, while most of the men of the village work in the oil refineries of Texas City, fifteen miles to the southeast. That certainly beats raising pears on the prairie.

There is a tradition in the South that once visitors get sand in their shoes they can never be happy away from the sandy shores. Perhaps it is not idle talk. After the rugged years of boyhood on the Texas coast I lived in Kansas City and Chicago, in Ohio and Michigan, in Philadelphia and Washington—and even in Brooklyn. But always I had one ear attuned to the soft cadences of Southern seas and Southern breezes. So I went back, not just once but many times. I read much about the Gulf regions in many books, lamenting the lack of a single volume, my own interest growing, until at last it became imperative that I try to write the colorful story of the whole curving shore.

II. The Valley

CONTINENTAL United States extends two long points to the south, 1,650 miles apart as measured over the highways, and between them the shore of the Gulf of Mexico describes a great arc of sand, swamp and mangrove-covered islands. The eastern

16

horn of this crescent is the southern tip of the Florida peninsula. Its capital is Miami, though the city is not at its most southern point. The western horn is the valley of the Rio Grande, the southmost point of Texas. Its capital is Brownsville, located on the Rio Grande twenty-two miles above the point where it enters the Gulf. The latitude of Miami is 25 degrees, 46 minutes and 37 seconds. Brownsville's latitude is 25 degrees, 54 minutes and 7 seconds. That is a difference of less than ten miles.

The two places have several things in common and many differences. Miami and its adjoining towns are situated on a narrow ridge of oölite rock between the Atlantic Ocean and the untamed Everglades, and have little productive hinterland. Brownsville is in a fertile alluvial valley, one of the nation's richest garden spots. Texans speak of it as "The Valley." If you belong to one of the local chambers of commerce you call it "The Magic Valley."

Here the Rio Grande flows almost due east to reach a seacoast that for a hundred miles extends a little west of north. "The Valley" extends some eighty miles up the river northwest from Brownsville and half as far to the north. It is a compact economic unit, and while Brownsville is its metropolis the neighboring towns of Raymondville ("The Onion Capital of the World"), Harlingen, San Benito, Edinburg, McAllen and Mercedes are important in the business of raising, packing and shipping each year enough citrus fruit and winter vegetables to fill a freight train 250 miles long. These towns are clean, with well-paved streets and highways; prosperous without ostentation. Streets and lawns are gay with date palms (which do not fruit here), fan palms, bougainvillaea, oleander, coral vine and orange trees.

The Valley contains more than 4,200 square miles and though the growing of winter vegetables is a major industry, here as in many other parts of the South, cotton is king. In spring and early summer long rows of lush green, spotted with cream-colored blossoms, stretch from highway to horizon. By early June the first bolls begin

Cotton is king

to open, and with hilarious ceremony the first bale of the season in the entire United States comes from the compress.

It is short staple cotton which matures early, and there is reason for this haste. A few years ago the pink boll worm threatened the entire cotton industry. The worm is propagated by eggs the adult insect lays in the stalks of the plant, where they spend the winter to hatch out early in the spring. Now there is a law that by midnight of a certain date every field of cotton stalks must be plowed under, or the grower faces a heavy penalty. This deadline for southern Texas is August 31, but as one goes north it is extended through September to early October.

Most of the cotton is shipped by water from Port Isabel, a man-made harbor on the outskirts of the city, which is connected with the Gulf and the Intracoastal Waterway by a straight channel seventeen miles long and thirty-two feet deep. This was completed in 1949, and here also is a fishing harbor, complete with unloading machinery, freezing and packing facilities. It is the base of operations for a fleet of 350 shrimp trawlers and vies with Key West as "The Shrimp Capital of the World." Taking shrimp from the prolific waters of the Gulf has in recent years become a multimillion-dollar industry, and trawlers equipped with powerful engines, expensive nets and sonar devices to locate shrimp beds as war vessels locate submarines, are to be found at almost every port along the coast. Mexico, anxious to obtain her share of the tasty crustaceans, has protested that U.S. boats have invaded her waters and the controversy has required adjustment at high diplomatic levels.

When winter lies heavy on the Central and Northern states the

Shrimp fleet at Port Isabel

residents of those regions get their vitamins from more than forty
varieties of vegetables grown in southwest Texas. String beans
planted in September and October are harvested in November and
December. Tomatoes are grown almost the year 'round. Lettuce and
potatoes are started in November and the harvesting begins in
January. Peppers, cabbage, spinach, strawberries—the list is as complete as a seed catalogue.

It is a wise carload of peas or potatoes that knows its destination
when it rolls away from its loading point in the Valley, for market-
ing winter vegetables is a big and hectic business. At any one of
several junction points between the Gulf coast and the North it
may be rerouted by shippers or brokers to where market conditions
may dictate. A car may start for Chicago but if a surplus suddenly
develops there it may be redirected to Philadelphia or New England. In some manner vaguely understood by the layman the lettuce
and tomato finally come together on the salad plate of the ultimate
consumer, who has small idea of where they came from or how they
got there.

Growing cotton or vegetables in the Valley, however, is not without its hazards, its losses, its heartaches and headaches. The farmers
there are subject to the ills that beset tillers of the soil everywhere.
Pink boll worms eat his cotton, blight invades the potato field, and
wilt strikes the tomatoes. Insectides and fungicides are bought by
the ton and dusted or sprayed to exorcise various evils.

But the chief threats to the farmers of the Valley are dry weather
and cold weather—droughts and freezes. Usually winter in the Valley means no more than a few light frosts, and ice is seldom seen
unless it comes from the refrigerator. In 1949 there was a freeze that
did considerable damage, and then in 1951 came the Big Freeze
(note the capital letters) that killed millions of orange and grapefruit trees. As if that were not enough, 1953 brought a drought so
severe that in places the Rio Grande River bed was completely dry
and the stream ceased to flow.

The citizens of the Valley, however, are a sturdy breed and little time was spent wringing their hands. In 1954 E. C. Breedlove, president of the First National Bank of Harlingen, wrote:

Even the most confirmed pessimist will admit now that the Big Freeze which knocked out so many millions of our orange and grapefruit trees has opened the way to putting the citrus industry on a firm, scientific, profitable basis. It eliminated trees and groves on marginal lands, lands not suited to citrus. It knocked out old trees, sickly trees, trees which for one reason or another were producing small yields, small fruit, or unpopular varieties. And our citrus growers, once the first shock was over, have been seizing on the opportunities the Big Freeze opened up to them. Better stock, disease free, is being used. Already great progress is being made in citrus' comeback in the Valley. It won't be many years until it is as great, or even greater, than before the freeze of 1951.

The key to the Valley's prosperity is water, and when the water fails its wealth remains locked in the soil. The average rainfall is 24.4 inches a year, but few years, like few people, are "average." The rain may not fall when it is most needed, or it may not come down at all. The answer is irrigation, and irrigation means the Rio Grande. Some lands are irrigated with wells but a driller may put down a well at considerable expense, only to find that he has tapped a vein of salt water. It is the river to which the grower must turn.

"The soil of this valley is richer than the valley of the Nile," said Ralph T. Agar, engineer and manager of Cameron County Water Improvement District No. 2. "All it needs is water."

Unfortunately the Rio Grande cannot compare with the Nile in volume of flow. As cultivation along its upper reaches has increased, greater demands are being made on its waters for irrigation. Furthermore, it is an international boundary and though its headwaters are in the United States, Mexico cannot be denied her share of its stream. So, like the stream in Ruskin's fairy tale, it has become "a river of gold."

Strictly speaking, the lower part of the Valley is not a "valley" at all, for the river is higher than the surrounding country, and before it was confined by levees it wandered all over Cameron County when the water was high. No place along its final stretch do streams flow into it from the north. This makes irrigation easy, for once the water is lifted out of the river it flows by gravity over the terrain that slopes at the rate of one foot per mile *away* from the river.

In 1944 the United States and Mexico signed a treaty which provided for an amicable distribution of the Rio Grande waters, and October 19, 1953, President Eisenhower and President Cortines, of Mexico, met to dedicate the Falcon Dam, 130 miles up the river. This great structure of rock and earth, 26,300 feet long and 150 feet high, will store the water in time of flood and release it in time of drought so that communities below may pump it out of the river to irrigate their crops. It is the first and largest of a series of dams to be constructed farther upriver. Much progress has been made since the first irrigation projects in the Valley were started in 1906, but there will probably be more litigation and legislation before the murky waters of the Rio Grande are used to the fullest extent possible.

Brownsville is a bilingual city. Many of the traffic signs and placards in store windows are in English and Spanish. The two languages are heard with equal frequency on the streets, and most of the clerks and waitresses are obviously Latins. Some of them live on the north side of the Rio Grande and are United States citizens. These include a number of Brownsville's social and business leaders. Others live in Matamoros, just across the river, and enter this country with passports, while some cross over with visitors' permits but these are good for only seventy-two hours and do not permit the bearer to be employed in the United States. Still others are probably "wetbacks" who crossed the river during the dark of the moon and are liable to deportation. But few of the Texans along the border are concerned about turning them in to the authorities. In fact you may be told that were it not for the "wetbacks" the Valley farmers would have a difficult time harvesting their vegetables and cotton.

Brownsville and Matamoros are connected by a railroad bridge and a highway bridge, the latter being the first structure across the

The Rio Grande and the international bridge between Brownsville and Matamoros

Rio Grande above its mouth. There is a constant stream of motor vehicle traffic, busses and foot passengers across the bridge, and a corps of courteous customs officials make sure that every entrant has proper credentials. It is all very routine, very democratic, and apparently without any racial tension whatever.

Monterey, Mexico, one of the most interesting cities in that neighboring republic, is 195 miles due west of Brownsville. Mexico City is 630 miles and lies almost due south. Both places can be reached by excellent roads.

For gentlemen who prefer blondes the Valley would be a poor place to look for romance. Dark eyes and black hair are everywhere predominant, while redheads and blondes are seldom seen. Perhaps it is the Spanish influence that makes the Valley break out in a rash of fiestas every year.

Most elaborate of the celebrations is "Charro Days," a four-day, pre-Lenten bust-out that begins in Brownsville and winds up in Matamoros. The *"charro"* is the traditional dashing gentleman horseman of Old Mexico, attired in tight-fitting riding trousers faced with white suede and silver, a heavily embroidered short jacket, flowing multicolored tie, an intricately woven serape across his shoulders, and the inevitable wide sombrero heavily decorated with silver completing the costume. His lady, the *"China Poblana,"* is dressed in a heavily sequined red and green skirt, a rose-embroidered blouse and silk rebozo, the national costume of Mexico.

Everybody dresses up as elaborately as his means will permit and the four days are given over to parades, dancing, music by brass bands and string ensembles, fireworks and general exuberance. But it is the children's parade that always steals the show, as hundreds of tots, decked in silk and embroidery of every color, march en masse with dignity and aplomb to the lilt of gay music.

The town of Weslaco, upriver from Brownsville, has an annual "Birthday Party" with a style show and a display of fruits and vegetables grown in the area. Pharr puts on an annual Valley Vegetable Show in December. The Texas Citrus Fiesta follows in January at Mission. Raymondville goes all out for an Onion Festival featuring the indispensable "Onion Queen." The Rio Grande Valley Livestock Show brings gay days to Mercedes in March, and on the Fourth of July the town of McAllen maintains a tradition of half a century with a fiesta that concludes with a gala bullfight in Reynosa, Mexico, just across the Rio Grande.

Brownsville was born of the war between the United States and Mexico in 1846–48. Both sides of the river were claimed by Mexico, but General Zachary Taylor, later to become president, had constructed an earthworks fortification at the present site of Brownsville and named it "Fort Taylor." On April 25, 1846, there was a clash between Mexican troops and a company of United States soldiers under Captain Seth Thornton about twenty miles west of Fort Taylor. Captain Thornton was taken prisoner and several of his men were killed. When news of the encounter reached President Polk he sent a message to Congress saying that "American blood has been shed on American soil, and war exists by act of Mexico."

This was no "cold war" and decisive action came soon. On May 8 General Taylor and General Mariano Arista faced each other in the Battle of Palo Alto within eight miles of where Brownsville now stands. The next day the armies met again in the Battle of Resaca de la Palma, only three miles away, and General Arista's guns shelled Fort Taylor from across the river. General Taylor hastened to the fort's relief but not until its commander, Major Jacob Brown, had been killed. Whereupon General Taylor immediately rechristened it "Fort Brown." These military actions cleared the Mexican troops from the north side of the Rio Grande and the river became established as the boundary between the two nations.

Fort Brown was developed into a large and well-equipped military post a few hundred yards north of where the original fortification had been built. Soon after peace with Mexico one Charles Stillman, who was born in Wethersfield, Connecticut, and later became a successful merchant in Matamoros, bought the land surrounding the military post and founded the city of Brownsville. His home, built in 1849, still stands. Elizabeth Street, the city's principal thoroughfare, was named for his bride.

When the Civil War broke out Brownsville was held by Confederate troops but Union ships patrolled the waters of the Gulf of Mexico. Cotton, worth almost its weight in silver in England, piled up in Brownsville. Much of it was hauled over the sand to the village of Clarksville, just above the mouth of the Rio Grande, and ferried across to the Mexican village of Bagdad from which point it eventually reached a Mexican port, thus evading the blockade. An October hurricane destroyed both villages in 1867 and today there is nothing to mark their sites in a wilderness of sand and marshland.

Cameron County can truly lay claim to being the scene of the last battle of the Civil War, and oddly enough the Confederates were victorious. A considerable quantity of cotton was stored in

Defaced historical marker commemorating the Battle
of Palmito Hill

Brownsville warehouses and the Federals who were established on
Brazos Island thought it would be an excellent idea to capture it.
No word of General Lee's surrender at Appomattox on April 9,
1865, had reached this far corner of the country, and on May 13 the
expedition started across the twenty-two miles of sandy wastes between Brazos Island and the cotton. But Colonel "Rip" Ford, a picturesque commander of the Confederate forces, heard of it and the
two detachments of troops met at Palmito Hill, fourteen miles east
of Brownsville. There was considerable shooting and 115 Union
soldiers were killed or wounded. The Federals concluded the cotton
was not worth the effort and returned to Brazos Island.

History, however, was not through with Brownsville and in 1906
its name flashed briefly on the front page of every daily paper in

the United States. Three companies of Negro soldiers, B, C, and D of the Twenty-fifth Infantry Regiment of the regular Army were stationed at Fort Brown. To wear the uniform of a soldier in the regular Army was a distinction that stirred their pride, and when on the night of August 13, 1906, they were denied admission to the town's saloons they rioted. Returning to their barracks a few of them got their rifles and proceeded to shoot up the town. A bartender was killed, a policeman wounded, and the citizens terrorized for several hours. When they got back to quarters their identities were lost and no one could, or would, point out the rioters.

President Theodore Roosevelt made a direct appeal to the members of the three companies, asking them to give up the culprits for the honor of the Army and the good name of their race. The answer was silence. Whereupon the President ordered the entire personnel of all three companies—250 men—discharged "without honor," and deactivated the military post.

Immediately the political fat was in the fire. In those days every Negro vote was axiomatically a Republican vote, and politicians in the North with Negro constituents were almost paralyzed, but not vocally. Senator Joseph B. Foraker, Republican, of Ohio, persuaded the Senate to pass a resolution calling for an investigation, which aroused Roosevelt, and he and the senator exchanged some heated remarks at the Gridiron dinner in January, 1907. This incident is supposed to have destroyed what chances Foraker may have had to get the Republican nomination for president in 1908. But the public excitement soon died down, and many Negroes as well as whites felt that the President had acted wisely in a situation that could not be ignored.

Another forgotten item of history is that it was in Brownsville that a young Army doctor, Lieutenant William C. Gorgas, began his great work of eliminating the scourge of yellow fever. Until early in the present century yellow fever was almost endemic along the Gulf Coast, flaring now and then into terrifying activity. Between 1769 and 1878 there were thirty epidemics of "yellow jack" in New

Orleans alone, and no city or village along the coastal area but paid toll in lives to this scourge of the tropics.

Young Dr. Gorgas, born in Mobile, was familiar with the history of yellow fever and anxious to study it, but he had never seen a case. Transferred to Fort Brown in August, 1882, not long after he had been commissioned in the Army Medical Corps at $133 a month, the young lieutenant found himself in the midst of a yellow fever outbreak among the troops, but because he was not immune (never having had the disease) he was ordered not to enter the fever ward or otherwise expose himself. Despite this he was caught, literally red-handed, performing an autopsy on a yellow fever victim. An order for his arrest was issued and almost immediately rescinded, but he was told to move his quarters to the section reserved for yellow fever patients. This suited the young investigator exactly, though in a short time he contracted the disease.

Another patient at the same time was Miss Marie Doughty, the young sister-in-law of Colonel William J. Lister, commandant of the post. The two were much in each other's company during their convalescence and were married two years later.

"It would be untrue to say that 'yellow jack' was the best man at our wedding," wrote Mrs. Gorgas in her later years, "but it would be perfectly true to say that in a sense he was an usher."

In the years that followed, Gorgas, ofttimes working against strongly entrenched prejudice, was eventually able to prove that yellow fever was carried by mosquitoes, and to give mankind control over a disease that had cursed it for centuries.

III. *The King Ranch*

Sᴛᴀʀᴛɪɴɢ north from Brownsville, U.S. Highway 77 runs for fifty miles through rich Valley lands, the towns of San Benito and Harlingen, and reaches Raymondville, the northmost Valley town and county seat of Willacy County. Leaving Raymondville the countryside changes abruptly, cultivated fields giving way to a flat landscape relieved only by endless stretches of live oak and mesquite thickets and prickly pear cactus. The highway parallels the Missouri Pacific Railroad, formerly the St. Louis, Brownsville & Mexico, and seems to end in a simmering haze on the northern

29

horizon. We have entered the cattle country and are on the western edge of the great south Texas oil fields.

The mesquite deserves a special chapter in the story of Texas. When mature it is a picturesque tree with a foliage of fine compound leaflets, and its fuzzy bean pods, resembling green beans of the garden, have some value as stock food. The trunk is covered with a heavy ridged bark and is frequently twisted into picturesque shapes, making it an attractive planting for lawns and patios. Mesquite will flourish on drought-stricken lands where nothing else but the ubiquitous prickly pear can compete with it, and thus offers some resistance to the sand and dust that blow when the land is dried out—and this country is dried out much of the time.

Until the present century the mesquite was confined largely to the courses of rivers and smaller streams and was looked on with a tolerant eye. Gradually it began to spread out into the open prairie and take over thousands of acres of grazing lands. In less than half a century it has extended its domain through a great part of western Texas and is pushing into Oklahoma. Ranchers have been forced to do battle with it and the issue is still joined. The experts of Texas' big Agricultural and Mechanical College have sprayed it with a variety of plant-killing chemicals. Sometimes the result is all that could be expected and the landscape is covered with lifeless tree skeletons. At other times this seems to have been achieved, only to have green buds appear after a dormant period, and soon everything is as it was. And sometimes the persistent mesquite just takes the poison spray in its stride and continues to flourish like the green bay tree of the Scriptures. No one yet knows what makes the difference, but soil moisture, atmospheric conditions, and even the time of day the spray is applied may have something to do with it.

A few miles out of Raymondville the highway enters Kenedy County, named for Captain Mifflin Kenedy, a pioneer of a century ago who was closely associated with Captain Richard King in the development of this area. It is cattle country, too sandy for cultivation, and includes the extensive Kenedy Ranch, part of the King

Ranch, and smaller holdings. The statistics of Kenedy County are interesting: area: 1,407 square miles; population (1950): 632; urban population: 0; rural population: 632; population: 6.9 per cent Anglo-American, 93.1 per cent Latin.

Passing through the little county seat town of Sarita (population, 1950: 200) the road enters Kleberg County, home of the King Ranch. Lying astride the county line is an inlet of tidewater with the baffling name of "Baffin Bay," which certainly is not what the early Spaniards called it. Nobody knows why this name from the Far North is found on the Texas coast. Various theories have been considered but none has the authority of history. This Baffin Bay of the South is also remarkable for being the third saltiest body of water in the world, the salinity of its waters being exceeded only by the Dead Sea and Great Salt Lake. Normally fish live in the waters of the bay, but sometimes there will be a heavy influx of brine and most of the fish will leave. Those that do not, go blind or starve to death.

Fifteen miles north of the headwaters of Baffin Bay is Kingsville, seat of Kleberg County and a busy burg wherein are located the business offices of the King Ranch. Here also is the Texas College of Arts and Industries and the home of the Border Poets Association. This group, organized in 1946, proves the people of the region are interested in culture as well as cattle. It is sparked by Dr. J. DeWitt Davis, head of the department of education, and includes students, faculty members, their wives, cowhands and anyone else who can write acceptable verse. Every year the group publishes a volume of poems written by its members, under the title of *The Silver Spur*.

Two of the biggest things along the coast of the Gulf of Mexico are the Mississippi River and the King Ranch. The river is the older, but the ranch celebrated its centennial in 1953.

The fences of the King Ranch enclose 840,000 acres, and the cattle in its pastures vary from 65,000 to 85,000 head, the number being reduced in times of drought. Among its 3,000 horses are two winners of the Kentucky Derby, others that have come in first on all the big-time tracks in the country, and some of the finest "quarter horses" to be found in the Southwest. Caring for all this and living on the ranch are eight hundred men, women and children, many of them descendants of Captain King's first ranch hands.

Not for size alone, however, is this ranch pre-eminent. Its chief title to fame is that for more than one hundred years, under the direction of men of unusual ability and vision, it has pioneered in new and better methods of livestock and ranch management, and cattlemen and consumers alike have benefited from this program. Santa Gertrudis beef cattle, a breed originated on the King Ranch, are to be found in twenty-seven states and sixteen foreign countries. Among the many "firsts" to the credit of the ranch management are:

Fencing the open range with board fences, then with barbed wire, and finally with woven wire fencing designed under the direction of the ranch owners.

Initiation of the work that led to the discovery that the cattle tick was the carrier of the "Texas fever," so fatal to the cattle of Northern latitudes, and development of methods of dipping and cattle rotation that have practically eradicated this pest.

Study and propagation of forage grasses suited to the region, culminating in "King Ranch Bluestem" and "Kleberg Bluestem," two of the best range grasses developed to date.

Determination that lack of phosphorus in the soil, and consequently in the grazing, was reflected in poorer cows, and so was especially detrimental to the calf crop; and lengthy experiment to find the best way to supply this deficiency.

Design of special machinery at considerable cost for use in uprooting mesquite thickets and returning the land to pasturage.

Scientifically controlled crossbreeding, line breeding and inbreeding to develop a high-grade beef animal congenial to warm climates; resulting in recognition by the U.S. Department of Agriculture in 1940 of the "Santa Gertrudis" as an established breed, the first beef breed to originate in the Western Hemisphere and the first new beef breed anywhere in two hundred years.

It is this last achievement that overshadows all the other accomplishments of the King Ranch, important though they may be, and has made it known to cattlemen around the world.

The ranch as it stands today is a monument to three men of remarkable enterprise who successfully directed its development. The first of these was its founder, Captain Richard King, who was born in New York City, July 10, 1824. Apprenticed to a jeweler as a boy, he was put to "baby-sitting" for his employer instead of learning the trade, and being dissatisfied with this arrangement he stowed away on a schooner and landed in Mobile, Alabama. His early years were spent as a sailor along the Gulf Coast, where he eventually became a pilot. During the war with Mexico he first piloted a government boat commanded by Captain Mifflin Kenedy, carrying supplies to troops under the command of General Zachary Taylor. Later he was given command of one of these boats and earned the title of "Captain King."

Thus began a friendship between two remarkable men. They established M. Kenedy & Co. in 1850, two years after the end of the war, and began operations in August of that year with two especially built steamboats and two or three war-surplus steamboats. In May, 1852, Captain King made a trip by horseback from his home in Brownsville to Corpus Christi, 165 miles up the coast, a trip that was to change the pattern of both men's lives and write an important chapter in the history of cattle raising in the United States.

Riding across the open prairie with only a few mesquite or a cluster of stunted live oak to break the long line of the horizon, King had a vision of the area between the Nueces River and the Rio Grande as a potential cattle-raising empire. The next year he purchased "three and one-half leagues" of land on Santa Gertrudis Creek, the present site of Kingsville. The Spanish "land league" was 4,428 acres, so this original purchase comprised about 15,500 acres. The sellers were the Mendiola heirs who held the land as a grant from the Mexican state of Tamaulipas. What with the land having been held first by Spain, then by Mexico, later by the Republic of Texas and finally by the United States, the good captain was to find that land titles were something of a mess, although these changes in government were not supposed to affect private titles. As he added to his holdings he sometimes had to buy the same piece several times, and the records show that one bit of acreage was paid for four times in order to quiet title. Early in his career as a landowner King retained the services of Stephen Powers, and later J. B. Wells, Brownsville attorneys who specialized in Spanish land titles, and for more than fifty years one or the other was attorney for the ranch. Jim Wells County, Texas, was named for the latter.

In 1860 Captain King interested his old shipmate, Captain Kenedy, in ranching and the two began to operate as "R. King & Company." This arrangement continued until 1868 when, for the sake of their heirs, the two men made an amicable division of their holdings. Two years after making his original purchase of land, Captain King married Miss Henrietta Morse Chamberlain, of Boonville, Missouri, whose father, a Presbyterian minister, had moved to Brownsville. The two captains sold their steamboat holdings to the employees of the company in 1874, and thereafter the river knew them no more.

An early biographer has said that when Captain King died in 1885 he left "a 500,000 acre ranch and debts of $500,000," a neat phrase that persists, but not in accord with the facts. The acreage figure is approximately correct but the debts were no greater than the current liabilities usually on the books of an enterprise of that magnitude. In the meantime he had brought into his service an enterprising young lawyer named Robert Justus Kleberg and had begun to entrust him with some of the ranch's legal business in near-by Corpus Christi. A romance sprang up between the good-looking attorney and the captain's daughter, Alice, but their wedding was postponed on account of her father's illness and did not take place until the year after his death. Mrs. King survived her husband by forty years, passing away in 1925 at the age of ninety-three. By the terms of her will the ranch, which had grown to 1,173,000 acres, was placed in a ten-year trusteeship. While she lived control of the ranch rested with her, but most of the problems of management and development she left to her son-in-law, and it was this lawyer turned rancher who guided the big venture through the second phase of its development.

When the Spaniard came to the New World he brought a gift of greater value than all the gold of the Incas and all the silver ever mined in Mexico. He brought cattle. The affinity between the Spaniard and his horned herds reaches back through the centuries. He is the original "cowboy." It is not just a coincidence that bull-fighting overshadows all other forms of entertainment in Spanish-speaking countries, and that the leading matador is a national hero.

Columbus brought a few cattle with him on his second voyage to the New World, but it was not until about 1690 that the first cattle to appear in the Texas region were brought in by the Spanish missionaries. The Indians were hostile. The missionaries were killed. The cattle survived. For a century and a half they roamed the Gulf coastal plains, and by a process of natural selection became the "longhorns" of song and story. Sometimes called "Mexican cattle," they were mostly horns, hoof and hide, and their flesh was anything but "prime." But they were a hardy breed, able to hold their own among the cougars and the coyotes, the mesquite and the mos-quitoes, and to triumph over long periods of drought.

Captain King stocked his ranch largely with cattle bought across the Rio Grande in Mexico and improved his herds as best he could by careful selection of his breeding stock. He had no Bureau of Animal Industry in a Department of Agriculture, no group of experts in a Texas A. & M. College, to call on for advice. He was strictly on his own. Furthermore it was not yet time for the curtain to fall on the rugged longhorn. For one thing, it was necessary to drive the marketable stock to the railroad at Abilene, Kansas, part of the way being over the famous Chisholm Trail. Rivers had to be forded, semi-deserts crossed, and the herds subsisted as best they could on the often scanty forage of the trail. The fat, short-legged beef cattle of today could never have taken it.

As the great railroad building boom in the United States gained headway after the close of the Civil War the need for rail connections in southwest Texas became more pressing. Captains King and Kenedy, never ones for halfway measures, began promoting and financing a road from Corpus Christi to Laredo, known as the Texas-Mexico Railroad. Rails did not reach Kingsville until 1904 when the St. Louis, Brownsville & Mexico line was constructed, Mrs. King donating the right-of-way where it crossed her ranch and some 75,000 acres in addition, and Robert J. Kleberg, Sr., serving as one of the original directors. It was the advent of the railroads that wrote the last chapter in the saga of the longhorns.

Between 1880 and 1885 the process of grading up these so-called longhorns was started by crossbreeding them with the British breeds of Herefords and Shorthorns in order to procure more and higher grade of beef per acre. Small herds of registered and pure-bred Hereford and Shorthorn cattle were also acquired over a period of years and added to the breeding herds. The British breeds, while more favorable from a market standpoint than the native Mexican cattle, did not prove themselves nearly so good range animals. They were not so prolific and suffered more from drought and insects. What was wanted was a type of beef animal that could stand the climate and reach a marketable condition on the grasses that the region afforded. In the first decade of the present century a few Brahman, or "Zebu," cattle had been brought to Texas from India, where they had developed in a climate entirely different from that of the temperate British Isles, and these showed themselves right at home in the Texas sun. This is the "sacred cow" of India and oddly enough it is raised there as a milk producer, as the Hindu will not eat its flesh.

In 1910 a neighboring rancher, Tom O'Connor, gave the King Ranch a half-breed Shorthorn-Brahman bull, black in color and of enormous size. During the next thirty years the geneticists were to have a field day with his offspring, and they finally achieved a geneticist's triumph. The story was the subject of a learned paper, not all of it intelligible to a layman, that was read before the Eighth International Congress of Geneticists in Stockholm, Sweden, in July, 1948, by A. O. Rhoad of the American Genetic Association.

A new type of plant or animal may be obtained by crossbreeding, say the geneticists, but the mating of the hybrids leads to undesirable complications. Unless a miracle happens the progeny of the crossmating deteriorates with succeeding generations. Starting under the direction of Robert J. Kleberg, the work of crossbreeding was continued under the most careful controls by his sons, the late Richard M. Kleberg and Robert Kleberg, Jr.

Only at rare intervals in the field of animal husbandry does there appear, somewhat mysteriously, a sire so prepotent that not only his immediate progeny, but all his succeeding generations, are stamped with his characteristics. Such were the stallions, "Byerly Turk," "the Darley Arabian" and "the Godolphin Barb," brought to England in the early 1700's to become the greatest progenitors of race horses of all time. Such was the unnamed colt given to Justin Morgan in Vermont in 1781 in part payment of a debt that sired the new and virile breed of "Morgan horses."

It was in the fall round-up of 1920 that a cherry-red young animal, essentially five-eighths Shorthorn and three-eighths Brahman, was branded with the "Running W" of the King Ranch. He looked like good breeding stock and so was not reduced to steerdom. They gave him the plebeian name of "Monkey" and in 1923 he was made part of the ranch's breeding herd. As soon as the calves of his get began to appear it was evident that here was a supersire. Soon Monkey showed that he deserved a place among the prepotent immortals. His Shorthorn parentage gave him the build and quality of a good beef animal. His Brahman ancestry enabled him to thrive

Santa Gertrudis steer with "Running W" brand

in the heat of the semitropic sun that drove less hardy animals into the shade of the mesquite. Most important of all, his progeny showed these same virtues and were able to transmit them when used in a grading-up program with cows of other breeds.

But the work of establishing a new breed was not concluded by the appearance of this remarkable sire. Wrote Robert Kleberg, Jr., in language best understood by the geneticist:

By using his [Monkey's] sons and grandsons on firstcross heifers, again on the doublecross resulting from mating firstcross bulls on firstcross heifers, and finally employing in-and-in line-breeding methods, the Santa Gertrudis breed has been evolved. These cattle, red or cherry-red in color, are very large, have excellent beef conformation, and carry a deep mellow covering of flesh. They are breeding remarkably true, both as to color and type. In 1940 the Santa Gertrudis breed was officially recognized by the United States Government as a distinct breed of beef cattle, only thirty years after the first exploratory use of the O'Connor bull.

With the fourfold object of further improving the breed, maintaining its standard of excellence, protecting the breeders from misrepresentation, and establishing a registry of the breed, 137 cattlemen met in San Antonio in 1951 and established the Santa Gertrudis Breeders International. The association now has about six hundred members. By its rules the cattle are judged on twenty-five points of excellence, and certified as "purebred," "accredited" or "rejected." Its 1954 publication contained the following interesting note:

Santa Gertrudis cows are excellent milkers, calve easily, and can nurse calves up to nine months readily. Santa Gertrudis cows "baby sit." Several cows will tend 30 to 40 calves while other cows are off in another part of the pasture grazing. This is a common occurrence and the cows themselves develop their own rotation system.

The King Ranch is really four ranches. The main holding includes the original Santa Gertrudis grant just west of Kingsville. Here are the headquarters buildings and here the breeding herds of horses and cattle are kept. To the east, across U.S. Route 77 lies the Laureles division along the shores of Baffin Bay and Laguna Madre. South of Santa Gertrudis is the Encino division, and to the southeast, lying partly along Laguna Madre, is the Norias division, generally referred to as "the lower ranch." More than three hundred miles of hard-surfaced roads are maintained by the ranch within its borders.

There is much to the ranch besides cattle. An extensive wildlife conservation program is carried out on the Norias division, and is regarded as an important part of the ranch operations. Deer, wild turkey and quail that half a century ago had almost disappeared from the region are now abundant enough to be used to restock other depleted areas. And there are horses, usually about three thousand of them, ranging all the way from Derby winners to the clever "cutting horses" used in handling cattle herds. In 1935 Robert Kleberg, Jr., became convinced that Texas could raise as fine animals as Kentucky, and imported a carload of racing stock from the bluegrass region. His judgment was spectacularly confirmed in 1946 when Assault, a King Ranch horse, won the "triple crown," consisting of the Kentucky Derby, the Preakness and the Belmont. His winnings that year totaled $424,000, and he was retired at the end of his racing career after having won $675,470 on the track. In 1950, Middleground, another King Ranch horse, carried the brown

Assault

and white of the ranch to victory in the Churchill Downs classic and the Belmont stakes.

Few things about the ranch suggest the "cowboy" as portrayed in the movies. Even the old-fashioned round-up has given way to progress, and instead of being chased through the brush and losing valuable pounds thereby, the steers are "rounded up" at various watering places when they come to drink. They are still lassoed and thrown for branding and castrating, but with a minimum of violence. Most of the "vaqueros," like the original cattle herds, trace their ancestry back to Spain via Mexico, but they are American citizens and the knowledge and love of cattle are in their blood. About 90 per cent of the ranch employees were born there, and many were accomplished cowhands when they were sixteen or seventeen years old. They live with their families in double-walled houses of brick, with tile floors and all modern conveniences.

At the end of the ten-year trusteeship created by Mrs. King in 1925, most of the ranch properties were incorporated and the shares distributed among the Kleberg families. Today it is more than just a big ranch. In a way it is an empire.

IV. *Corpus Christi*

Sheltered from the open waters of the Gulf by Padre and Mustang islands, and hard by the bay that receives the flow of the Nueces ("New-ACES") River, is Corpus Christi, one of the most versatile cities of Texas. It is 125 airline miles due north of Brownsville. In its immediate hinterland are cattle ranches, oil wells, and wide fields of cotton, grain sorghums and winter vegetables.

The visitor from the North may be puzzled by the mammoth

grain elevators in a country where he sees neither corn, wheat nor oats. They are storage and shipping points for millions of bushels of grain sorghums grown locally, and for wheat grown in Kansas, Colorado and even southern Nebraska. From Corpus Christi these products are shipped all over the world.

Grain sorghums, called "combine milo" by local farmers, belong to the maize family and bear a heavy head of small grains at the top of a stalk two or three feet tall. When milled and the brown husks removed they yield a pure white starch, dextrin, sugar and syrup. Much of the crop is processed in the big plant of the Corn Products Company just outside the city. This grain enables many farmers to harvest two money crops a year. All cotton must be harvested and plowed under by August 31, and often the field is immediately planted to milo which may be combined before cotton-planting time the following year. Heavy fertilization is necessary for such a program.

Between Corpus Christi and Kingsville is a large industrial plant with weird towers, tanks, pipes, retorts and what not rising against the skyline. It belongs to the Celanese Corporation of America and here natural gas from near-by wells is converted into acetic acid, acetone, menthanol and other chemicals and shipped in tank cars east, west and north to be used by many industries, principally in the manufacture of plastics. This is the outpost of a rapidly expanding industrial empire that stretches along the Texas coast from Corpus Christi to Beaumont and Port Arthur, and it is the combination of cheap oil and gas with barge and ocean transportation that is sparking Corpus Christi's rapid expansion. In 1920 it had a population of 10,522. Thirty-five years later the figure stood at 160,000.

Corpus Christi might be called the new city with an old name. More than a hundred years before the Pilgrims landed at Plymouth Rock, Alonzo Alvarez de Pineda sailed into what is now Corpus Christi Bay and gave it that name but attempted no settlement because of the hostile Karankawa Indians. Its modern history began when a colorful and adventurous character, Colonel Henry Lawrence Kinney, landed on the bay shore in 1839, probably in a foul mood because Daniel Webster had recently refused to allow the colonel to marry his daughter.

The colonel began his career by hiring a private army of forty men, arming them, and opening a trading post. The army was necessary because at that period the land between the Nueces River and the Rio Grande was disputed territory when anyone thought the control of the empty acres was worth disputing. Mirabeau Lamar had just succeeded Sam Houston as president of the new Republic of Texas and whether the Nueces or the Rio Grande was the international boundary was not to be settled for nine years. The trading post did a thriving business with Americans, Mexicans and Indians by maintaining a position of "armed neutrality." On one occasion when threatened by an organized Mexican force thirty of Kinney's "army" deserted, but he made a show of resistance, exploded some buried bombs to make the enemy think the area was mined, and saved his skin and his store.

By 1845 trouble was really brewing. Texas was getting ready to join the United States and Mexico had threatened war if the wedding took place. Kinney, who had acquired large landholdings south of the Nueces, was anxious that his titles and his Mexican neighbors be disturbed as little as possible. General Zachary Taylor, then unknown outside the Army, was in command of troops at Fort Jessup, Louisiana, and President James K. Polk, influenced possibly by Kinney's wire-pulling, ordered him to move his forces to Corpus Christi to be ready for whatever might develop.

St. Joseph's Island is a sliver of sand just north of Mustang Island and here on July 25, 1845, General Taylor's troops planted the first United States flag to fly in Texas. With the arrival of the soldiers, who soon numbered four thousand, the little trading post town began to boom. Among the junior officers was Lieutenant Ulysses S. Grant. Another who arrived a short time later was Lieutenant Robert E. Lee, not to mention General Taylor's son-in-law, Colonel Jefferson Davis. A list of the young officers of the expedition reads like a roster of generals, North and South, of the Civil War which was to follow.

Word that the Congress of the United States had accepted the proposed constitution of the state of Texas on December 9, 1845, alerted the troops, and February 16, 1846, the flag of the Republic of Texas was hauled down and the Stars and Stripes raised in its place. Trouble was breaking out along the Rio Grande and after a stay of more than seven months in Corpus Christi General Taylor started south with his troops March 11, 1846, to win glory as "Old Rough and Ready," to win a war—and the presidency of the United States.

The passing of the soldiers seemed to be the end of the little boom town, but Kinney bestirred himself, sparing neither energy nor money—and he had plenty of both—to justify his faith in the region. In consequence it became a starting place for the California gold fields, being the nearest Atlantic tidewater point to the California coast. Prosperity returned and the municipality was organized in 1852. But the rancher, trader and adventurer of the Nueces–Rio Grande region came to an anticlimactic end. He spent large sums in an unsuccessful attempt to establish a colony in Nicaragua, got into difficulties with Central American politicos, and returned to Texas broke and discredited. On a visit to Matamoros in 1865 he became mixed up in a street fight between two local factions and was shot through the heart.

Under the impetus Kinney had given it Corpus Christi continued to prosper. In 1870 sheep ranching was begun in Nueces and Duval counties and shortly a million sheep were grazing on land that had been purchased for as little as twelve cents an acre. In 1880 Corpus Christi had the largest wool market in the United States. But about that time the open range began to disappear behind fences, markets were less favorable, and by 1886 90 per cent of the sheep had disappeared.

A new era had begun. Cattle took the place of sheep, railroads crossed the prairies, water-borne traffic increased and invested capital became established. Soon there appeared on this sun-drenched stage another character, as colorful as Colonel Kinney but from a very different background. She is remembered as Mrs. Clara Driscoll, rich, handsome rather than pretty, educated in New York and France, talented, and with a personality like a tropical hurricane. She was born at St. Mary's, Texas, near Corpus Christi, April 2, 1881. Her father had made a fortune as a rancher and investor and this was to be swelled later by oil. She had one brother, Robert, Jr., who never married. These two men as bankers and industrialists did much for the development of the region, but today in Corpus Christi "Driscoll" means "Clara."

At the age of twenty-four she wrote a successful novel, *Girl of La Gloria*. The next year she scored again with *The Shadow of the Alamo*. This was followed by a musical comedy, *Mexicana*, that had a successful run on the New York stage. She was married in 1906 to H. H. ("Hal") Sevier, Texas newspaperman and legislator, then on the staff of the New York *Sun*. The wedding took place in St. Patrick's Cathedral, New York City, and was followed by dinner at Delmonico's. The couple had no children and in 1937 they were divorced. Hal died three years later.

Clara reclaimed the name "Driscoll" but kept the title "Mrs." Mature, experienced, wealthy, she gave her full attention to Texas, for which she had an abiding affection. When the historic Alamo in San Antonio was about to be engulfed by tall buildings and filling stations she made an unsuccessful attempt to interest the state legislature in its preservation and finally put up $65,000 of her own money to save it. Eventually the legislature made the site a state park and refunded her money. According to the *Texas Almanac*, published by the Dallas *Morning News*, this was done "largely through the efforts of the Daughters of the Republic of Texas and Mrs. Clara Driscoll, who, as a schoolgirl, began her fight to save the Alamo grounds."

This same D.R.T. built a beautiful clubhouse in Austin but when the mortgage became due they were unable to finance it. So Clara

Mesquite trees at their best in a Corpus Christi patio

wrote out a check for $92,000, Governor Lee O'Daniel proclaimed October 4, 1939, "Clara Driscoll Day," and the occasion was observed with proper pageantry and eloquence. These spectacular contributions were not the full measure of her generosities, however. Hospitals, churches and a variety of charities were helped by her. She was a great friend to John Nance ("Cactus Jack") Garner and spent considerable money promoting a "Garner for President" boom in 1940.

Always salty of tongue, contemptuous of sham, generous to friends and defiant to foes, she was good newspaper copy and legends grew up around her. One story may be accepted as a fact beyond quibble. Angered at a Corpus Christi hotel proprietor, she flashed a scornful look at him and said: "I'll build a hotel here so high I can spit on yours!" Build it she did, and the Robert Driscoll hotel, eighteen stories high, stands today, one of the finest hostelries in Texas. From its spacious roof one might indeed spit on all of Corpus Christi when the wind is right. When Clara died in 1949 she left a large part of her wealth for the establishment of the Driscoll Foundation Children's Hospital, the greatest of many monuments to this remarkable person.

Corpus Christi is the annual meeting place of one of the most active literary groups in the United States, the Southwest Writers' Conference, organized and conducted by the By-Liners, a group of local professional women writers. Since its first meeting in 1944 its attendance has grown to nearly 400, and it has attracted not only most of the great Texas writers but famous authors, editors and publishers from all over the country as well. The Conference registration counts members from thirty-seven states and nine foreign countries, and through the years members have sold more than $100,000 worth of manuscripts, a cultural and financial record in which even our largest cities could take pride.

Situated on the south shore of Corpus Christi Bay is the United States Naval Air Station, the largest installation of its kind in the world, covering 17,527 acres. This is an advanced training base, most of its personnel coming from Pensacola after receiving basic training there. During World War II and the Korean War more than forty thousand pilots were trained here and its graduates saw action in every combat area. The station was established in 1941 and grew rapidly in importance, one reason being that there are but eighteen days out of the calendar year when flying conditions here are not normal.

With but few exceptions the Corpus Christi Station is strictly

"Brown Shoe Navy," the "Black Shoe Navy" having but a small representation. Observing that the uniform of the airborne Navy called for brown shoes, while the surface or water-borne gobs wore black, the recruits hit upon that method of differentiating them and it has become semiofficial. Unification has really been effected here, for details of the Marine Corps, the Army and the Coast Guard are all "aboard the CCNAS." Even though he is an airman the recruit learns to speak of being "aboard" the station, and if he goes upstairs he is "on the second deck." What the Naval Air Station means to the economy of the area is illustrated by its payment annually of some $8,456,000 for fuels, $953,000 for milk, meat and groceries, and $596,000 for utilities.

Stretching along the south Texas coast from just above the mouth of the Rio Grande to Aransas Pass opposite Corpus Christi, a distance of 130 miles, is one of the longest, narrowest islands in the world—Padre Island. Some maps show Padre's north end terminating at Corpus Christi Pass and Mustang Island extending twenty miles beyond. But storms have filled the pass with sand and today a well-paved highway without any fill runs across what was once a channel to the Gulf. The entire stretch is usually referred to locally as Padre Island and at no point is it more than four miles wide. The fishing docks and Coast Guard base of Port Aransas are at the northern end. Between the island and the mainland lies Laguna Madre.

The island has a history comparable to its length. Before the coming of the Spaniards it was a land favored by the savage Karankawas and many Indian artifacts have been found along its shores, including flint arrowheads and hatchets that must have been obtained in trade with tribes to the north or west. Louis E. Rawalt, who in addition to being Audubon warden for the region is also regional vice president of the Texas Archaeological Society, has made a notable collection of such objects.

When the Spaniards arrived in the early 1500's they called it "Isla de Blanco" because of its white sands, and later maps list it as "Isla Santiago." Some of its area contains only wind-blown sand dunes as barren as the Sahara but other parts provide a fair pasturage when there is sufficient rain for grass and drinking water, and cattle have roamed there for two hundred years.

Charles IV of Spain in 1792 granted the island to Padre José Baille, a high church official whose headquarters were in San Antonio. The padre visited the island occasionally but left its management to his nephew who ran considerable cattle there. When Mexico became independent of Spain the padre's title to the island was challenged. A long legal battle followed and Padre Baille's ownership was finally established shortly before his death. In the meantime the island came to be referred to as "The Padre's Island," and Padre Island it is today.

Venturesome motorists have driven the entire length of the island but it is not a trip to be undertaken lightly. Port Aransas at the northern tip is the only permanent settlement on it, and the highway from there to the Corpus Christi causeway is its only road except for the hard sand of the beach. Long regarded as little more than wasteland, Padre Island has recently begun to "boom" and future maps may show it traversed by an improved road and dotted with vacation resorts. Fishing piers have been built out into the Gulf, where the casual angler can usually get some kind of action while his wife nurses a sunburn in one of the cabanas that have been built along the beach.

Louis E. Rawalt, National Audubon Society warden, sat in his small boat which lay idly in the half-mile stretch of shallow water of Laguna Madre between South Bird Island and Padre Island, fourteen miles south of Corpus Christi. A hundred yards away a group of solemn white pelicans preened themselves in the morning sun, the black primary feathers of their wings making a striking contrast with their otherwise white plumage. Along the shoreline almost-grown reddish egrets bickered with each other and their neighbors of many species, while on the higher background great blue herons stood like sentinels atop their nests that crowned the stunted yuccas.

But it was the terns that stole the show—royal terns, Caspians, Cabots, Forsters, with here and there a "least tern" representing its division of the family. Some sat on the sand at the edge of the water, their streamlined black-crowned heads pointing into the gentle Southern breeze. Most of them were on the wing, however, and a common sight was a tern with a small fish in its orange-colored bill being pursued through an amazing series of aerial acrobatics by another bird intent on stealing the tidbit. All the while their shrill screams and scoldings tortured the air.

"The nesting season is about over now and the noise is not so bad," said Rawalt. (It was early July.) "A few weeks ago you could hardly carry on a conversation this close to the island. Not so many terns now nest on the island as a few years ago, many having gone to the spoil banks created when the Intracoastal Waterway channel was dug. This year's count showed 600 nesting royal terns, 450 Cabot terns, 132 great blue herons, 117 reddish egrets, 16 snowy egrets and but 4 Louisiana herons. As might be expected on this part of the coast, the largest colony was that of 3,500 laughing gulls."

The laughing gull which is found in great numbers all along the Gulf Coast is not so named because it has a sense of humor, but because beaches and harbors echo with its cackling cry that sounds like a burst of sardonic laughter.

The brown pelican, like some species of seagulls, has become half-domesticated. Around our Southern harbors he sits humped up on the pilings waiting for the discards of a fishing trip, or diving into the near-by waters for a luckless fish to the delight of the tourists. But his big white brother is not so sociable. The brown pelican has a wing spread of six and a half feet, the white can stretch his wings a full nine feet. Moreover the white pelican never dives for its food, but catches it in shallow water.

"A flock of white pelicans will form an arc in the shallow waters offshore," said Rawalt, "and with great splashing will advance together until thousands of small fish are driven in to where the water is only a few inches deep. Then the birds scoop them up in their great yellow pouches. When this takes place during the hatching season a few birds will be left to take care of the small ones while the parents are away. I have seen such a guardian take after a straying nestling and maneuver it back to the rest of the kindergarten, just like a dog keeping a flock of sheep together. South Bird Island is the only place along this coast where the white pelican nests, and this year we had sixteen hundred nesting birds here.

"I have sat here for days and weeks watching parent birds feeding and training their young and it is a fascinating spectacle. When young terns are taking their first swimming lessons near the shore a strong wind may start blowing them out into the lagoon. Under such conditions a parent bird will swoop down, catch a bill full of feathers on the little fellow's back, and start towing it shoreward, the load being too heavy to lift. If the wind is too strong for safety to be reached with one effort the older bird will let go after several yards have been gained, circle a few times, and then repeat the process until Junior is safe.

"Another interesting performance is the mating dance of the great blue herons, a bird standing about four feet high and often mistakenly called a crane. In the mating season five or six male birds will form a circle about a single female and put on a show for her. First they stand very straight, their long necks stretched, their yellow bills pointing to the sky, and their wings partly spread. Then they go into a sort of dance routine, flapping their wings and moving in a circle about the lady but never approaching her. This performance is repeated several times until the female signifies her choice by walking up to one of her suitors. The two stand face to face and very close for a moment, their wings open and their necks stretched to the utmost. It is really beautiful. Then they fly away. As soon as they are gone the remaining males engage in a free-for-all fight in which some feathers may fly but no lives are lost."

Shore birds feed almost altogether on small mullet, menhaden, and similar noncommercial species. Most fishermen have learned this and no longer consider the birds as competitors. Abundant food and a variety of shore conditions make the Gulf Coast a paradise for shore birds of many species. Some, such as gulls, terns, herons, and a colony of roseate spoonbills on San Antonio Bay, are permanent residents and nest here. Others, including several species of ducks, geese and the few whooping cranes that are left in the world, spend the summer in Northern states or Canada raising a family and come to the Gulf Coast in winter. To protect the birds from wanton destruction the National Audubon Society and the Fish and Wildlife Service, U.S. Department of the Interior, have established wildlife refuges at strategic points around the entire perimeter of the coast where competent wardens having police authority keep a constant eye on their feathered charges. The Texas Game and Fish Commission is also active in this work of conservation.

The gregarious habits of most waterfowl are a great aid in this task. For some reason which ornithologists have not yet fathomed they will select an island, apparently no different from a score of others in the same region, and decide to establish thereon an avian metropolis. Such places are South Bird Island, a few miles south of Corpus Christi, and Lydia Ann Island, a few miles north, where Warden Vernon N. Johns stands guard against unwarranted intrusion. The southernmost refuge is the Fish and Wildlife Reservation at Laguna Atacosa, twenty miles north of the mouth of the Rio Grande.

Every warden of more than a few seasons' experience can tell unhappy stories of refuges invaded by wanton killers who break eggs, shoot or club birds, and seem to enjoy senseless destruction. Such a raid may result in the birds abandoning the entire nesting site, and perhaps the extinction of the colony. Too often the offenders are "sportsmen" whose idea of sport is to shoot anything that runs or flies. Percentage-wise these persons are few. Those who are arrested are haled into the nearest Federal court where the judge looks them over with an unsympathetic eye, and the local press makes news of the resultant fine or jail sentence.

During the fall duck shooting is allowed and duck blinds dot the coastal marshes in many places. In summertime these are usually occupied by a pair of nesting herons. It is the nesting grounds that the conservationists are particularly anxious to protect, and for this reason the program has the support of genuine sportsmen.

Turning basin of Houston's famous ship channel

V. *The Burgeoning Coast*

Noʀᴛʜ of Corpus Christi the Gulf Coast begins its
gentle swing to the east, indented by several large bays of irregular
outline—Corpus Christi Bay, Aransas Bay, Copano Bay, San Antonio
Bay, Matagorda Bay and Galveston Bay. Except for the latter two
these bays connect with one another and are the route of the Intracoastal Waterway. Long sandy peninsulas or islands, such as Padre,
separate them from the Gulf.

Federal Highways 77 and 59 are the most traveled routes between
Corpus Christi and Houston, two hundred miles up the coast, but
State Route 35 stays closer to the shore, leaving it only to cross the
peninsulas between the several bays. It passes through a region of
rapid industrial development, not only affecting south Texas, but
also indicating a shift in the national economy. The reason is to be
found in easy access to raw materials such as sulphur, salt and
aluminum-bearing ores, cheap fuels in natural gas and oils (also

the source of a weird array of new chemical compounds), cheap water-borne transportation, and a salubrious climate.

Approaching the town of Aransas Pass, twenty-five miles from Corpus Christi, one sees in the distance on the right the great aluminum plant of the Reynolds Metals Company. It is incongruous to look across wide acres of cotton where Negroes are harvesting the crop and see in the background what looks like a large slice of Pittsburgh, where aluminum foil is being turned out by the acre. Less than an hour's drive brings into view the still larger smelter plant of the Aluminum Company of America. A little farther on are the even more stupendous plants of the Dow Chemical Company in the vicinity of Bay City and Freeport. The aluminum companies get bauxite, from which aluminum is extracted, from Jamaica by ship or from mines in Arkansas by barge. Rumor is rife that General Motors is planning to erect a plant somewhere along the coast to manufacture the aluminum parts used in its cars.

There is also a yarn told locally that in the early days of World War II Washington authorities were insistent that the Dow Chemical Company, never one to give much publicity to its operations, inform them how long its supply of raw materials would last. After considerable delay, runs the story, the government busybodies were told that so long as the Atlantic Ocean kept the Gulf of Mexico full and so long as the Gulf waters washed the shores of Texas, so long would the company have a supply of raw material. It is not, however, as simple as that. While the company does extract chemicals from sea water it also uses many other sources in the manufacture of its myriad products.

The aforementioned industries are only a part of those that dot the flat countryside from Corpus Christi to the Houston-Galveston area. Oil refineries and many smaller installations are also in the picture. So much so that some residents say that in another generation this will be an industrial region second to none in the United States.

"The great problem of industry here, as almost everywhere, is water," said Cary Smith, editor of the Bay City *Tribune*. "The

Colorado, the Brazos, the Navidad, and other streams large and small bring down water to the Gulf, but greater demands are continually being made on them and their waters are being impounded by dams for use in the big plants. Already the water table has been perceptibly lowered in some places and we are getting worried. Rice is an important crop around here and it cannot be grown without irrigation. It would be tragic for industry to come in at the expense of the land."

The landscape along Route 35 is as flat as a tabletop but along its two hundred miles and more it offers a variety of interest. Leaving Aransas Pass (named by the Spaniards in honor of Our Lady of Aranzazu) the road is bordered by wind-and-sand-tortured live oaks. Then it enters a fertile area with wide fields of cotton and milo on the left and narrow Aransas Bay on the right. Abruptly the rich soil is left behind and mesquite and prickly pear stretch to the horizon, to be succeeded in turn by wide reaches of salt marsh. A long causeway crosses the waters between Aransas Bay and Copano Bay. Beyond it the road runs through rich pasturelands where red Herefords and white Brahmans stand knee-deep in grass. Then come hundreds of acres of milo fields. This is the big ranch established by Tom O'Connor, one of a number of Irish immigrants who came to this part of the Texas coast in the early 1830's and did much to develop it. It was another Tom O'Connor of the same family who gave the King Ranch a half-Brahman bull that figured in the development of the Santa Gertrudis breed.

Riding along the shore of Aransas Bay one can see across its waters the low outline of St. Joseph's Island. No highway connects it to the mainland, for it is the private estate and game preserve of "Sid" Richardson, colorful and wealthy Texas tycoon, who with his fellow Texan, "Clint" (Clinton W.) Murchison, was very much in the public eye a few years ago because of their part in helping their good friend, Robert Young, get control of the New York Central Railroad.

At Port Lavaca on Matagorda Bay a narrow road leads down the bay shore to the little village of Indianola, which is marked in

Texas history as the spot where a group of German colonists landed
December 11, 1844. They had come direct from Bremen and were
under the direction of "The Society for the Protection of German
Immigrants." This society had been formed by twenty noblemen in
the interests of the peasantry, then much afflicted by taxes and
military service. Prince Carl of Solms-Braunfels, commissioner general of the society, had preceded the immigrants and arranged for
them to settle along the Guadalupe River. Others followed the first
arrivals and this colony had considerable influence on the early
development of Texas.

Bay City, seat of Matagorda County, is an old town with wide-
spreading live oaks festooned with moss suggesting South Carolina
or Georgia. Its newspaper, the Bay City *Tribune,* celebrated its
hundredth birthday in 1945. Twenty-one miles south of it is the
little town of Matagorda, one of the earliest settlements of the
region, but prosperity has passed it by. Near by some maps will
show the little village of Gulf, now referred to as "Old Gulf." There
is little to mark this site that was once the greatest sulphur-producing
point along the coast. Sulphur is obtained by sinking a well four to
six hundred feet, melting it with a jet of live steam, and forcing it
to the surface in liquid form with compressed air. When the deposits at Gulf were exhausted the producers found another supply
thirty miles to the north and established the town of New Gulf,
where sulphur is now being produced.

Freeport, unlike most towns on the Texas coast, is not situated
on a bay but faces the Gulf from the right bank of the Brazos River.
It is a shipping point of considerable importance and here the Dow
Chemical Company has its own docks, besides which there is a
public dock that has recently been enlarged. Sulphur plays an
important part in its economy, as do cattle and grains, but the Dow
Company is its "sugar daddy."

Between Freeport and Galveston, forty miles northeast, there is
no settlement on the coast. Houston, "The Oil Capital of the World,"
is fifty-eight miles north of Freeport and its principal trading center.

VI. *Houston*

Cɪᴛɪᴇs have personalities much as do individuals. New Orleans and San Francisco are not like Chicago or Kansas City; Boston and Philadelphia are yet another type. Houston, Texas, is in a category by itself and has changed so much in the last few decades that it is hard to catalogue.

Some wag has said that "Houston is not a wine and violin town. It is a whisky and trombone town." That is true only in part. It has been called "The Chicago of the South," which also is partly true. The *Texas Almanac*, published by the Dallas *Morning News*, says Houston is "Texas' most populous city, with 52.5 percent increase, 1940 to 1950; first city in the South." Such a city must "have something" and Houston has several things. The greatest of its several assets, however, has been the character of the men who have organized and directed its destinies during the present century. Its metropolitan population in 1900 was 44,633. Today the figure is well over a million.

"A list of men who have contributed most to Houston's development would include several who have also won distinction in national and international fields," said Roderick J. Watts, managing editor of the Houston *Chronicle*. "Other cities have produced men of great ability and wealth, but what distinguished this group was the way they worked together for whatever was best for Houston. This does not mean that they did not have their disagreements. Sometimes there were wide differences of opinion and loud arguments, but when the chips were down there had evolved a program on which they could all unite.

"Foremost in this group was the late Jesse H. Jones, known generally as 'Mr. Houston' and probably Texas' greatest citizen since General Sam Houston. He envisioned the development of the Houston Ship Channel and was the first chairman of the Houston Harbor Board which brought deep water fifty miles inland to Houston. Mr. Jones was foremost in movements to bring new enterprises to the Gulf Coast; as a philanthropist he provided scholarships for hundreds of students in more than fifty colleges and universities, and he contributed generously to civic projects.

"There was William Marsh Rice, who founded and endowed Rice Institute, one of the finest seats of higher learning in this country. George Hermann, a poor Swiss immigrant, came to Houston, accumulated a fortune, and on his death left it all to the city. His name is perpetuated in Hermann Park, Hermann Hospital and Martha Hermann Square. M. D. Anderson, of Anderson, Clayton &

Company, the world's largest cotton firm, left a fortune of $25 million to the Anderson Foundation for health and education, a sum that has since grown to $40 million. His partner, W. L. Clayton, spared neither time nor money in developing Houston into a world trade center.

"Hugh Roy Cullen, oil man and philanthropist, benefactor of the University of Houston, established a foundation that has been given $160 million for worthy projects. Any list of Houston's first citizens should also include George W. Strake, oilman and Catholic lay leader; J. S. Abercrombie, George and Herman Brown, Judge J. A. Elkins, and certainly Oscar F. Holcombe, now serving his eleventh two-year term as mayor, who has guided the city during the period of its greatest growth."

One incident will illustrate the spirit of Houstonians. In 1900 when the city was little more than a "cowtown" the Federal government approved a project to dredge a twenty-five-foot channel from downtown Houston to Galveston Bay. As is wont in government operations this work dragged along for ten years and was still far from completion. So a committee of businessmen went to Washington in 1910 and told the powers there that if Uncle Sam would get on with the work Houston would pay half of the balance needed. This was such an unheard-of procedure that it almost called for a Senate investigation, but the offer was accepted and the channel was completed in 1914. In August, 1915, the port of Houston was officially opened, and the SS *Santilla* arrived as the first large ocean-going vessel to dock in the turning basin inside the corporate limits of the city.

Houston was "born" the same year as the Republic of Texas and near the same spot. Hostilities in Texas' fight for freedom from Mexico began in October, 1835, and ended at the Battle of San Jacinto April 21, 1836, when General Sam Houston commanding seven hundred Texans attacked General Santa Anna, President of Mexico, routed his army of fifteen hundred and took the general prisoner.

The smoke had hardly cleared from the battleground when two enterprising real estate men from New York, Augustus C. Allen and John K. Allen, concluded that a site on Buffalo Bayou, eighteen miles from the scene of the battle, would be a good place for a town. They bought up a quantity of land for a dollar an acre, named the town Houston for the popular hero, and started the same kind of promotional ballyhoo that had lured them to Texas from New York in 1832.

The name of the new settlement and its location near the famous battlefield, along with some pressure from the Allens, induced the Texas legislature to make Houston the first capital of the new republic. The town prospered despite inflated currency, recurring yellow fever epidemics, and the ills common to all frontier ventures. The place was officially incorporated in 1837 and in the first municipal election James S. Holman, with twelve votes, became Houston's first mayor. His opponents, Francis R. Lubbock and Thomas W. Ward, received eleven and ten votes respectively.

Two years later, amid loud cries of pain from the Gulf Coast, the state capital was moved to Austin, but Houston continued to grow steadily and in 1840 the city's Chamber of Commerce was incorporated, making it one of the oldest organizations of its kind in the United States. Texas entered the Union in 1845 and moved out again on March 3, 1861, when the state legislature ratified the constitution of the Confederacy, and the Stars and Bars became the sixth flag to fly over this part of the Gulf Coast. It had been preceded by the flags of France, Spain, Mexico, the Republic of Texas and the United States. The Confederate colors remained over Houston until June 19, 1865, when General Gordon Granger of the Union Army landed at Galveston and proclaimed the freedom of all slaves in Texas. The Negroes of the Houston area still celebrate "Juneteenth" as the anniversary of their liberty.

In the early days of reconstruction Houston suffered with the rest of the South from the chaos of carpetbaggers, Ku Klux Klan, and disrupted trade. An even more bitter blow fell in 1867 when the city had the worst yellow fever epidemic in its history. When reconstruction ended in 1874 Houston received a new charter and the city began to creep out over the surrounding plain of Harris County. Railroads were stretching their lines across the prairies and winter vegetables were shipped from the area to Chicago, Denver, St. Louis and other cities of the North. Ex-President Grant came down to open a new Union Railroad Station in 1880 amid great acclaim, and reconstruction was complete. A few years later Edwin Booth played *Hamlet* to a packed house in Pillot's Opera House.

No one knew it at the time, but Santa Claus was soon to come down the chimney with the greatest gift in all the hectic history of Houston. Perhaps it should be said he was about to come *up* the chimney.

Over in Jefferson County in the little town of Beaumont, eighty-seven miles east and north of Houston, a persistent young man named Pattillo Higgins had the crazy notion that oil could be found under a slight elevation in the prairie called "Spindletop," distinguished only by foul water and bubbles of escaping gas. The "experts," who in the future were to be confounded on several occasions, looked over the ground and shook their heads. John Archbold, who with John D. Rockefeller was making millions out of Pennsylvania oil, is reported to have said he would drink all the oil found west of the Mississippi.

Higgins persisted with his singular idea, and with assurances of great wealth to follow persuaded three of his friends to help him finance a well in 1892. The number three seemed bad luck. They sank three wells, found no oil, and gave the promoter the brush-off. Finding no more local support Higgins advertised in Eastern papers and thus interested an Austrian immigrant, Captain Anthony Lucas, who had a little money. They drilled again and on January 10, 1901, a gusher of oil blew the top off the derrick. Ironically it was called the Lucas gusher. Higgins had to sue for his share of the profits and though he spent the rest of his life in the oil business he never made a fortune from it. But he did receive from the citizens of

Beaumont a testimonial giving him full credit for his discovery. He died in June, 1955, at the ripe age of ninety-two.

"The discovery of oil on January 10, 1901, at Spindletop whirled Texas into one of the most exciting and glamorous periods of its entire history," says a Houston Chamber of Commerce publication, "and destined Houston to become one of the great ports and industrial cities of the world. On November 6, 1904, the 'Moonshine' well near Humble, was brought in, opening Harris County's first big oil field and the wave of oil development swept throughout the area. The year before Harris had become the wealthiest county in the state, its commerce largely based on agriculture. The coming of 'black gold' brought new industries, new money and new expansion to the fast-moving city on the bayou."

Today there are more than four thousand "oil fields" in Texas. The term needs clarification. It has nothing in common with a "cornfield," and is not a matter of acreage. All oil development and production in the state is strictly controlled by the Texas Railroad Commission and is also subject to Federal controls. Officially an oil "field" is a single deposit or pool, referred to by oil men as a "horizontal." The first well to be drilled in a new field is allowed a larger production quota than later wells in the same field as an encouragement for new explorations. Fields that have an actual or ultimate recovery of one hundred million barrels of crude oil are known as "major fields," of which Texas has forty-eight.

The rapid development of drilling that followed the Spindletop discovery brought chaos and the wasting of many millions of barrels of crude oil. Except for tank cars there was no means of transporting it to Northern and Eastern markets. Local industry began using oil instead of coal for power and often got it for a fraction of a cent per barrel. Automobiles were regarded as a rich man's toy to be stored away in the winter and road maps were still in the future, so there was only a limited market for gasoline. The industry was to suffer from this overproduction for a long time. When the East Texas field was brought in, October, 1930 (again where geologists said there was no oil), there was a great hassle which culminated in Governor Ross S. Sterling ordering out the National Guard and stopping all oil production in that area. Out of that grew a proration program that is now in force throughout the state.

Along with the production of oil came natural gas, at first regarded as a nuisance. Until the middle twenties it was only used locally, but later in that decade pipe lines began to carry it to Northern markets. Today Texas natural gas is piped to every major section of the country except New England and the Pacific Coast. Being very "rich" in heating units it is often mixed with manufactured gas for consumers in large cities.

Most natural gas is recovered from oil-producing wells where it was once burned to get rid of it. Today this is no longer permitted and every such well must be equipped to conserve its gas. There are also wells that produce only gas. Before the gas is put through the big pipe lines for the North it is processed to remove valuable by-products, many of which would lessen its value as a fuel. A big industry has also been built up from "sour gas," a gas so impregnated with sulphur and other elements that it is unadaptable as a fuel. This, by one of several processes, is converted into carbon black and sent to manufacturing plants by carload and shipload. It is extensively used in the manufacture of rubber, paints and a wide variety of products.

"The Age of Plastics" might be a general term for a new type of development that hit Houston about 1940. In the next ten years its population more than doubled, due largely to the great demand for unpronounceable chemical products used in the manufacture of everything from false teeth to automobiles. These products have opened new and apparently unlimited products for derivatives of petroleum and natural gas, of which the Houston area has an abundance. The Texas National Bank of Houston has put out an attractive brochure for its big-time customers listing "Manufacturers of Chemicals" and "Chemicals Manufactured" in the Texas Gulf Coast area. The roster contains the names of one hundred manufacturing firms, sixteen of which have their home offices in New York City, with Chicago, Philadelphia, Pittsburgh, Cleveland and even San Francisco being represented. The list of organic chemicals begins with "acetaldehyde" and 190 items later winds up with "zinc dimethyldithiocarbamate." Thirty-two inorganic chemicals are added as a sort of afterthought.

Harris County, with Houston near its southern border, contains more people and more cattle than any other of the 254 counties in the state. It ranks thirteenth in area and contains 1,730 square miles, which provides room for a lot of cows. The census bureau divides its population into 90.5 per cent urban, 8.8 per cent nonfarm rural, and 1.2 per cent farm rural, with 178 acres as the size of the average farm. The story they tell in Houston is that folks in the money—and there are a lot of them—have become very enthusiastic about owning a fine herd of Jerseys, Herefords, Santa Gertrudis or other breeds, and with a piece of ground that may be ten acres in extent or maybe as much as two hundred acres, have gone into the cattle-raising business. If the venture shows a loss at the beginning a lot of it can be written off, come income tax time, and in the meanwhile the nucleus of a very fine herd is formed.

With characteristic energy Houston has developed the entertainment of conventions into big business, and more than a million badge-wearing delegates flock to it every year. It claims "more air-conditioned convention accommodations than any comparable city," with six thousand downtown hotel rooms and twelve hundred motel rooms near by. The largest hostelry is the Rice Hotel with a thousand rooms and dining rooms where twelve hundred guests can be served at a single sitting.

Five miles south of downtown Houston is the Texas Medical Center, covering 160 acres, probably the most complete installation of its kind in the country. Long discussed as a possibility, the Center began to develop in 1941 when the state legislature authorized the establishment here of a cancer hospital as a branch of the University of Texas. Baylor University moved its college of medicine here from

Dallas in 1943 and the Center now includes five hospitals, in addition to several clinics and training schools for nurses and doctors. Its affairs are administered by the Texas Medical Center, Inc., which was "formed exclusively for benevolent, charitable and educational purposes."

Rice Institute, founded by the late William M. Rice in 1912, is Texas' largest private educational institution not church connected. It is unique in that its student body is limited to fifteen hundred and only scholarship students or those passing competitive examinations are admitted. This and its carefully chosen faculty give some justification for Houstonians calling it "The Harvard of the South." Its principal courses are the liberal arts and engineering, with a recent accent on nuclear physics.

Like other cities Houston has a traffic problem, but is developing a series of "freeways" to alleviate it. One section already reaches from the center of the city southward, six lanes wide and leaping over cross streets, connecting with the high-speed route to Galveston. Construction of a "belt line" to detour through traffic around the city has started, and radiating freeways from the center of the city will connect with it.

Such is the Houston of today—rich without snobbishness, sophisticated without smugness, and as friendly as an overgrown pup. But now and then a bit of the old "cowtown" background crops out. Recently two of its citizens engaged in a gun duel in the streets but time had dulled their aim and though one was wounded neither was killed. They were promptly arrested but it developed that the one who was the better shot could not be prosecuted unless his opponent would file charges against him. This the wounded man with true Western spirit refused to do. Each could be held for a misdemeanor, but as such a charge carried no prison sentence it seemed inadequate. So both were turned loose by the thoroughly disgusted police.

(*Houston* Chronicle)

VII. *Galveston*

Eᴄᴇᴘᴛ for Key West at the tip of the Florida Keys, Galveston is the only city on the Gulf Coast that is open to the sea and not sheltered on the shore of a bay. It sits on the eastern end of an island thirty miles long which for the most part is an undeveloped sandy waste. Within its environs is small triangular Pelican Island to the east, just across Galveston channel, along both sides of which are wharves and shipyards.

A fine four-lane divided freeway leads out of Houston to Galveston, fifty-two miles southeastward, arching over crossroads that lead to Alvin, Alta Loma and Hitchcock a few miles to the west, and

Dickinson and the busy port of Texas City on Galveston Bay to the east. The flatness of the land is relieved only by scattered oil derricks and tree-bordered bayous. Galveston County is only one-fourth the size of Harris County, but it has more than twenty-thousand acres under irrigation by wells where rice and winter vegetables are grown.

At the southern end of the mainland the highway crosses a coastal marsh and enters Galveston over a two-mile causeway spanning a narrow arm of Galveston Bay. This bay is the deepest indentation along the Texas coast, stretching a long arm fifty miles to the north where it receives the waters of Trinity River. The narrow arm that separates Galveston Island from the mainland is West Bay. These waters divide Galveston County into three parts: the mainland, the island, and a thirty-mile-long peninsula to the east separated from the mainland by East Bay. On the western end of this peninsula, opposite Galveston, is the old settlement of Bolivar Point, and the ship channel from the bay to the open Gulf lies between them.

The traveler who comes to Galveston by way of Corpus Christi and Houston is in for a surprise. Here is none of the stir or sense of urgency characteristic of most Texas cities. There is less traffic on the streets and the pace is slower. Latins, so evident in Corpus Christi and scarcely less so in Houston, are seldom seen here, but there are more Negroes. The causeway leads into Broadway, a tree-bordered boulevard that continues across the island to the beach and is the city's principal north-south thoroughfare. Here and there, sedate and aloof, stands a fine old residence but its architecture is suggestive of McKinley's administration, and most dwellings are cubelike, two-story frame buildings with the inevitable "gallery" (porch or veranda, depending on where you are from) on the first floor and usually another at the second level.

The somberness is relieved by the tall, flourishing oleanders that grow in every yard and line every street, their profuse blossoms of white, pink, red and intermediate shades giving color to the city the greater part of the year. Local horticulturists have catalogued sixty varieties of this blossom, which was first brought to Galveston on a trading schooner in 1841.

The shopping center of Galveston, its banks, and most of its business offices are contained in a section not more than seven blocks each way. Modern structures like the W. L. Moody Bank, the American National Insurance Company Building, or the Jean Laffite Hotel bear a smart and modern appearance, but most of the business buildings like most of the residences seem old and tired. Along Rosenberg Street, a wide thoroughfare that marks the northern boundary of the business area, three buildings several blocks apart cast their shadows over older and humbler dwellings. They are the large yellow brick courthouse, a beautiful six-story post office, and a gleaming eight-story Union Depot that harbors the offices of the Gulf, Colorado & Santa Fe and other railroads. Across Twenty-sixth Street immediately behind the imposing post office is one of the most unsightly Negro slums to be found in all Texas.

Yet there is money in Galveston—lots of it. They tell you proudly at the Chamber of Commerce that it is the world's greatest shipping point for sulphur, "leads the nation in the export of cotton, and is among the top-ranking ports in the export of grain and other commodities." Houston has a greater over-all tonnage, but Galvestonians say that were it not for Houston's large export of petroleum products it would rank second to Galveston. Within half an hour after casting loose from a Galveston pier a cargo vessel may pass Bolivar Point and be in the open Gulf. But it takes a day and a half to negotiate the narrow channel between that point and the port of Houston.

The most beautiful thing in Galveston other than its oleanders is a wide, gently sloping beach where the long rollers from the Gulf of Mexico curl and break into foam against the tawny sand. It makes the island one of the most popular resorts in the South, winter and summer, for vacationers from Houston to the Canadian border and beyond. The beach lies at the foot of a massive sea wall, more than eight miles long and four feet above the highest tide ever recorded, erected following the hurricane of 1900 at a cost exceeding nine million dollars. A wide roadway and ample parking space skirt the top of the wall, while between its footing and the water vacationers have plenty of space to loll under beach umbrellas or stretch on the sand and get a fashionable tan. Hotels and motels, adequate but not elaborate, provide housing for the classes and the masses. The largest of these, the Galvez, was rebuilt following the hurricane and has long been a landmark.

The story of modern Galveston begins in 1836 but the island has a colorful past that reaches back to the earliest days of the European

Isle Pier dominates one of the loveliest bathing beaches in Texas

(*Houston* Chronicle)

in North America. It has been well established that the first of these
to leave his footprints on its sands was the Spanish explorer,
Alvar Nuñez Cabeza de Vaca, who, with a few companions, was
shipwrecked here in 1528 while trying to get to Mexico after disaster had overtaken the expedition in Florida. In the narrative of his
adventures he called the island "Mal Hado," the island of ill fate.
A century and a half later Ferdinand de La Salle, French nobleman
and one of the greatest explorers of all time, landed here while trying to find the mouth of the Mississippi, and went inland to meet
his death by treachery on the banks of the Trinity River. Almost
another century passed and this time the Spaniards were back. Don
Bernardo de Galvez, Spanish governor of Louisiana and later viceroy
of Mexico, landed on the island and named it for himself.

Though the island was named for Señor Galvez its history is more
closely associated with the career of the freebooter and privateer,
Jean Laffite, the courageous and colorful character who was never
quite inside the law and never quite outside it. Says Stanley Clisby
Arthur in his remarkable biography of the man: "Countless are the
legends clustering about the name of Jean Laffite, suave buccaneer
of Barataria, but none of them for fantastic improbability equals the
cold truth of his exploits at the long sandy island named Galveston.
The actual story of what took place there has long been a secret,
as is true of many other parts of this man's checkered life." It was
Mr. Arthur who proved by signatures on old documents that the
name of this adventurer was "Laffite," and not "Lafitte," the latter
being the name of a different and numerous family in New Orleans.

The story of the Laffites centers around New Orleans and the
Galveston chapter does not begin until after Jean and his followers
had fought valiantly under General Jackson at the Battle of New
Orleans, had been pardoned for all offenses by President Madison,
and had resumed his raids of Spanish commerce. The "fantastic
improbability" of his Galveston exploits is due to the fact that while
continuing to prey on Spanish shipping and co-operating with the
Mexican revolutionists seeking independence from Spain, he was at

the same time in the pay of Don José Cienfuegos, captain general of Cuba, as an intelligence agent with a secret code number, pledged to help rid the Gulf of Mexico of the buccaneers and privateers that were looting Spanish ships! In view of the fact that the dominant passion of Jean Laffite's life, and with reason, was hatred of Spain, his role in Galveston is exciting but not surprising.

Arriving in Galveston in March of 1817, Laffite found a group of revolutionists already established and was soon in command. By the end of the year his followers numbered more than a thousand, some of them motivated by patriotism, but many ready to slit any throat for a few doubloons. His orders were to attack none but Spanish ships and to kill only when opposed. It was a riotous group over which the freebooter ruled but in the main he held them in check and established an orderly town which he called Campeche. On more than one occasion a blood-letting follower was hanged for disobedience of orders, and once when a U.S. Navy vessel called to demand the surrender of a man who had looted a plantation, Laffite showed the commander the man's body already swinging from a tree.

The United States would have broken up the raiders of Galveston earlier but for the interference of the Spanish minister in Washington who protested that the land west of the Nueces River belonged to Spain. But eventually the commerce of the Gulf became so demoralized that Washington determined to act. Early in January, 1821, Lieutenant Lawrence Kearny, USN, commanding the brig *Enterprise,* called on Laffite at Galveston and told him that at the end of sixty days all the men, ships and goods must be off the island or the place would be bombarded. Laffite, who never opposed the United States government, said he would comply. The following March Lieutenant Kearny returned. Laffite entertained him and the officers of the *Enterprise* with all courtesy. Then in their presence he put the torch to his own house, the "Maison Rouge," and sailed away from the burning village, exchanging salutes with Lieutenant Kearny.

Sailed away—to where?

For a century and a quarter it was a mystery. Historians usually said he disappeared into Central America and died there a short time later. But he was to live for thirty-five years more and die far from the tropics. We must wait until we get to New Orleans to learn the truth.

Galveston Island remained deserted until 1830 when the Mexican government established a customshouse there, but it did very little business. No one else arrived until a group of refugees sought shelter there in April, 1836, prior to the Battle of San Jacinto. One of these was Gail Borden, who had been a pioneer farmer and surveyor in Texas for ten years. Following the defeat of Mexico and the organization of the Republic of Texas, Colonel M. B. Menard established his claim to "a league and a labor of land" (4,587 acres) on Galveston Island and with nine associates formed the Galveston City Company in 1841, a corporation that was not liquidated until 1944. Sam Houston, the first president of Texas, appointed Gail Borden the first collector of the port at Galveston, and it was while living there that he began to experiment with methods of preserving milk that eventually made his fortune and gave his name to the mighty milk business that survives him.

With good cause Galveston lays claim to more than twenty-five Texas "firsts" including the Galveston Artillery Company, organized in 1841 and the state's oldest military unit; the first golf course in 1898, and the first city commission form of government in 1901. It seems the city is more interested in its past glories than in its future opportunities.

Although Galveston sustained a crippling blow when the storm of 1900 devastated it, that catastrophe hardly accounts for its failure to keep step with the expansion in population and business of towns and cities around it. Other cities including San Francisco, Chicago and Baltimore have been struck down only to recover rapidly and eclipse their former glories. A book, *Galveston in 1900*, written by William C. Chase soon after the hurricane that year, gives an account of the disaster and concludes the narrative by saying: "With no desire to add one iota to Galveston's importance as a port . . . but simply to state the truth and emphasize an undeniable fact, it is beyond all doubt that no port in the south has so brilliant a future as Galveston." The port is there, the most accessible on the Gulf, but the prophecy has not been realized.

When General Robert E. Wood, chairman of the board of Sears, Roebuck & Company, wrote an article for the *Reader's Digest,* September, 1948, on "The Gulf Coast—Our New Frontier," he named thirteen cities and towns—Houston, Brownsville, Corpus Christi, Texas City, New Orleans, Pensacola, etc.—but made no mention of Galveston, although that city was shown on the map accompanying the article.

In July, 1955, the Associated Press released a comprehensive story of a survey of twenty-eight Texas cities by its member papers. It showed the average population of that group had increased 29.2 per cent since the census of 1950. Two, Victoria and Midland, had doubled in that time. Corpus Christi had jumped from 108,053 to 155,000, or 43 per cent; Houston (metropolitan area) from 806,701 to 1,023,000, or 28.8 per cent; Orange from 21,100 to 31,000, or 47 per cent. Galveston grew from 66,568 to 71,590, which was but a fraction more than 7.5 per cent.

Galveston is "The City That Might Have Been." In addition to its fine port it is served by six railroad lines. Natural gas and oil are at its doorsteps; rice and green pastures can be seen from atop its moderately high buildings. It has six banks, and the bank clearings approximate $345 million a year. Yet a sense of apathy seems to hang over the place. Why?

The answer is not to be found in books or statistics, but a brief interview with almost any well-informed citizen within a radius of 150 miles will give a clue. Bluntly it is this: For two generations or more Galveston has been controlled by a group of wealthy men who did not welcome competition. Their slogan might have been, "What's in it for me?" Outside capital does not like such a setup.

Big business in the city is the export of cotton, grains, sugar and sulphur; the waterfront is controlled by the Galveston Wharf Company, and there is scant room for a newcomer or the enterprising young-man-on-the-make unless he is willing to throw in with the powers that be. It is natural that businessmen of the Texas coastal region are reluctant to be quoted on this situation, but off the record they will make the foregoing observations sound like understatements.

"I have talked to cotton men, not just one but several," said one. "They have told me they would prefer to ship their cotton from Galveston, as it is their logical port. But unless they meet the terms of the men in control there they are out in the cold. Consequently many of them take their business to Houston instead."

The death of William Lewis Moody, Jr., at the age of eighty-nine was duly noted in the August 2, 1954, issue of *Time* magazine, which referred to him as "one of the U.S.'s ten richest men (estimated total assets: $400 million) . . . who controlled vast tracts of Texas land, including Galveston Island which flourished for years as the gambling mecca of the southwest, and such miscellaneous enterprises as the $364 million American National Insurance Co., 33 hotels and tourist courts, two banks, both Galveston newspapers, and eleven ranches." But the following year the July 17 issue of the Houston *Chronicle* headlined a significant omission: not one of the yearbooks issued by five of the biggest U.S. corporations mentioned the passing of this Galveston titan.

The founder of the Moody fortune, W. L. Moody, Sr., was born in Virginia in 1828, got a law degree at the University of Virginia, and came to Galveston shortly after the Civil War. A *History of Galveston, Texas* in the Rosenberg Library in Galveston tells of the activities of some of the city's early financial organizers with remarkable candor, considering that its publication must have been approved by their successors. Its flyleaf contains the notation: "By S. C. Griffin, A. H. Cawston, managing editor and publisher. Published in Galveston, 1931." Its first 106 pages are labeled "Narrative."

The remaining 277 pages are "Biography" and contain some of the stickiest laudatory personal sketches to be found in print. The "Narrative" includes the revealing story of the Gulf, Colorado & Santa Fe Railway, among whose early directors was W. L. Moody, Sr., wherein Galveston County was first permitted to subscribe $500,000 in bonds to aid the project. When the money ran out before the road's completion the county was induced to sell its stock to the railroad's reorganizers, again including Mr. Moody, for only ten thousand dollars. In addition "the company received generous land grants from the state, amounting to 10,240 acres for every mile of road constructed, a grant that eventually included 3,259,520 acres of land."·

Construction was resumed and the reorganized railroad was. completed, hooking up with the 'Frisco railroad at Paris, Texas, and the Atchison, Topeka & Santa Fe at Purcell, Oklahoma. Now the road had connection with two of the country's largest systems, the promoters had three and quarter million acres of land, and the "Narrative" boasts that the road has never been in the hands of a receiver. Business boomed, freight piled up on the wharves, the Moody fortune was on its way to the four hundred million mark—and Galveston County had ten thousand dollars!

The saga of the Gulf, Colorado & Santa Fe may help explain why Galveston is "The City That Might Have Been." Such a beginning is not encouraging to independent investors, and there is no indication that the situation has changed very much.

VIII. *Disasters*

EтснED deeply into the history of Galveston County are two of the worst disasters ever visited on a community in the United States. One was truly "an act of God"; the other can be charged only to governmental stupidity. The first was the Galveston hurricane of September 8, 1900, that took a toll of not less than 5,000 lives and possibly as many as 7,000. The second was the explosion of a shipload of ammonium nitrate fertilizer in Texas City Harbor, April 16, 1947, killing 576 persons and maiming or burning at least 4,000.

The story of hurricane destruction along the Southern coasts is as old as their history, but only as communities were established and properties improved did the loss of lives and values begin to appear in statistics. The Texas coast does not lie as directly in the path of these storms as does south Florida, but enough of them blew through that region in the 1800's to acquaint the population with the need for taking them seriously. A storm is not a hurricane until its winds reach a velocity of seventy-five miles an hour, and the winds of most recorded hurricanes do not exceed one hundred miles an hour, which is a lot of wind. Within this range there may be a considerable difference in storms. Some are accompanied by terrific downpours of rain, others will have so few clouds that sun or moon will occasionally beam down on the havoc the wind is wreaking. A large hurricane may be a whirling mass of air four hundred miles in diameter and not necessarily violent as hurricanes go. A smaller one may have half that diameter and be more destructive within its range. Always within its center is the "eye," a place of dead calm where barometers have recorded the lowest pressures known to meteorologists.

As a hurricane moves over the face of ocean or gulf it may create a gigantic wave, so that in striking the shore the water will create more havoc than the wind. That is what happened in Galveston and that is why the city has constructed a mighty sea wall, so that if the situation is repeated the force of the water will be broken.

On September 4, 1900, the United States Weather Bureau learned that a tropical storm was building up in the Caribbean and the southern waters of the Gulf of Mexico, and so notified the cities and towns along the coast. Lacking present facilities of airplane and radar the bureau could not predict its course as accurately as could be done today, but the warnings were repeated on the fifth, sixth and seventh.

Saturday morning, the eighth, the wind was from the north at Galveston but as the day wore on it shifted to the east and rapidly increased in violence. This began to pile the surf on the beaches and some of those in seaside cottages started leaving them and seeking a haven with friends more securely situated. Still there was no panic and not much apprehension. The city had seen high water before in 1875 and again in 1886. The last train to reach the island arrived at 2:10 P.M. after experiencing great difficulty in crossing the two-mile wooden bridge over the bay because the water covered the tracks. A little later vessels which had broken loose from their moorings smashed through the railway and highway bridges across the bay, carrying away the telegraph and telephone lines to the mainland, and the city was isolated.

The census of 1900 had credited Galveston with a population of 37,789, all packed together at the eastern end of a thirty-mile island. Of these one in six was never to see another sunrise.

By four o'clock the rising wind and raging seas were battering down the buildings along the shoreline, and hurling their timbers like great battering rams against the buildings farther up the beach. Before the people could realize what was happening disaster was overwhelming them. Many who had scorned to seek safety now braved the turbulent waters too late, only to be swept away like May flies in a mill race. Too often it made little difference, for in hundreds of instances a house that had seemed higher and stronger than others and had been sought out by neighbors, yielded at last to the terrible onslaught of sea and wind and its scores of refugees were engulfed in the maelstrom.

Only in the central part of the city and in the industrial area where many of the structures were of brick or stone was there an opportunity to outlive the storm. In the little two-story brick Union Station at the foot of Twenty-second Street a group of forty of fifty persons, mostly strangers to each other, became acquainted through the terrible intimacy of death. Driven from the first floor by the invading waters they huddled through the night on the second floor of the quivering structure. There was nothing they could do but wait. And while they waited they sang:

> Jesus, Lover of my soul,
>   Let me to Thy bosom fly,
> While the nearer waters roll,
>   While the tempest still is high.

The force of the storm began to break in the windows, so the men braced them with papers held in place by pieces of furniture or by straining hands. There was no panic. An old man sat in a corner holding a barometer, shaking his head as the indicator dropped lower and lower.

Out over the city and along the flat shores of the mainland someone was dying every second. Survivors were to tell later that after a building had collapsed, and they had found temporary haven on a floating piece of wreckage, their greatest danger was from the flying debris that hurled scores back into the water or battered them to pieces.

> Hide me, O my Savior, hide,
> 'Til the storm of life is past,
> Safe into the haven guide,
> O receive my soul at last.

A hurricane does not blow with a steady force. There is no other wind like it. The voice of the storm will drop to a sobbing moan, and straining ears hope that the worst has passed. Then with redoubled force the screaming air will rise to a shrill crescendo, and when nerves seem to have reached the limit of what can be endured a greater gust will bring new tortures. Even the most unimaginative will begin to feel that the storm is a malignant, living Thing. There is nothing that can be done, once the storm has struck. To venture out into it is to court death. And it is difficult to endure in silence, so the little group in the depot raised their voices in familiar hymns:

> Other refuge have I none,
> Hangs my helpless soul on Thee.
> Leave, oh leave me not alone,
> Still support and comfort me.

In the files of the U.S. Weather Bureau there is a remarkable report. It is that of Isaac M. Cline, local forecast official, written a few days after the storm. The report begins with a simple recital of barometric pressures, wind directions and velocities preceding the disaster. It tells of the early violence of the hurricane when the recording instruments were blown away, and continues:

At 8:30 P.M. my residence went down with about fifty persons who had sought it for safety, and all but eighteen were hurled into Eternity.

Among the lost was my wife, who never rose above the water after the wreck of the building. I was nearly drowned and became unconscious, but recovered though being crushed by timbers, and found myself clinging to my youngest child who had gone down with myself and wife. Mr. J. L. Cline joined me five minutes later with my other two children, and with them and a woman and child we picked up from the raging waters we drifted for three hours, landing 300 yards from where we started.

In the Union Station the old man's barometer registered 27.90 at 10:00 P.M. Questioned, he answered simply: "I think we are lost."

> All my hope on Thee is stayed,
> All my help from Thee I bring;
> Cover my defenseless head
> With the shadow of Thy wing.

But the storm was defeating itself. Along the Gulf shore 1,500 acres had been swept clean of the 2,636 buildings they had contained. Much of the wreckage was piled in a miles-long windrow, twenty-five feet high in some places, and this began to serve as a bulwark against further destruction. During the next few days three thousand bodies were to be taken from this mass of debris. Soon after midnight the wind began to abate and although the water remained turbulent it began to recede. The old man watching his barometer was at last rewarded. The needle trembled, stood still, and started to climb. "It's over! It's over!" he shouted.

By sunup the wind had dropped to twenty miles an hour. The first persons to venture forth estimated there must be five hundred dead. Three men left Galveston at eleven o'clock Sunday morning to tell the rest of the world what had happened and to get relief for the survivors. They found a small, damaged twenty-foot steam launch and managed to get it working well enough to get them across the rough waters of Galveston Bay as far as Texas City. That small town was as badly hit as Galveston so they walked across the prairie to a railroad track, got possession of an old-type hand car, and pumped it fifteen miles. They reached Houston at 3:00 A.M.

Wreckage on Galveston Island after the hurricane

Monday, from which point messages were sent to President Mc-
Kinley and Governor Sayers.

The storm was over but a terrible problem faced the survivors.
The dead lay everywhere, floating in the water, lying on the beaches,
enmeshed in the wreckage. Surviving police and sheriff's deputies
hastily organized to prevent looting, and these were soon supple-
mented by National Guardsmen. Rumors flew about that seventy-
five persons had been shot while robbing the dead, but whether this
estimate is too high or too low will never be known. Certain it is
that the complete story of the disaster would reveal human nature
at its best and worst. Benumbed survivors were to tell stories of
the living raped and robbed, and the dead mutilated by vandals
and ghouls; of corpses found with fingers cut off and ear lobes split
so that finger rings or earrings might be quickly removed. Accounts
published soon after the storm said many of the looters had slipped

into the stricken city with the first relief forces, coming from places as far distant as Houston, Austin and New Orleans. There is no official record of these crimes, for those caught robbing the living or the dead were not arrested—they were shot on the spot and their bodies added to those of the innocent victims of the storm.

Accepted forms of burial were out of the question as the hot tropic sun began to hasten disintegration. Something must be done and quickly. Hundreds of bodies were loaded on barges and towed out to sea where they were weighted and sunk, but this method proved inadequate. Orders were given that the dead should be burned or buried where found and this was done, many being burned because too often a grave would fill with water before a body could be lowered into it. Some were buried in mass graves on higher ground.

Food, clothing, medical supplies and money poured in from a sympathetic nation. The last victim was found and the last bit of wreckage cleaned up. Along the shoreline of the mainland almost as far as Hitchcock, fifteen miles distant, a long row of wreckage was piled up consisting of everything imaginable—furniture, food, clothing, merchandise of all sorts, lumber, boats large and small, and here and there a gruesome reminder of the great death toll.

How many lives were lost in Galveston and vicinity? Any answer must consist in a large part of conjecture. Whole families and groups of families were wiped out. A conservative estimate is that six thousand were lost in the city, to which must be added the victims among twelve hundred truck farmers and dairymen who lived on the island west of the incorporated district, and the lives snuffed out in the scattered settlements along the coast.

Such is the record of one of the great disasters of all time, although another, almost as heartbreaking, was to occur nearly half a century later in Texas City, just across the bay.

World War II had ended. The countries in Europe that had been occupied by enemy forces were desperately in need of food, and were lacking in facilities to produce their own foodstuffs. The United

States government, moved by a generosity it was later to deny its own distressed citizens, moved to meet the emergency. It sent food and necessities of all kinds to the stricken peoples, and it sent ship-loads of fertilizer to enable them to speed their own crops.

On the morning of April 16, 1947, the French steamship *Grand-camp* was tied up at Pier O in Texas City, a town on the mainland shore of Galveston Bay, ten miles from the city of Galveston. It is strictly an industrial center, given over almost entirely to the refine-ment and shipment of petroleum products. In the ship's hold were 380 bales of cotton, 9,334 bags of shelled peanuts, and a large con-signment of balls of sisal twine picked up at other ports. There were also 2,300 tons of fertilizer in 100-pound paper bags—46,000 of them —labeled "Fertilizer, ammonium nitrate 32.5%." It was waiting to take on another 700 tons before proceeding to Europe. The am-monium nitrate had been specially treated with a mixture of petrolatum, rosin and paraffin to make it suitable for fertilizer. This had been done by the Federal government in its surplus ordnance plants, and the resultant mixture was known as "Fgan."

At Pier A, five hundred feet from the *Grandcamp,* lay the Liberty ship, *Highflyer* with 900 tons of Fgan in its hold and its turbines down for repair. At near-by Pier B another Liberty ship, the *Wilson B. Keene,* was loading flour for France. Previous to this date some 700,000 tons of Fgan had been shipped abroad without incident, which in view of what happened later was due more to good for-tune than good management.

Soon after the stevedores resumed loading the *Grandcamp* at 8:00 A.M. smoke was noticed coming from one of the holds. How the fire started will never be known. The "careless cigarette" theory was advanced but no evidence was found to support it. A quantity of waste paper and wood had been laid at the bottom of the hold to protect the cargo, and fire may have started there. Hand fire ex-tinguishers using soda ash compounds and buckets of drinking water were used on the smoldering mass but the smoke continued to increase. The ship's fire hose was brought out, but the first mate

(*Houston* Chronicle)
Texas City waterfront the day after the explosion

refused to allow it to be used lest the water harm the cargo. Instead, tarpaulins were placed over the hatches and battened down and live steam turned into the hold, creating ideal conditions for what was to follow.

Soon the hatch covers burned off or blew off and at 8:33 A.M. a fire alarm was turned in. Twenty-seven men of the Texas City Volunteer Fire Department responded and the crew was ordered off the ship. Near-by chemical plants sent their fire-fighting crews and equipment and fireboats were ordered from Galveston, in the hope that the flames could be kept from spreading.

By nine o'clock the *Grandcamp* was a roaring furnace. Nobody suspected that it was full of an explosive compound and the crowds pressed against the fire lines to watch the spectacle. Twelve minutes later the ship exploded and seconds later an even more violent explosion seemed to center in the air high above where the *Grandcamp* had been. Black smoke blotted out the sun and two airplanes were shot out of the sky like ducks. The chief of the fire department and his twenty-six men disappeared in the holocaust. Balls of burning sisal twine were scattered over a wide area, spreading the fire to the surrounding chemical plants. Some of them landed five miles away. Windows were broken in Galveston; the shock was felt in Palestine, Texas, 160 miles distant, and was recorded on the seismograph in Denver.

Within seconds the waterfront of Texas City was a scene of horror. Shattered bodies of men, women and children lay everywhere. A mother holding her baby suddenly found it lifeless. Some persons disappeared completely, no identifiable portion of them ever being found, and this was true of most of the firemen. Those who still lived looked unbelieving at the stumps of limbs that had been torn away. Frightened, screaming children ran bleeding from shattered schoolrooms. Near-by tanks of benzene, ethyl, propane and benzol were broken, their contents ignited, and many who had survived the violence of the explosion found themselves engulfed in a flaming sea. There is no point in continuing the terrible narrative. The figures tell the story: 576 dead, of whom only 398 could be identified; not less than 4,000 wounded or burned.

Army, Navy and Coast Guard detachments braved the fires that raged over a wide area, as did fire companies from Galveston, Houston and Alvin. The ship *Highflyer* was burning fiercely with the nine hundred tons of Fgan in its hold. Four tugs at great risk to their crews got lines to it and tried to tow it into the bay, but it was so badly wrecked it could not be moved. It burned for four hours and then blew up with two explosions as had the *Grandcamp*. Forewarned, the near-by dockside was deserted, but one death and twenty-four injured resulted. The explosion broke the steamship, *Wilson B. Keene*, in two and hurled the stern portion three hundred feet. For two days the inferno continued, and then the flames sullenly subsided.

Relief for the survivors was rushed from all over the country, as is usual in such crises. The American Red Cross spent $478,246.85 for emergency relief and $723,845.53 for rehabilitation, a total of $1,202,092.38.

To what extent was the United States government responsible for the Texas City disaster, and what was and is its obligation to pay for the losses? The record is clear. All the following information and quotations are from House Report No. 1386, 83rd Congress, 2nd session, under date of March 24, 1954. It is the report of the Committee on the Judiciary, a subcommittee of which went to Texas and held hearings there, after the U.S. Supreme Court in a four-to-three decision held that the case for relief was not covered by the statute

Monsanto Chemical Company's plant at Texas City, a pile of twisted steel

(*Houston* Chronicle)

under which the action was brought. That left the plaintiffs no hope except through Congressional action.

"For reasons to be stated later in the report," says the document on page one, "the committee is of the considered opinion that the United States Government is wholly responsible for the explosions and the resulting catastrophe at Texas City; that the disaster was caused by forces set in motion by the Government, completely controlled or controllable by it."

Under the subtitle, "History of Court Litigation," the report notes that actions against the Federal government were instituted under the Federal Tort Claims Act (passed in 1946) in the U.S. District Court for the Southern District of Texas. There, the judges sitting without a jury found negligence on the part of the government and rendered judgment in favor of the plaintiffs. It quotes from the District Court's decision as follows:

Record disclosed blunders, mistakes and acts of negligence, both of omission and commission, on the part of the defendant (the U.S. Government) its agents, servants and employees, in deciding to begin the manufacture of this inherently dangerous fertilizer. And from the beginning of its manufacture on down to and after the day of the Texas City disaster, it discloses such disregard and lack of care for the safety of the public and of persons manufacturing, handling, transporting, and using such fertilizer as to shock one. When all the facts in this record are considered one is not surprised by the Texas City disaster, i.e., that men and women, boys and girls, on the streets, in their places of employment, etc., were suddenly and without warning, killed, maimed or wounded, and vast property damage done.

This decision was carried to the six judges sitting as the Court of Appeals for the Fifth Circuit. These judges reversed the decision of the District Court, and the case then went before the U.S. Supreme Court. The committee report continues:

The United States Supreme Court, by a decision of 4 judges to 3, 4 being a majority since 2 judges did not sit, affirmed the decision of the Court of Appeals. . . . [It] held that the Federal Tort Claims Act did not apply to the type of governmental action involved in the Texas

City disaster litigation. . . . The Supreme Court did not go into the question of whether or not the Government was at fault; it did not hold the government free from negligence. It simply held that even if it was to assume that the Government was negligent there could still be no recovery because the courts, on account of the wording of the Torts Claims Act, were without power to grant relief.

(*Note:* This by a 4 to 3 decision!)

The particular fertilizer which blew up at Texas City had been produced at three of the Army ordnance plants reactivated by the government for the fertilizer program. It was shipped by rail, under government bills of lading, from ordnance plants in Nebraska and Iowa to the French Supply Council as consignee in Texas City. Under the subhead, "Government's Knowledge of Dangerous Characteristics of Fertilizer," the report says:

The government knew it had a good fertilizer in Fgan. It also was aware of the fact Fgan possessed certain dangerous qualities. Ammonium nitrate, the basic ingredient of the fertilizer Fgan, had a formidable reputation for treachery. Over the years it had caused, through explosion, considerable destruction of property and lives. For example, at Oppau, Germany, in 1921, 5,000 tons of ammonium nitrate, even though diluted with more stable ammonium sulphate, exploded with a loss of 586 lives, injury to 2,000 persons and the substantial wiping out of the entire town of Oppau. And in Kensington, England, in 1896, ammonium nitrate exploded while being heated in an iron retort to produce nitrous oxide for dental use, and destroyed the plant.

After summarizing the tremendous loss of life and property because of the explosion, the committee tells how it investigated the possibility that a carelessly handled match or cigarette might have caused it, adding:

The committee considers as a more reasonable explanation—one recognized by the government itself—that the coated Fgan (which generated its own heat), being hot and tightly confined in a great mass in the hold of the *Grandcamp* without proper ventilation, ignited spontaneously and exploded. As one Bureau of Mines' expert who investigated the disaster testified, these explosions were a classic example of simple factors of mass, heat, density and confinement.

Perhaps the most incredible statement in the document is found on page 12. It reads:

If additional evidence were needed to buttress the above statements as to the cause of the disaster, it need only be pointed out that part of the Fgan which was on the docks at Texas City awaiting stowage at the time of the explosions was later shipped by rail to the port of Baltimore, Md., where it was stowed aboard the steamship *Ocean Liberty* for shipment overseas. On July 28, 1947, at the port of Brest, France, that Fgan exploded and completely demolished the *Ocean Liberty*.

That might be called learning the facts of Fgan the hard way!

Thirty-nine volumes of testimony, more than 33,000 pages were taken, and with this outspoken report of its own committee at hand the Congress was in a position to act. Congressman Clark W. Thompson, of the Ninth Texas District which includes Texas City and Galveston, introduced a relief bill in the House in 1954 and a similar bill was laid before the Senate. The House bill passed but in the Senate the bill came up too late for thorough consideration and the measure it eventually passed was regarded as inadequate by its sponsors. There was no time for a conference and the measures died with the 83rd Congress.

When the 84th Congress convened in 1955 Congressman Clark started all over again and eventually a measure known as Public Law 378 was approved by the President on August 12, 1955. Its first paragraph reads: "The Congress recognizes and assumes the compassionate responsibility of the United States for the losses sustained by reason of the explosion and fires at Texas City, Texas, and hereby provides the procedure by which the amounts shall be determined and paid."

The act places the responsibility for settlement of the claims on the Secretary of the Army. It limits to $25,000 any single payment for death, injury or property loss, and no attorney or agent may receive more than 10 per cent of the amount awarded a client, any contract to the contrary notwithstanding. No insurance company shall be reimbursed for loss claims paid out. The Army first estimated that close to $50 million would be involved but recent studies have reduced that estimate by more than half. A total of $35 million was set up in the Federal budget to cover the cost. As this is written, nine years after the tragedy, the Judge Advocate General has a staff of some forty persons in Galveston County reviewing claims and forwarding them to Washington for settlement. The act requires that a full report of all claims filed and all payments made shall be submitted to the Congress at the end of two years.

Belated justice is injustice. While lawyers and legislators discussed "pro" and "con" for nine years the widowed mothers had to go to work to take care of the mortgage on the home, or to educate their children who were growing up without a father. Cripples found their earning power gone and private charity had to assume the burden of supporting those incapacitated by governmental bungling. In the meantime the United States paid handsome sums to Japanese fishermen burned by atomic ashes and sent aid to foreign citizens impoverished by war—all since the blood was washed from the Texas City wharves.

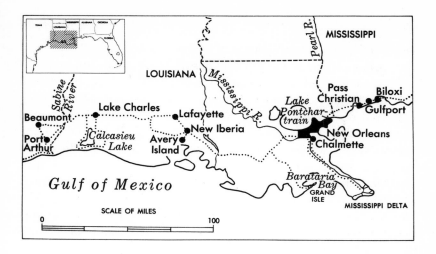

IX. *The Rice Country*

THE accepted route from Galveston eastward is via the freeway to Houston and then over U.S. Highway 90, through Beaumont to New Orleans. If you are asked to spell "Beaumont" with three letters, the answer is "o-i-l." About all that could be said of the place at the turn of the century was that it was the seat of Jefferson County. But when, on January 10, 1901, the Lucas gusher blew the top off the derrick it was truly "the shot heard 'round the world," and the results were almost as important for the economy of the United States as for Beaumont.

The opening of the Spindletop field, as it was called, put this country in the position of the world's leading petroleum producer, a position it has never relinquished. New methods of deeper drilling and reactivating old wells have kept the region in the forefront of production, and the county's annual output approximates nine mil-

93

lion barrels. Its second source of income is from 65,000 acres of rice, making it one of the top counties of Texas in this industry.

Beaumont, which had a population of 94,000 in 1950, has moved into the 100,000 class since that year, and notwithstanding its big industrial development it is a city with smart retail and residential districts. With Port Arthur and Port Neches, all located on the Sabine-Neches waterway and only fifteen miles apart, the Beaumont area is a single economic unit with a population of more than 200,000. Jefferson County has 90.4 per cent of its population listed as urban, the highest in the state, and only 9.6 per cent rural. The Lamar State College of Technology was established as a coeducational school in Beaumont in 1923 and now has a faculty of 125 and an enrollment in excess of 2,500.

The traveler intent on following the coastline will not go through Beaumont, but will cross the entrance to Galveston Bay on the free ferry the Texas Highway Department maintains between Galveston and Bolivar Point. This is State Highway No. 87, an interesting and not overcrowded route, that parallels the coast for seventy miles between Bolivar Point and Sabine Pass at the extreme southeast corner of Texas. There are no crossroads and no cultivation along this route, which for about half its distance runs within a few yards of the beach and is never more than a quarter of a mile from it. Until the last few years it was all but deserted but now frame cottages on high stilts house hundreds of summer vacationers along its shore.

There is but one drawback, and that is millions upon millions of mosquitoes. They do not bother the motorist while traveling, nor do they interfere with a stroll along the beach, but to disturb the grass by the roadside or beachside is to bring them out in such hordes that even the most frantic slapping is futile. For thirty miles the road follows a peninsula between the Gulf and East Bay, which is an arm of Galveston Bay. This is still Galveston County. Cattle, mostly Brahmans, graze in lush pastures on either side. There is good fishing in the bay and in the Gulf, and future road maps will show villages strung along the route.

Once the end of the bay is passed the roadway begins to run within a stone's throw of the Gulf, while on the left the flat grasslands of the McFadden Ranch, one of the first established in south Texas, stretch away to the north. Here and there along the lonesome beach groups of terns sit with their heads pointing into the breeze, dowitchers, sandpipers and other shore birds run along the edge of the surf, and farther out a brown pelican sails lazily above the dimpling water, into which he dives occasionally to capture a luckless fish. It is an unspoiled scene.

At the end of this stretch where the highway turns abruptly north toward Port Arthur and Orange, is the little settlement of Sabine Pass. In the center of the crossroad is a large granite boulder, placed there by the United Daughters of the Confederacy, "commemorating the feat of Dick Dowling and his 42 Irish patriots.

"On September 8, 1863," the legend continues, "an army of 15,000 Federals attacked the small force at the pass. The brave little garrison under Lieutenant Dick Dowling without the loss of a man disabled and captured three of the gunboats and 350 prisoners."

Sabine Pass itself is a narrow body of water connecting Sabine Lake with the Gulf. A narrow road leads southward from the village to the extreme point of land and a tiny fishing settlement called Jetty. Its only claim to importance is that here the pilots board incoming vessels to take them up to Port Arthur, Orange and Beaumont. On the far side of the pass and the lake are the marshy shores of Louisiana, accessible only by boat.

Soon after turning north at the Dick Dowling monument there comes into view the great "tank farm" of the Gulf Oil Company, where rows and rows of oil tanks cover hundreds of acres. A little farther on, the route passes through a forest of weird, giant machinery where the company has an enormous refinery. It is the heart of a mighty gasoline-producing system, but do not run out of gas here, for there is not a filling station in sight. On the other side of town a similar array of tanks and towers marks the site of the Atlantic refinery.

Seven miles beyond Port Arthur looms the highest highway bridge in the South, where Route 87 spans the Neches River. Its roadway is 183 feet above the water. Beyond the bridge is Orange, a settlement of some thirty thousand, named for an orange grove that flourished along the Sabine River a hundred years ago until it was killed by a freeze. The town has some interest in oil but relies more on small manufactures and the rice fields of its hinterland.

At Orange Route 87 joins with U.S. No. 90, and just east of the town the highway crosses the Sabine River over a bridge almost as high as that spanning the Neches, and enters Louisiana. The Sabine is a natural boundary as well as a political one, for once across it the landscape changes abruptly. Groves of southern pine border marshlands near the river, some of the trees standing gaunt and lifeless where the flood waters have killed them. Farther on are sweetgum and hardwoods, interspersed with rice fields. Not more than half the land is cleared. Thirty-nine miles beyond Orange another high bridge appears, spanning the Calcasieu ("KAL-ka-shu") River, and the motorist is in Lake Charles.

This is the heart of rice country of the South, and Lake Charles, with the sizable town of Crowley fifty miles eastward, are the nuclei of this little understood industry.

All the average American knows about rice growing he learned from the pictures in the *National Geographic* magazine, showing a water buffalo dragging a wooden plow through a flooded paddy field, with a bare-legged mama following behind sticking green shoots into the muddy soil. Yet, without the aid of water buffalo, the United States produces about ninety million bushels of rice annually in seven states, half of which it exports, and the acreage is continually increasing. This crop figures not only in our national economy but is of international importance, although it is but 2 per cent of world production. For more people are dependent on rice

for sustenance than on any other food, and the rice eaters are the "problem children" of the world today.

This, then, is a brief story about rice in the United States.

Coming up the Texas coast from the mouth of the Rio Grande, the traveler sees the first rice fields near Corpus Christi. Before Houston is reached they are much in evidence, and eastern Louisiana is primarily rice country. Arkansas has considerable acreage in the flat lands bordering the Mississippi River, and Missouri and the state of Mississippi are beginning to plant rice in a small way. California gets into the act with plantings in the Sacramento and San Joaquin valley. One reason for this expansion is the crop control program of the Federal government. With his acreage of corn, wheat and other crops limited by this policy the farmer seeks another use for his land, and if it is reasonably level and water is available for irrigation he may turn to rice. When enough of them do that and a large rice-growing community develops, the government puts a limit on the amount of rice they may grow!

There are so many "angles" to rice growing that it is seldom a one-man enterprise. Often it is split three ways between the landlord who owns the land, the "waterlord" who furnishes the water, and the tenant who does the actual farming. Such a triumvirate must agree on how the expenses of seed, fertilizer and weed-control chemicals will be divided. The waterlord's share is usually one-fifth of the crop if the irrigation is all he contributes. There are several varieties each of short, medium and long grain rice and a decision must be made as to which is best suited for any specific piece of land.

To insure an even depth of water when the field is flooded it must be carefully surveyed and "contoured." Small "levees" are then constructed, dividing it into strips or "cuts," each high enough to hold five or six inches of water. The land is plowed and harrowed and the seed planted with a grain drill, frequently one that deposits a row of fertilizer beside or under the row of seed. Large operators now often use "water planting" instead of drills, flooding the field slightly and sowing the seed by airplane. About one-fifth of the Gulf Coast acreage is sown this way. The planting season extends through April and May, although under some circumstances it may begin in March and continue well into June.

Rice fields are submerged during the growing season, not only because rice grows best under such conditions but also as a measure of weed control. The water is never allowed to cover the young shoots. Certain kinds of weeds flourish with the grain nonetheless, and usually the fields are sprayed with a mild solution of 2,4D, strong enough to kill the weeds without injuring the narrow-bladed rice. This is done by airplanes, and they are also used to give the crop a top dressing of fertilizer.

Rice requires a growing period of 120 to 180 days, depending on the variety and the weather. Approximately thirty-six inches of water are necessary during this period, and as Louisiana normally receives but sixteen inches of rainfall during the growing season the rest must be supplied by irrigation, either from wells or irrigation canals fed by rivers and smaller streams. An irrigation well is no puny thing but is most commonly a ten-inch pipe sunk to a depth of from one to four hundred feet, and operated by a pumping unit in excess of a hundred horsepower. Such a well will irrigate 200 to 250 acres. Where surface water is used it may travel twenty-five to seventy-five miles from river to rice field. This water is supplied by a private agency and its volume is accurately measured.

Two or three weeks before the rice is ready to harvest the water is drained from it. This water is returned to the streams clearer and richer than when it was taken from them. Industrial development has complicated the irrigation problem in some regions where industrial wastes have polluted the waters, or where dredging ship canals has allowed sea water to seep into low lands and render them unfit for agriculture.

A few years ago rice was harvested with a binder and shocked in the field until ready for threshing. Today nearly all of it is harvested with a combine that threshes it as it cuts it and dumps it into a tractor-drawn "rice buggy," a bin on pneumatic tires, that carries it from the field. The cost of machinery is a big factor in rice culture, requiring a capital investment equal to about seventy-five dollars an acre. From the farm the rice goes to a drier, a tall, elevator-like structure, where its moisture content is reduced in natural gas ovens from 20 or 25 per cent to 14 per cent. There it is sold, usually to the rice millers.

Rice milling is as complicated a process as flour milling, but follows an entirely different principle. A flour mill takes the bran and "shorts" from the grain kernel and reduces the remainder to a fine flour. A rice mill also extracts certain by-products, but in a manner to preserve the whole grain so far as is possible. The first process in rice milling is to remove the husk or "hull" from the grain, which is done by passing it between two flat "stones," one of which is revolving rapidly in a horizontal plane. These are not the old-fashioned millstones, but large disks of carborundum. The upper one whirls so rapidly that the grains are stood on end and the end of the hull cracked so that the next machine, a "chaffer," is able to separate the kernel and the hull. Rice hulls are very hard and are usually burned, as they have no value as stock feed or fertilizer, but recent experiments have shown they can be made into cheap bricks that are very resistant to radiation, so they may become a factor in the new atomic world.

The grain as it comes from the chaffer is called "brown rice" and mixed with it is a powdery substance called "stone bran," which is removed by the next process. This bran is sold to the large stock feed companies. Next an aspirator or "bran duster" removes a still finer powder, called "polish," that clings to the kernels, and when they emerge from this process they begin to resemble the rice of commerce. But whole grains, half-grains and smaller bits are all mixed together and must be put through other machines before each type is segregated. In fact, rice grains come from the mill as nine different products. The "head rice," or whole grains, are the most valuable and are graded "first head" and "second head," according to the percentage of broken grains they contain. The next smaller size finds ready market as "brewer's rice" and actually has the highest nutritional value of any rice product. as it contains a high percentage of seed germs.

From a hundred pounds of rough rice as it comes to the mill, the miller gets approximately sixty-four pounds of whole and broken kernels, sixteen and a half pounds of bran and polish, and nineteen and a half pounds of hulls.

The fine "polish" removed in the milling process has nothing to do with the "polished rice" of commerce. This latter product is made by adding a small amount of corn syrup and talc to whole grains of head rice to give them a shiny appearance. It is really "gilding the lily," because it quickly comes off when the housewife washes her rice (as she should do) before cooking it.

There is a great deal more to rice growing than rice, for the business is tied up tightly with the beef cattle industry. Rice takes so much nutriment from the soil, even when fertilizers are used, that it should not be grown on the same field oftener than one year in three or two years in five. The most productive rotation plan is to use the fields on off-years as pasturelands. Flooding the fields during the rice-growing season does not kill the native grasses, nor the "red rice" which has found its way into the rice country as an undesirable alien. Following the rice crop the fields offer good grazing and the herds keep the red rice down so that it does not seed. Beef strains such as Angus or Brahman are usually pastured on the land for two or three years before it is resown to rice.

It follows that in a rice-growing region there is only about a third of the available acreage in rice at any time. A farmer with 1,000 acres of land will have only 330 acres in rice and the rest in grass. This in part accounts for the fact that rice growing does not have much to offer the small landowner unless he is prepared to lease enough acreage to operate on a fairly large scale.

Although Lake Charles, with seventy thousand inhabitants in the city and suburbs, has more than thirty rice mills in its trading area that ship their products from its port, it is far from a one-industry town. With fifty-four producing oil wells in the area it has shared in the oil boom of the coastal region and the expansion of chemical industries that followed. The lake itself is just a wide place in the Calcasieu River marking the western boundary of the town. On the opposite shore is the $60 million plant of the Olin Mathieson Chemical Corporation that turns out soda ash, caustic soda, ammonia and fertilizers by boatload and trainload. Swift & Company has one of its most modern packing plants just east of the city. The local Association of Commerce proudly points out that the effective buying income per family is $8,393 annually.

A ship channel thirty-five miles long and thirty-five feet deep through the lake and the lower Calcasieu River connects the city with the Gulf and the Intracoastal Waterway. It has a unique history. Shortly after World War I the people of Calcasieu Parish (County), unable to interest the Federal government in dredging such a channel, voted a bond issue of $7,500,000 and dredged the river themselves. The port was opened in 1926 and its operation was so successful that Uncle Sam financed a channel across the lake, adding considerably to the capacity of the port which now handles more than fourteen million tons of cargo annually.

The city of Lake Charles had its beginnings a century ago as a center of a cattle and lumber industry. The stands of southern longleaf pine have long vanished but the cattle are still here. It is not a bilingual city, as is Brownsville, nor so much so as Corpus Christi or Houston, but the French influence is very apparent. The telephone directory is full of names such as Breaux, LeBleu, Chaumont, Thibodeaux, Gaspard, Fontenot, etc.

Just east of the city is the extensive installation of the Lake Charles Air Force Base, where the 806th Air Division of the Strategic Air Command is located. This is the great offensive arm of the Air Forces of the United States. The Division comprises two tactical wings, each composed of three bomber squadrons equipped with Boeing B-47 Stratojets, the most potent bomber in the world today. Designed to carry nuclear weapons to enemy targets anywhere in the world, it can reach altitudes of forty thousand feet at speeds in excess of six hundred miles an hour. Although these B-47's can carry a bomb load of twenty thousand pounds three thousand miles without refueling each tactical wing has a tanker squadron attached for air refueling, so that they could fly around the world nonstop.

The gleaming aluminum giants can be seen from the highway, arriving or departing for maneuvers, or ranked in shining rows beside the hangars. But to get past the guards at the gate is something else. Don't try it unless you have business there!

Two narrow roads, one from Lake Charles and one from the town of Sulphur four miles to the west, lead down to the Gulf shore,

Mixed bathing in the soupy mud of Louisiana's Holly Beach

thirty-five miles south. At the beach they are connected by a stretch of twenty miles of gravel road, the only highway along Louisiana's 985 miles of coastline except for a short stretch along Grand Isle, south of New Orleans.

The road leading south from Sulphur runs most of the way through salt marshes, more water than land. At its southern end on a cluster of insecure stilts is a group of summer cottages called Holly Beach. There is nothing like this beach anywhere else on the Gulf Coast, for its sands along the waterline are covered with several inches of black slimy mud. A bather can get out in the surf and wash off the clinging goo, but must splash through it again when he returns. The place will never rival Miami Beach. Driving east along the beach the motorist crosses the Calcasieu River on a free ferry and enters the little town of Cameron, seat of Cameron Parish. This far-out-of-the-way place was never heard of by the rest of the country until the big oil companies began drilling oil wells out in the waters of the Gulf. Now it is a supply depot for the seagoing oil industry, along with Grand Isle at the southwestern end of the state.

Bounded on the west by Sabine Pass and Sabine Lake which separate it from Texas, and on the south by the Gulf, Cameron Parish is the most inaccessible in the state, and though one of the largest its population is but 6,300. Cameron has no municipal government and no mayor. The sheriff is the local boss. The town has a second industry, that of processing pogies into fish oil and fertilizer. Pogies are a species of menhaden, too full of bones to be edible, but rich in oil. They abound in uncounted millions off the Louisiana waters and during the summer a large fleet of trawlers are kept busy netting them and bringing them to the processing plant in Cameron. The oil is used principally in soap making, the solid matter makes excellent fertilizer, and the smell is something never to be forgotten.

Continuing east through Cameron toward the small village of Creole, fourteen miles distant, the traveler is due for a surprise. Here, seemingly out of place in a land of oil and fish oil, are a number of well-kept farm homesteads set back under rows of live oak trees that cannot be less than seventy-five years old. Around them are pastures where beef cattle graze on lush grasses. It is an old community, French as is all this part of Louisiana, and thrives on this bit of high, rich soil with miles of marshland on one side and the open Gulf on the other.

At Creole the road turns north through the salt marsh, back toward Lake Charles. Where these little-used highways cross the Intracoastal Waterway traffic is served by free ferries that pull themselves along a cable stretched from shore to shore like a spider on its web. A gasoline engine provides the power and the craft's capacity is eight cars per trip. When a barge tow comes along the waterway one end of the cable is slacked off and it sinks to the bottom while the barges pass over it.

A short distance north of the waterway the road passes an unusual sight, a lake several acres in extent filled with lotus, the broad green leaves standing well out of the water and the large, delicately pink blossoms smiling at the sun. No other highway along the coast offers such a spectacle.

As one approaches Lake Charles from the south the land becomes firmer and soon there are rice fields and pastures on each side of the road as far as one can see. From the low grassy "levees" in the pastures it is evident that they were once sown to rice and as soon as they have been "rotated" will again be put under cultivation.

From Lake Charles fifty miles eastward to Crowley the general scene can be described in two words: rice and cattle, cattle and rice. En route there are rice mills at Jennings, where venerable oak trees shade no less venerable residences; at Mermentau, where a high bridge spans Nezpique Bayou; and at Estherwood, two miles farther on.

Crowley calls itself, with reason, "The Rice Capital of the United States," for while Lake Charles handles a lot of rice and a lot of other things, Crowley is pretty much all rice. Large rice driers, mills and storage elevators line the railroad tracks, and here every fall is held a great "Rice Festival" with a queen, parades, accordion contests, a jumping contest for frogs (from near-by Rayney) and dancing in the streets. From Crowley U.S. Route 90 continues east to Lafayette and then turns south to New Iberia. But a state road south from Crowley and then east through Kaplan and Abbeville to the same point is just as good, and keeps closer to the Gulf—which is not very close. For it is along here that mud flats and salt marshes push the arable lands farthest from the shoreline.

Abbeville, while not in the famous "Teche (rhymes with 'mesh') country," is an outpost of that unique region. As the seat of Vermilion Parish it has a large white stone courthouse of classic design that dominates the town. Here are large homes which, if not a hundred years old, belong to the architecture of that period, and all about them are spreading oaks so close together that the sunlight has difficulty in reaching the lawns beneath.

Just east of Abbeville the first fields of sugar cane appear, stretching from Vermilion Parish to the levees of the Mississippi, and along here the last of the rice fields are passed. It is a poor town in this region that does not have an annual festival, fair or hoop-la of some sort, and each year Abbeville chooses a King and Queen of Dairyland, stages a Dairy Festival, and everybody has a grand time. Farther along the road, Delcambre (it rhymes with "welcome") is the site of the annual "Iberia Shrimp Festival and Annual Fair." This town lies at the head of a shallow channel leading to the Gulf, and many of the 150 or more shrimp boats operating out of the town are built there.

(*Carrol and New Iberia Chamber of Commerce*)
The "Evangeline Oak," St. Martinville

X. *Sugar Cane and Evangeline*

IT is New Iberia, "The Queen City of the Teche," capital of "The Evangeline Country," and entirely surrounded by sugar cane, that strikes the keynote of romanticism so characteristic of this part of the South. This is the result of circumstances, happy and unhappy, that had their beginnings far away and more than two centuries ago. It is generally believed (at least in southern Louisiana) that the true facts are these:

In the early 1600's a number of the French peasantry settled in Nova Scotia where their community was known as Acadia. In 1713 France yielded the country to England, and considerable unrest followed. So Governor Laurence in 1755 called on all Acadians to swear allegiance to the British Crown or be deported. Six thousand of them refused and were banished with inexcusable brutality, all men over ten years of age being deported separately from the women. Many families thus parted were never united. Some four thousand of the Acadians settled along the Teche and neighboring bayous and their descendants are still there. Such is established history.

Living in Acadia at that period were two young persons engaged to be married, Emmeline Labiche and Louis Arceneaux. They were put on different ships but both made their way after many hardships to a French fort in Louisiana, known as Poste des Attakapas, which later became the town of St. Martinville on the Bayou Teche, six miles from New Iberville which also is on the bayou. Louis arrived first but by the time Emmeline arrived three years later, still treasuring her wedding gown, her sweetheart, despairing of ever seeing her again, had married. They met under the canopy of a great oak tree in a churchyard hard by the bayou. This bitter climax to the long years of travel and search broke Emmeline's heart, and she died soon after.

Three-quarters of a century pass. Edward Somin, a native of St. Martinville, is a student at Harvard. In the course of his sojourn there he told the story of the unhappy Acadians to his professor of modern languages, whose name was Henry Wadsworth Longfellow. In 1847 Dr. Longfellow wrote a poem which began:

> This is the forest primeval. The murmuring pines and the hemlocks,
> Bearded with moss, and in garments green, indistinct in the twilight,
> Stand like Druids of eld, with voices sad and prophetic.

It was the story of *Evangeline*.

Although Emmeline Labiche was certainly the prototype of the poet's "Evangeline" and Louis Arceneaux that of "Gabriel," the two

Bayou Teche

narratives have many differences and a different climax. Longfellow
had the sweethearts miss each other by tragically narrow margins
several times, cleverly prolonging the suspense. Finally Evangeline
becomes a nun in a charity hospital where one day she recognizes a
patient dying in her arms as her long-sought Gabriel.

New Iberia and St. Martinville share the fame that Longfellow's
widely accepted poem brought to them more than a century ago.
But for him they would be just two other towns along the Teche.
In St. Martinville is the "Evangeline Oak" where Louis (Gabriel)
gave the bad news to Emmeline (Evangeline). Outside the near-by
church is a bronze figure of a young woman seated, and on the
granite base is carved both "Evangeline" and "Emmeline Labiche."
This statue was donated by the cast which in 1929 made the motion
picture *Evangeline,* with Dolores Del Rio in the title role. Across
the Teche is the quaint shop of Monsieur André Olivier, which bears

the legend, "Evangeline Enshrined Here." In the rear of his store this dedicated descendant of refugees from Nova Scotia has a collection of Evangeline memorabilia, and here he will leave a customer to deliver an impassioned lecture on that remarkable character, who was part fiction and part fact.

The telephone directory of New Iberia, much the larger of the two towns, contains an Evangeline Café, Evangeline China Market, Evangeline Funeral Home, Evangeline Hotel, Evangeline Life Insurance Company, Evangeline Mattress Company, Evangeline Theatre and the Evangeline Wholesale China Company. Oddly enough the visitor will find it impossible to buy a copy of Longfellow's poem anywhere along Main Street, though M. Olivier has them for sale in his St. Martinville store.

It was the coming of the Acadians that gave the name "Cajun country" to this part of Louisiana, and "Cajun French" to the patois spoken here. It is not unusual in this and neighboring parishes to find persons who cannot speak a word of English, although their forebears have lived here for two centuries. This is true of many Negroes, and it is rather startling for the tourist to ask directions of an old Negro who looks as though he might just have stepped out of the cast of *Uncle Tom's Cabin,* only to have the old fellow look at him uncomprehendingly and mutter something in unintelligible French. Soldiers from this region who reached France during World Wars I and II were at first unable to understand Parisian French, but soon became accustomed to the different accent.

The first settlers here were Spanish. The French came later, many being here when the Acadians arrived. As the Iberian peninsula in southwestern Europe is occupied by France and Spain, so the mingling of the races here gave the parish and the town the name "Iberia."

Situated along the western side of the sugar-cane-producing area, New Iberia contributes to the fun-making season by having a three-day "Sugar Cane Festival and Fair" each September, just before the harvest begins. It starts with a serious note when high church dignitaries formally bless the crops, and the first night concludes with a street dance, called "Fas Dodo." There is a children's parade, a parade for King Sucrose and Queen Sugar, and a parade organized by the Negroes and led by "Queen Brown Sugar."

Sugar cane has been raised in southern Louisiana ever since a French planter began experimenting with it in 1795, but with the coming of power machinery the method of cultivating and harvesting it has undergone a radical change. Planting begins early in September when two stalks of cane are laid in the bottom of furrows, the ends of one row of stalks opposite the middle of the other, and the furrows are then filled. In a short time a green shoot springs up from each joint, or "node," so that the canes stand about six inches apart in the row. Winter frosts will not hurt the young shoots, although a freeze will set them back. In the early spring the canes start to grow in earnest and during the growing season the fields are heavily fertilized with a liquid form of anhydrous ammonia, which is 82 per cent nitrogen. By October, thirteen months after planting, the crop is ready to harvest. In a good year the usable part of the cane will be six or seven feet long with a top more than half that length.

Harvesting is done by a large machine that cuts the cane a few inches above the ground, cuts off the top, and lays the canes parallel on the ground. Another machine, usually an attachment to a tractor, gathers the stalks and lifts them into a tractor-drawn wagon. If the mill is near by the tractor will haul the wagonload to it, but in most instances the cane is taken to a near-by point on the highway where cranes lift it into a large truck which takes it to the mill.

At the mill knives cut it into small lengths and it is then put through crushers which extract the juice. This is put through evaporating ovens and the resulting product is "raw" or brown sugar. Many of the mills carry the process no further but ship it to bakeries, candy manufacturers or pharmaceutical companies. Some of it is shipped in liquid form. Formerly all raw sugar was sacked for shipment but recently much of it is loaded in bulk into paper-lined freight cars which at their destination are gripped by giant machines which tip them on their sides and pour their contents into a hopper.

A ton of cane will yield about 165 pounds of raw sugar, in addition to 7 gallons of "blackstrap" molasses. This blackstrap is much in demand as cattle feed, especially for dairy herds, where it is often mixed with silage at the time the silos are filled. The cane fiber left after the juice is extracted is used in the manufacture of coarse papers and cardboard. Some of it is shredded, baled and sold to poultry raisers who find it excellent covering for floors of chicken houses. After it is used there for a time it is again baled and sold for fertilizer.

The first crop of cane from a new field is the "plant crop." The next year another crop is cut from the same planting and this is the "first stubble crop." The following year the "second stubble crop" is harvested, and then most planters agree it is time to start over again. Each stubble crop must be heavily fertilized but the fields are never irrigated. After the second stubble is harvested the field is plowed and sowed to soybeans or Clemson peas. This crop is not harvested but is turned under for "green manure" and the ground replanted for cane. The grower thus harvests three paying crops every four years.

New Iberia lays claim to being the "sweetest, saltiest, pepperiest" city in the world. The first claim is due to its location in the sugar cane area. The other superlatives are to be found on three neighboring islands, Avery, Jefferson and Weeks. On Avery Island is a large, ivy-covered factory that puts out the famous Tabasco sauce, made from hot peppers grown there, and on it and the two adjoining islands are mines five hundred feet deep from which solid rock salt is mined. In addition Avery Island is the site of a "jungle garden" filled with native and exotic plants and trees and a "bird city," one of the oldest wildlife refuges along the Gulf Coast.

The three islands, which are connected with the mainland by a causeway, are a geologic formation unique in this part of the world. Each is a great dome of pure salt thrust up from the bowels of the earth when the lower part of the North American Continent was being formed. Before the European came the Indians were making salt from the brine found on the tops of these hills, that are higher than the mainland to the north. Later centuries have covered them with a tropical growth that has been disturbed but little. Early settlers obtained salt here intermittently but large-scale development did not begin until shortly after the Civil War. Now they are operated under lease to large salt-producing companies.

Back in the 1840's Edmund McIlhenny was associated with the Avery family that owned the salt works when a friend who had been in southern Mexico gave him some pepper seeds from that region. Having a taste for hot Mexican dishes, McIlhenny planted the seeds on Avery Island and eventually invented a condiment from the peppers that he and his friends enjoyed. About that time the Civil War and the subsequent occupation of New Orleans by the Union forces interrupted the growing business, and the Averys and McIlhennys moved to Texas. They returned to find the old home overgrown with tropical vegetation, but the peppers had seeded themselves and were flourishing. Cultivation began again and when a large New York grocery house got a sample of the sauce and began to order it by the barrel, the business was made.

The peppers are grown on the island after being sprouted in greenhouses, and at harvest time are carefully culled, placed in oak barrels, sealed with a layer of fine salt, and left to stand for three years. At the end of that period the making of the sauce is completed and the product is shipped all over the world.

McIlhenny was an ardent lover of wildlife and became much concerned when the rage for egret feathers threatened the extinction of the snowy egret which abounded in the islands. With others he was instrumental in getting the Federal government to outlaw the plume business, and today "Bird City" is a nesting place for many species of waterfowl and a refuge for many more on their migratory flights. Another member of the family, the late Edward Avery McIlhenny, born on the island, was a naturalist of wide reputation and served in that capacity with Admiral Peary's 1893 expedition to the Arctic. He added to the island's natural beauty by landscaping and by importing trees and shrubs from the distant tropics, so that today it is a delight to the casual visitor and a treasure island for the botanist.

From New Iberia U.S. Route No. 90 ambles to the southeast through the cane fields as close to the Gulf shore as it is feasible to build a highway; through Jeanerette, Baldwin, Franklin, Garden City and Patterson, to Berwick—all spaced along the Bayou Teche like beads on a string, and all completely surrounded by fields of sugar cane. In every town and often between towns derricks beside the highway show where the cane is loaded on big trucks which carry it to the mills, whose tall smokestacks are seldom out of sight along this road. The countryside has an air of quiet prosperity; frame houses, usually white, are set back in neatly clipped lawns edged with flower beds of shrubbery. Here and there a genuine Southern "mansion" looks out from a grove of immense moss-hung live oaks, eloquent of an era that has all but vanished. There is much in this region to remind the visitor of the "Deep South" of Georgia, the Carolinas and tidewater Virginia, but the Eastern states suffer by comparison. Perhaps it is because in recent years sugar cane has been a better money crop than cotton or tobacco.

Berwick and Morgan City are on opposite sides of the Atchafalaya ("A-CHAFF-a-la") River through which, geologists say, the waters of the upper Mississippi once flowed to the Gulf. Here it has a depth of 127 feet at mean low water, which hardly equals the 200-foot depth of the Mississippi at New Orleans. The Atchafalaya starts 138 miles upstream where the Red River joins the Mississippi, and at times of threatened flood great spillways pour the waters from those two streams into the Atchafalaya to reduce the hazards of a break in the levees.

As the highway nears Berwick and Morgan City the cane fields and oak trees give way to willows and marshland, but approaching

Houma, forty miles farther on, the land is a few inches higher and cane fields crowd the highway on one side as Black Bayou flows sluggishly along the other. Houma is the southmost point of U.S. Highway No. 90 in Louisiana, and here the route makes a right angle turn and heads northeast for New Orleans, seventy miles distant. Houma, named for an Indian tribe that still has a few members in this area, was at one time the center of a large business in muskrat pelts, the many bayous and canals in the area furnishing ideal homes for those busy rodents. But excessive trapping threatened them with extinction and conservation laws now restrict the pelt industry.

Twelve miles from Houma is Raceland on "the longest street in the world," as the highway along Bayou Lafourche is frequently called. It is less than an hour's drive from here to New Orleans, but the visitor interested in exploring the curving shore of the Gulf will turn south on "the longest street," which stretches from Napoleonville, thirty miles to the northeast, to Golden Meadow, forty-five miles in the opposite direction. Beyond Golden Meadow, the highway leaves the bayou and eventually terminates at Grand Isle. ("Glamorous, exciting Grand Isle!" says the Vacation Guide to Louisiana's Deep South.)

Leaving the New Orleans road at Raceland and taking State Highway No. 1 along Bayou Lafourche, the motorist sees fewer and fewer cane fields as the strip of arable land between the bayou and the salt marsh narrows. The villages crowd the road and the road crowds the bayou, one settlement merging into another, which gives an impression of one town a block wide and miles long. Oil derricks, which have been scarce for the last hundred miles, now appear in clusters. Banana plants line the bank, not the banana of commerce but a small semitropic variety. Gradually the bayou widens and shrimp trawlers and other fishing craft become more numerous.

Beyond Golden Meadow the last small houses and scrub willows disappear. In front and on either side stretches a flat, green, deceptive landscape. This is the "trembling prairie" that is neither land nor water. Come back in a millennium and it may be one or the other. The thousands of acres of marsh grasses are laced by shallow lakes and waterways, sought by hunters of waterfowl during the shooting season and by fishermen the year round. The broad Bayou Lafourche and the narrow road beside it stretch away southward toward a cluster of oil derricks, stark amid the watery wastes. Here the road crosses the bayou over a high bridge and soon swings away to the right, leaving the bayou to continue its lonely way to the Gulf.

It is a good road, made by dredging a canal and piling the dirt up for a highway, as the Tamiami Trail was constructed across the Florida Everglades, but this is a more monotonous region. At last a line of low trees and a few small buildings appear across the field of interminable green, the car rattles across a wooden bridge, and the traveler is in Grand Isle. ("One of the beauty spots of the deep south of Louisiana," says the brochure.)

It is an anticlimax for one who believes everything he reads. The only really attractive cottages on the place are for employees of the oil companies. The others are mostly jerry-built and on stilts, and all are heavily screened against mosquitoes. There is no modern filling station. (Tourists for a day should carry chamber pots. A restaurant proprietor asked a customer not to use much water when flushing the toilet!) But it is the long beach of dark, solid sand, which might be attractive, that is the most disappointing. Hardly a square yard of it but is littered with discarded beer cans, shattered remains of crab feasts, the charred fragments of forgotten campfires, and a scattering of debris of various sorts. This is regrettable, because with care it could be as pleasant a place as the beaches of Padre Island.

Looking southward over the Gulf one sees the derricks and platforms of the "seagoing oil rigs." Here is taking place a most unusual industrial development, for the oil sands hide their wealth deep, unaffected by surface conditions. Across the sparkling water the derricks and anchored platforms are but misty outlines against the horizon, and some are too far out to be seen from shore. Probably more money has been spent on such development than the oil so far recovered has been worth, but new machinery and new methods are being tried out for this type of production, and the companies putting up the money believe the great gamble will pay off.

Having exhausted the possibilities of Grand Isle there is no place to go but back—back over the quaking prairie, back past the shrimp trawlers, back to the cane fields and the mossy oaks of Raceland. There one may leave the longest street, and taking Route 90 again, cross the Lafourche and head for New Orleans. It is not an exciting road. The highway has been raised by digging a deep ditch on either side, and these are lined with willows and other water-loving flora. Through them the motorist gets an occasional glimpse of marshland, or more solid terrain where cattle are grazing.

Soon a railroad trestle begins to rise out of the willow trees to the left, getting altitude for the leap across the Mississippi. The automobiles, capable of climbing steeper grades, continue on the level until the stupendous structure of the Huey Long Bridge is in sight. The highway approach rises rapidly until it is on the same level with the railroad, and car and train, side by side, roll across the mighty stream far above its muddy waters, confined on either side by levees. The road slants down beside the railroad trestle and the motorist is in "The Crescent City."

XI. New Orleans

NEW ORLEANS occupies a unique place among the major cities of the United States. Philadelphia, New York, Boston, also established in the eighteenth century, were parties to the War of Independence and were important centers in the new republic as soon as it was established, while distant New Orleans remained under Spanish rule. As the republic developed and extended westward the city at the lower end of the Mississippi was growing also, and becoming increasingly important to the economy of the upper valley from Pittsburgh westward, but it was almost a quarter of a century before the Louisiana Purchase in 1803 brought it into the United States.

Thus "The Crescent City" entered the Union as a mature, influential metropolis, with a background of French and Spanish development almost a century old. Other cities, such as San Francisco and St. Louis, had their beginnings before they became a part of the United States, but they were hardly more than trading posts at the time of the change in sovereignty. New Orleans, however, had been the capital of a territory as large as that of the original thirteen colonies, though with a much smaller population. When she joined the family of states she was as well known in Europe as Boston or Philadelphia, she had an aristocracy and a culture that rivaled that of those two cities, and she was inclined to look down her Gallic nose at her new Northern kinfolk.

In the century and a half that followed New Orleans has become completely integrated with the rest of the United States economically and commercially. It is a very busy city. After New York it vies with Houston as the second largest port (some say Houston is second in tonnage while New Orleans is second in value of shipments). But outside of the countinghouses the city retains the lightheartedness and love of pageantry that still give it some of the flavor of Paris and Madrid. There is no disloyalty in this, but because of it the city has an added interest and charm for the visitor.

While proud of its past New Orleans shows no tendency to live on the glories of bygone days, and keeps fully abreast of the changing times. It is constructing a new bridge across the Mississippi near the heart of the city at a cost of $65 million and another across shallow Lake Pontchartrain to the north was opened to traffic in June, 1956. These are being financed by bonds that will be liquidated by toll charges. Its International Trade Mart, a nonprofit enterprise opened in 1948, is unique as a global market place. Here in a building as modern as this morning's newspaper, are displayed products from all forty-eight states and thirty foreign countries. Twelve foreign governments have official agents there and others are represented by their industrial firms. More than six hundred lines of merchandise are offered, including everything from heavy machinery to toilet articles. Buyers and sellers can in a short time complete contracts that would otherwise require transoceanic travel or volumes of correspondence. A bronze tablet in the foyer reads: "International Trade Mart. Erected 1946–1947. Dedicated to World Peace, Trade, and Understanding."

A block away from the International Trade Mart, housed in a ten-story building, is the International House, established in 1943. The two institutions are not rivals but are complementary. International House is a membership organization, a sort of international club, where American and foreign buyers and sellers meet for their mutual interests. It has no merchandise displays, but provides private offices, bilingual stenographers, interpreters, maps and trade information covering the globe. Its luxurious lounge, two general dining rooms, six private dining rooms and similar appointments make it a mecca for those engaged in international trade.

Like much of the Gulf Coast to the west of it, New Orleans' prosperity is largely dependent on oil. Large administrative buildings put up by the big oil companies—Texas, Humble, Standard, Gulf, Pan American, Shell—dominate its skyline. There are 150 oil fields within a hundred-mile radius of the city and a billion cubic feet of natural gas are produced in the area every day. New wells are continually being drilled in the region, but the greatest activity is out in the Gulf where operations are being pushed farther and farther from shore. An odd result of this is the fillip it has given to the fishing industry. For some unknown reason—perhaps it is curiosity—fish are attracted by the oil rigs and platforms, not only at night when they are lit by flares, but in the daytime as well. In consequence commercial fishermen are taking record hauls and sports fishermen make fabulous catches.

Although both New Orleans and Houston are focal points for the oil industry there is considerable difference in their development. Houston is the center of an expanding petrochemical empire where petroleum products are broken down into new molecular combinations, such as are used in the world of plastics. New Orleans has few plants of that type and its petroleum is almost wholly converted to gasoline, lubricants and fuel oil.

The largest industrial plant in the New Orleans area is the $145 million Kaiser Aluminum Works astride the battlefield at Chalmette, where General Andrew Jackson defeated the British under General

Pakenham, January 8, 1815. Its principal output is aluminum pig refined from ore brought from Jamaica. At the eastern edge of the city is Chrysler's new $70 million tank engine plant and on the other side of town is American Cyanamid's multimillion-dollar installation for the production of nitrogen. These are but a sampling of the city's industrial expansion in the last decade.

When the Intracoastal Waterway, which ties the Gulf Coast together from Brownsville to Pensacola, reaches the levee along the west bank of the Mississippi at New Orleans it is raised by locks to the river's level and continues eastward. New locks are under construction to take care of the increasing barge traffic.

But it is not to see thirteen miles of deepwater terminals, aluminum plants or oil company offices that thousands and tens of thousands of visitors flock to New Orleans, winter and summer. Their lodestone is the old French Quarter—the "Vieux Carré"—and the pre-Lenten Mardi Gras, most notable of the festivals, parades, carnivals and such staged annually by American cities.

The Vieux Carré, French term for "old square," lies at the heart of downtown New Orleans and is thickly encrusted with tradition. To understand it requires an understanding of its beginning.

The Spaniards were the first to see the lower Mississippi and the coast where its waters finally reach the Gulf. It may have been an obscure adventurer, Alonzo Alvarez de Pineda, who first looked on the great delta as he claimed in 1519, though his story is doubted. Certainly Cabeza de Vaca and some of his companions of the De Narváez expedition drifted past there in 1528 before being wrecked on Galveston Island. But it was Hernando de Soto, pillager of the Inca Empire, wealthy captain and explorer, who in 1541 carried the banner of Charles V of Spain across the "Father of Waters" after a two years' trek from the spot where he and his six hundred followers had landed on the Florida coast. The next year he died, probably close to the present Louisiana-Arkansas line on the river, and was buried beneath its waters. His surviving soldiers followed

Delicate iron grillwork in the Vieux Carré

the stream down to the Gulf, being the first Europeans to sail past the present site of New Orleans.

Spain's hold on the river was tenuous at best. Her several expeditions to what was then known as "The Floridas" had been universally disastrous and she made no formal claim to the river or its delta. So when in 1682 Robert Cavalier, Sieur de La Salle, came down the river from the French possessions in Canada and claimed its entire valley for King Louis XIV of France it became the French territory of "Louisiana." But La Salle was not to escape the curse that had fallen on the Spaniards before him. Returning to France in triumph he was shown every honor at court and returned in 1684 to found a colony in the new possession. He missed the mouths of the Mississippi, landed in Matagorda Bay on the Texas coast, marched inland, and somewhere along the Trinity River was murdered by a disgruntled group among his followers, an ignominious end for one of the ablest and most romantic figures in history.

France, sensing the opportunity that Spain had missed, sent out another colony in 1699 under Pierre Le Moyne, Sieur d'Iberville, and his younger brother, Jean Baptiste Le Moyne, Sieur de Bienville. Headquarters were first established at Fort Biloxi, near the present Mississippi town of that name, and later on Mobile Bay, but before much progress had been made orders came to move the capital to a site on the "Fleuve Saint-Louis," as the French then called the great river, and to christen it "Nouvelle-Orléans," in honor of the then regent of France, Louis Philippe, duc d'Orléans. D'Iberville had died in the meantime and young Bienville had succeeded to the governorship. He selected as a site for the new city "one of the finest crescents in the river," and the soubriquet "Crescent City" still clings.

So the city of New Orleans was founded by Bienville in 1717, and not in 1718 as some historians have it. Eighty convicted saltmakers, banished for evading the salt tax in France, were among the first arrivals and they erected the first buildings. In March, 1721, an engineer laid out the first streets of the town site, almost square, facing southeast toward the river. It is there today—the old square, the "Vieux Carré."

A visitor's first sight of the Vieux Carré may be disappointing. The streets are only thirty-eight feet wide, including the narrow sidewalks. The buildings, seldom more than three stories high, are generally shabby. Small shops selling exquisite lingerie and perfumes sit next to hardware stores, warehouses or the locked doors of some forgotten establishment that have not been opened in a decade. But there are antique shops displaying old furnishings of rare beauty; art stores where examples of every school, medieval and modern, may be seen; shops where one may buy or sell cameos, candelabra, tapestries, figurines, bracelets and bric-a-brac, sometimes arranged in orderly display and sometimes looking as though a dump truck had been upended and left them there. It is a place to linger.

A place to linger and to eat. There are "smart" restaurants in New Orleans where expensive food can be eaten to the accompaniment of sounding brass and more-than-tinkling cymbals, but they are not the ones for which the Vieux Carré is noted. Here are eating places with international reputations, but their decor is as quiet as their foods and wines are excellent. Unless a visitor knows just where he is going it is easy to pass them by, for no glaring neon signs proclaim their presence and no doorman uniformed like a lieutenant general stands outside.

Most of these places have their "specialties" although their menus offer a variety of dishes. Antoine's is known for its "oysters Rockefeller"; Arnaud's "shrimp Arnaud" is different from shrimp-anything-else; La Louisiane has a distinctive Creole cuisine. Broussard's, Galatoire's and D'Orleans are other places not to be missed by those who enjoy "adventures in gastronomy." The list might be extended.

For a proper appreciation of the Vieux Carré the stranger should have a guide, or walk its narrow streets with guidebook in hand. Scores of authors have written scores of books about the place but none is more informative or more authentic than *Old New Orleans,* by Stanley Clisby Arthur, newspaperman, biographer and historian, who as executive director of the Cabildo had access to the old records of the days of French and Spanish rule.

The buildings put up by the French in the early and middle 1700's were mostly one-story structures of brick walls laid between heavy upright timbers. In 1762 the colony was ceded by France to Spain, although it was not until 1769 that the Spanish took full possession. Building then began to take on a more substantial character, bricks brought from Europe as ballast in sailing vessels replaced wood, and tiles were used for roofs instead of cypress shingles. Few of those early buildings remain, however, for in 1788 and again in 1794 disastrous fires swept the city and most of the old buildings now standing were erected after the latter date.

When fire wipes out the heart of a city there is a gain as well as a loss. Outmoded buildings and those that have fallen into decay are replaced by new structures designed for present needs. So the city that quickly sprung up after these holocausts was solidly built and much of it is still serviceable after a century and a half. The rebuilding was done during the Spanish regime and the early days of American sovereignty, but many of the builders were French and the French style is dominant.

Common to all residences was the courtyard or "patio" (the word is from the Spanish), concealed from the street by the surrounding buildings and entered by an arched passageway. In more pretentious structures this was wide and high enough to permit a carriage to enter. The outside walls were flush with the sidewalk and often the first floor was the business establishment of the family that occupied the upper floors. These patios, paved with brick and perhaps enclosing a fountain and a small garden, are still among the more attractive spots in the old city. A narrow balcony or "gallery" (the word is from the French) projected from the second floor over the patio and in many instances a similar structure extended over the sidewalk on the outside. These galleries were enclosed by iron railings and their variety and artistry are outstanding features of the architecture of the Vieux Carré. The oldest of these decorative pieces are of wrought iron and were made in Spain, often after designs sent over by the builder and embodying his monogram. Grillwork made after 1830 usually was of cast iron and was made in England. Souvenir dealers today sell bits of decorative ironwork to the tourist trade but the ancestry of some of these pieces is suspect.

Most notable of the buildings in old New Orleans is the St. Louis Cathedral with its three slender spires. It faces the Mississippi River across Jackson Square, once called the Place d'Armes but rechristened in honor of the hero of the Battle of New Orleans. This is the third church to stand on that site. The first, a simple building erected in Bienville's time, was demolished by a hurricane in 1722. The second, a pretentious adobe-covered structure, was burned in 1778. The present building was completed in 1794 and had not been thrown open for services when the great fire of that year swept the city. It narrowly escaped destruction for buildings on both sides of it were burned; so it stands intact today, having undergone several additions and improvements in the century that followed.

"The Very Illustrious Cabildo" was not a building but was the legislative assembly of the Spanish colonial government. The foundations of the present building known as "The Cabildo" were laid in 1795 and the triangular pediment above the main entrance bore a carving of the royal arms of Spain. After the Louisiana Purchase by the United States the design was changed to an eagle with the shield of the Union on its breast. Like the near-by cathedral it is the third such building to occupy this spot, the two previous structures having been burned.

It was in this very building that the formalities of the transfer of the province from Spain to France took place November 30, 1803, and twenty days later in a similar scene the title passed from France to the United States; no doubt the quickest turnover of so large a property—almost a million square miles—in all the history of real estate transactions. The large room on the second floor of the building where these formalities took place is still known as the *Sala Capitular.*

Now under the direction of the Louisiana State Museum, the Cabildo houses a priceless collection of paintings, costumes, furniture and other memorabilia of the era of French and Spanish occupation, a delight to the casual visitor as well as the antiquarian. Here also are the old records, now crumbling with age, of real estate transfers, mortgages and court procedures, described in formal French or Spanish and meticulously written with quill pens, telling of the days when pesos and piasters were the mediums of exchange.

Outstanding among the museum treasures is a gilded death mask of Napoleon, the first of five or six made by Dr. François Antommarchi, the physician attendant on the exiled emperor at the time of his death on St. Helena Island in 1821. The doctor offered the masks to the French government but it was not interested. When he visited his daughter in New Orleans in 1834 he gave one mask to her and it was eventually acquired by the state from her family. In 1932 an attempt to steal the mask was frustrated when the culprit was caught leaving the building and since that time it has been displayed in a heavy glass case.

Even the most casual reference to the Vieux Carré must include such famed spots as the Old Absinthe House, the Haunted House and Laffite's Blacksmith Shop, for writers of fact and fiction have built them into legends. The Old Absinthe House is a two-story structure at the corner of Bourbon and Bienville streets, with arched doorways and the inevitable iron-railed gallery. Its foundations were laid in 1806 and it was built as a combination residence and storehouse for goods imported from Spain. The property has never changed hands since that year and belongs to the heirs of the original owners now living in Spain. It became a "coffee house" in 1861 and one Cayetano Ferrer of Barcelona, Spain, was employed as chief bartender. He concocted an absinthe frappé, using a secret formula, and the place became popular. In 1874 Ferrer leased the place and christened it "The Absinthe Room." It soon became a New Orleans landmark and during the latter part of the century began to be pointed out as "The Old Absinthe House."

The Haunted House has been raising goose pimples on the credulous for more than 120 years—longer than that if some stories are to be believed, but researches have proved that the house, a substantial three-story structure at 1140 Royal Street, was not built until 1832. The story begins with Marie Delphine Macarty, a vivacious daughter of one of the leading families of New Orleans. In 1800 she married a young Spanish nobleman who died four years later. A second husband died in 1816, and the twice-widowed

Delphine married Dr. Leonard Louis Nicholas Lalaurie, a native of France who had emigrated to New Orleans. They built the house on Royal Street and it became at once a center of gay social life.

All this ended suddenly on April 10, 1834, when an aged Negro cook set fire to the house when the owners were absent. Neighbors rushed in to save what they could and found several slaves chained in their rooms. The fire was brought under control and no one died, but a newspaper account the next morning so inflamed the populace that a mob formed and started to tear the mansion to pieces. It was necessary for soldiers to come to the aid of the sheriff before the place could be saved. In the meantime Madame Lalaurie and the doctor fled the city in their carriage and took refuge with friends. Soon afterward they sailed for Paris and never returned to New Orleans. But when Madame Lalaurie died in 1842 her body was secretly returned to New Orleans for burial.

The Lalaurie house was saved from the flames but it became the focal point for weird tales that never lost anything in the telling. In them chains clank, screams echo through the building, and a brutally whipped young slave girl jumps from the roof to the courtyard at midnight. Even today there are fearful persons who will not walk past the place after dark.

The story told of Laffite's Blacksmith Shop at 941 Bourbon Street is that here with a smithy as a "front" the Laffite brothers, Jean and Pierre, disposed of slaves and other property hijacked from Spanish ships. The most careful search of the activity of the Laffites fails to reveal any tale about such a place or the necessity for having a blind. But the quaint one-story building with its dormer windows is one of the oldest in the city, having survived the fires of 1788 and 1794. It is of brick-between-the-posts construction, such as was used by the early French settlers, and may be two hundred years old.

The festivities associated with Mardi Gras begin in January with masked balls, receptions and such gala affairs, but these are given by organizations that have no other purpose, admission is by invitation only, and they are in no sense public functions. "Mardi

(Bureau of New Orleans News)

Gras" is an Old World term and literally means "Fat Tuesday" which is French for "Shrove Tuesday," the day before Ash Wednesday and the beginning of Lent. As that date approaches the tempo of the city increases. There are brilliant night parades of marchers led by a masked "king," the kings ruling the parades as the queens rule the balls.

The high point of the celebration is reached at noon on Mardi Gras Day when "Rex," King of the Carnival, rides unmasked at the head of the greatest parade of all. Groups and individuals in fanciful costumes follow in his wake, there is dancing in the streets, while residents and visitors, rich and poor, surrender to the spirit of festivity.

The carnival is strictly of Creole origin, and this is a good place to emphasize that a "Creole" is a person of French or Spanish ancestry or a mixture of the two, but without a drop of Negro blood, as some erroneously suppose. The Creoles are the aristocrats of New Orleans and were so before it became a part of the United States. It was a group of young Creole gentlemen who in 1838 organized the first masked parade as a part of the Mardi Gras holiday which until then had been restricted to indoor festivities. For many years the merrymaking was confined largely to residents of New Orleans and its environs, but with the advent of the excursion train, the automobile, the tourist agency and the motel, Mardi Gras has become a national affair.

A story of New Orleans without some reference to the "scarlet women" who have paraded its levees would be to serve sole without a sauce. Other cities have often been characterized as "wicked" but the indiscretions of New Orleans always have had an aura of high excitement. This phase of New Orleans life had an early beginning, for soon after landing on the Gulf Coast D'Iberville wrote to Louis XIV to "send me wives for my settlers, for they are running in the forests after the Indian girls." The royal response was to send a shipload of women who could most easily be procured, along with a midwife that was immediately nicknamed "Madame Sans-Regret." Few of the girls married and most of them continued the life they had learned in Paris.

This led to loud protests by the wives of the officers in the colony, so the king bestirred himself and sent the "casket girls." These were mostly orphans or daughters of poor parents, and were guaranteed to be virtuous, not by the king but by their priests and mother superiors, which was more convincing. Each girl had a "casket" that contained a dowry from the king, four sheets, a blanket, two pairs of stockings, six headdresses, and a pelisse. They were met in New Orleans by the Mother Superior and taken to the convent of the Ursulines there. They made good wives, business fell off in the Indian-haunted forests, and casket girls continued to arrive in the colony over a period of twenty years until 1754. In later years many of their descendants were proud to say that grandmother, or perhaps great-grandmother, had been a casket girl.

New Orleans continued to grow with no more vice than might be found in any seaport town, until there developed in the early 1800's a group that had its counterpart nowhere else in the United States. They were the "quadroons," and the "quadroon balls" became a famous institution. Strictly speaking a quadroon is a person with one-fourth Negro blood, but the term was generally applied to any-one lighter than a mulatto, or half-Negro. Many women of mixed parentages were to be found among the common prostitutes of the city, but "quadroon" as used in New Orleans came to mean a woman of mixed blood who was the mistress of a white man. Stirring tales have been told of their beauty, and most of them undoubtedly were beautiful. If they were not they did not get the job.

These women of dubious ancestry first appeared in New Orleans when the revolt of the slaves in Santo Domingo in the 1790's forced the French aristocrats to flee. Many sought refuge in New Orleans, bringing their dusky mistresses along with them. These quadroons of legend were not slaves and were strictly "kept women." They knew all the social graces, they were educated under a mother-teaches-daughter system, they spoke excellent French, and fre-quently were accomplished musicians. Mostly they lived in small houses on Rampart Street at the western limits of the Vieux Carré where all expenses were met by their "protector," and to him they gave their undivided loyalty. A census taken in 1788 shows there were fifteen hundred "unmarried women of color, all free" living along Rampart Street. That year the Spanish governor, Estevan Miró, had passed an ordinance making it a misdemeanor for any of them to appear in public wearing plumes, silk or jewels. Their head-dress in public was limited to the colored handkerchief or *tignòn* usually worn by Negro women.

For three-quarters of a century it was a poor Creole dandy who did not have a dusky paramour along the ramparts. Sometimes this association ended with his marriage, often it did not. It is not surprising that men found such companionship more interesting than that of the secluded Latin women, brought up in the strict atmosphere of a convent, taught embroidery and a few "social graces," and never allowed to get more than an arm's length from the chaperone.

Restricted as they might be in their appearances on the streets, the women born under the bend sinister came into their own at the quadroon balls and they made the most of it. Dressed decorously after the latest mode, sparkling with jewels and carrying the inevitable fan, they danced with unsurpassed grace or flirted discreetly as they sipped their wine. These balls were conducted with all the decorum that characterized the most exclusive white soirées; there were no Negro men nor white women present, but the gatherings had a purpose. It was there the mothers brought their daughters, perhaps a shade whiter than themselves, in the hope of finding for them a "protector" who would install them in another little house on Rampart Street. No bargains were closed in the ballroom, it was solely for display of the merchandise, and the young Creole gentleman who was interested in some dusky virgin restrained himself until discreet inquiries and proper arrangements were made for the new venture. The young gentlemen did not take these associations lightly. It was a time when dueling was in high favor, and more than one fatal encounter had its origin at a quadroon ball.

This situation continued until the 1860's, but after the Civil War the balls rapidly declined in character and within a decade they had ceased entirely.

Much more violent is the record of common prostitution in New Orleans, and like such a record in any metropolis it is a story of political corruption, crime and bloodshed. But New Orleans managed to give a few new twists to this scarlet saga which is as old as civilization. Throughout the nineteenth century the rest of the country looked on this "City of Sin" with amazement sometimes tinctured with envy, and that period might be divided into the flatboat era and the steamboat era.

The Louisiana Purchase in 1803 coincided with and accelerated the great shift in population from the Atlantic seaboard to the Ohio and upper Mississippi valleys. The great "Father of Waters" now flowed untroubled by international intrigue from the forests of the North to the Gulf of Mexico—a new highway to new markets. Its muddy current offered free transportation to anything that would float, and almost everything that would float appeared on it during the ensuing half-century, laden to the waterline with bales, boxes and bottles. Out of this trial and error came the flatboat, an oblong barge of rough timbers destined to be broken up for lumber as soon as its cargo had been unloaded in New Orleans. It was marked by a long oar, or sweep, at each corner to be used in warding the boat off sand bars and snags and allowing some control in the muddy currents. Because of this feature they were known as "broadhorns."

These craft were manned by the toughest characters that ever appeared on the American scene, cowboys and gold prospectors not excepted. They had to be tough for the meanderings of the Mississippi offered harbor to wreckers and river pirates who did not hesitate to board a flatboat and murder all on board if conditions favored. This exciting pastime was also practiced by Indians along the western shore of the river during the early days. The flatboat crewman slept on the open deck wrapped in a buffalo hide when he had the time, ate boiled meat from a big stewpan around which he and his fellows gathered, and scorned to drink anything but Monongahela rye whisky, of which there was always a free supply on board. Otherwise he would not have joined the crew. When a flotilla of broadhorns tied up at the New Orleans levee the lid blew off with a bang that shook the town.

It is not surprising that the aristocratic Creoles of the Crescent City usually held their Northern countrymen in contempt, for the advance guard from the republic to the north was largely made up of roistering rivermen. Only when businessmen from the Northern cities moved to the rapidly expanding metropolis and brought their families with them did this feeling of bitterness begin to abate.

The force of *gens d'armes* composed principally of discharged Spanish soldiers and mulattoes that had been organized in 1803 to police the city were helpless against the flatboat men. In 1806 a new *garde de ville* was formed but the river boys disarmed them and beat them up at the first encounter. Tchoupitoulas Street near the levee and a few blocks south of the Vieux Carré was the tough Tenderloin early in the century, but too often the invaders only paused there long enough to get thoroughly fired up, and then invaded the more respectable quarters, wrecking bars and restaurants, and on one occasion completely demolishing a small circus.

But if the organized police could not handle the tough boys, the dive keepers with their bartenders and prostitutes took their measure. As the river trade increased this unsavory group pushed out along Girod Street to a section called "The Swamp" where lawlessness held undisputed sway and the police let them severely alone. Here was no attempt at "gilded vice." Boards laid across kegs served as bars, beds or gaming tables. If a riverman was lucky enough to win at a crooked faro or roulette game he was blackjacked before he could leave the district with his winnings. If he did not give all his money to his girl companion she took it from him when he was in a drunken stupor. If he protested his body would soon be floating down the river. There were never any inquests or investigations. Inevitably such a cesspool was a harbor for thieves, pickpockets and crooks of every hue who preyed on the rest of the city continuously.

The man who wrote "finis" for The Swamp and flatboat crews probably never heard of them. His name was Robert Fulton and he designed and partly financed the *New Orleans*, the first steamboat to navigate the Mississippi. It was built in Pittsburgh and arrived in New Orleans January 12, 1812. Within a decade steamboat traffic on the river was commonplace and in two decades the flatboat had almost disappeared from that stream. New Orleans breathed more easily.

The steamboat marked the beginning and the Civil War the end of what has been called the golden age of New Orleans. Sugar and cotton, produced by slave labor, and a water-borne traffic that literally covered the harbor waters with every type of craft, brought wealth to the city in spite of corruption in state and local politics. Gambling and prostitution flourished, but except for a few unpopular reformers nobody seemed to care, even when these activities began to encroach on the Vieux Carré. In 1857 an ordinance was passed under which houses of prostitution would be allowed to operate after receiving a license signed by the mayor. A few of these were issued but an enterprising madam who paid the $250 fee and then took the matter to court succeeded in having the law declared unconstitutional.

When Admiral David G. Farragut sailed up the Mississippi and captured New Orleans April 25, 1862, the curtain fell on the prosperity of the city and cannot be said to have raised until a new century had dawned. With the coming of peace the commerce of the city was gone, the enormous investment in slaves had evaporated, carpetbaggers had taken over the government and ex-slaves sat in the legislature. But the bagnios remained for the madams were quick to reach a *"rapprochement"* with the new regime.

Basin Street, the reputed birthplace of jazz, no longer appears on the maps of the city except for a very short section of that once notorious thoroughfare. It ran parallel to Rampart Street, the western boundary of the Vieux Carré. It was never given over to Negroes but it was the Grand Avenue of the red-light district that grew up around it after 1870. Here the term "gilded vice" was no mere figure of speech. Two- and three-story "mansions" lined the street, with stone steps leading up to carved doorways and bay windows looking out on the busy traffic. Inside the parlors were furnished with imported rugs, overstuffed chairs, marble-topped tables, and all the expensive and terrible bric-a-brac of the mid-Victorian era, while over all hung a crystal and gold chandelier. This magnificence might be duplicated in other cities, such as the famous "Everleigh Club" in Chicago, but the New Orleans entrepreneurs showed an originality rare in the Deep South: they advertised for business.

Mme. Emma Johnson, better known as the "Parisian Queen of America," needs little introduction in this country. . . . Everything goes here. Pleasure is the watchword. Emma never has less than twenty pretty women of all nations, who are clever entertainers. Aqui si habla Espanola. Ici on parle Français. Phone connection. 331–333 N. Basin.

Countess Willie V. Piazza, 315 Basin Street, is one place in the Tenderloin District you can't very well afford to "pass up." The Countess Piazza has made it a study to try and make everyone jovial who visits her house. If you have the "blues" the Countess and her girls can cure 'em. She has, without doubt, the most handsome and intelligent Octoroons in the United States. . . . The Countess wants it to be known that while her maison joie is peerless in every respect, she serves only the "amber fluid."

Mme. Lulu White, cor. Basin and Bienville streets. No where in the country will you find a more popular personage than Madame White. . . . To see her at night is like witnessing the late electrical display on the cascade at the late St. Louis Exposition.

These gems of the copywriter's art appeared in the *Blue Book,* a complete directory of the red-light area, which came out in several editions during the first decade of the present century. The 1906 issue contained 100 pages in which were listed 22 houses and 422 girls. Of the latter 318 were white, 58 colored and 46 octoroon. The *Blue Book* had been preceded by a *Green Book, or Gentleman's Guide to New Orleans,* published in 1895, and the *Red Book* a few years later. Copies of these are now eagerly sought by collectors.

Basin Street enterprises, however, were not dependent on books of green, red or blue to exploit their attractions. There sprang up in New Orleans from time to time several "newspapers" the columns of which were given almost wholly to sensational crimes and juicy items of interest about Basin Street.

Nettie Garbright, who for a number of years kept a sporting house at No. 139 Customhouse Street, and retired to private life, is back on the turf again, comfortably situated at No. 1537 Customhouse Street.

Eunice Deering, who presides at the swell mansion, No. 341 Basin Avenue, corner Conti, has increased her staff and is ready for the Carnival business. In this mansion nothing but swell women are to be seen.

Miss Josie Arlington is suffering with a bad cold, but she is on deck all the same attending to business.

Josie Arlington was the most spectacular madam of her time, a title held by Kate Townsend, Abbie Reed and "Queen" Gertie Livingston of an earlier day, and her four-story "mansion" at 225 Basin Street was the most expensively furnished bordello in the district. Josie, whose real name was Mary Deubler, was a native of New Orleans and had been a good-looking but brawling prostitute since she was seventeen. She had, however, a keen business sense and after managing a place successfully on Customhouse Street she acquired the Basin Street property in the late 1890's and presided there for ten years, making a considerable fortune in spite of the fact that she became known as "the snootiest madam in America."

In her latter years Josie became melancholy, purchased a two-thousand-dollar lot in Metaire Cemetery, and erected thereon a fifteen-thousand-dollar tomb, the copper door of which bore the figure of a kneeling woman. She also bought an expensive home on Esplanade Street and lived there after leasing her Basin Street business. Three years later she died. Within a few months the city put up a traffic light near the tomb. The red glow it cast over the resting place of the scarlet woman excited so much curiosity and comment that the color of the light was changed. Then her heirs removed Josie's bones to a vault and sold the tomb for a tidy sum. "*Sic transit gloria mundi.*"

From 1897 until it was abolished the segregated district of New Orleans was known as "Storyville," and an odd story it is. By 1890 the manner in which uncontrolled prostitution was taking over the city became an acute problem and various remedial measures were proposed and rejected. Alderman Sidney Story, a broker, made

an extensive tour of European cities at his own expense to study
their methods, and on his return introduced an ordinance provid-
ing for a segregated district taking in part of the French Quarter
and including Basin Street. This was passed and immediately real
estate prices and rents inside the prescribed area doubled, while
properties to be evacuated fell in value accordingly. Screams of
anguish arose from the madams, the girls and their backers, but
there was nothing to do but move. They immediately christened
the new area "Storyville," much to the alderman's distress, and the
name stuck.

As Storyville it soon became the most widely known red-light
district in the country and a major point of interest for visitors. The
area reached its peak of prosperity and notoriety around 1910 and
received its death blow in 1917. With the entry of the United States
into World War I Secretary of War Newton D. Baker and Secretary
of the Navy Josephus Daniels issued orders forbidding prostitution within five miles of a military or naval establishment. That
meant Storyville. Mayor Martin Behrman went to Washington,
where he made a formal protest. There he learned the only question
was whether the city would close the place or the Federal government would do it. So the city adopted an ordinance making prostitution illegal after midnight, November 12, 1917. The women were told
they could remain, but there must be no red lights and no business.
Details of police and firemen stood guard as the zero hour approached but their services were not needed. The patrol wagons
rolled back to the station houses empty. Exactly two hundred years
after its founding, prostitution in New Orleans was outside the law.

Within the three parishes that comprise Greater New Orleans the
Mississippi River follows a tortuous course, mainly eastward, and at
one point for a short distance it flows directly north. After a few
more convolutions it heads in a southeasterly direction for the Gulf
of Mexico into which it enters 110 miles below the city, not in the

grand manner befitting such a stream, but in a spattering of divided and subdivided "passes" through the half-submerged alluvial plain it has built up through the centuries. The main ship channels are through South Pass and Southwest Pass.

A concrete highway follows the west bank for almost a hundred miles, which is as far as the levee extends. Halfway down is a free ferry that connects with the lower end of a similar highway on the east bank, by which one may return to the city. These highways along the river have little in common with those that parallel the Bayou Teche and Bayou Lafourche. The latter traverse the rich sugar cane country and are dotted with prosperous-looking villages, but the Mississippi's last long stretch is largely through marshy wasteland and few tourists are met with. A highway map shows a number of villages spaced along the route—Jesuit Bend, Diamond, Happy Jack, Homeplace, Empire, Triumph—but most of them are hardly "wide places in the road" and have not bothered to put up roadside signs so the stranger may know which one he is passing through.

Yet the journey is not without a charm of sorts. The road is seldom more than a hundred yards from the river, but the traveler never gets a glimpse of it for it is on the other side of the levee. Willows border the roadway and through them the motorist occasionally catches glimpses of cattle pastures, but most of the landscape is marshland. There are no fields of rice or cane, and for long stretches not a house of any kind is in sight. By one of those freaks for which Old Mississip' is noted the land takes on a more stable character along the lower part of the route. Here are a number of small orange groves, and fig trees flourish in almost every dooryard. At one point there were extensive plantings of oranges until a severe freeze in 1947 killed most of the trees. Most of the groves have since been replanted and are just beginning to bear.

Near the end of the highway at what is known as "Plaquemines Bend" are the remains of Fort Jackson on the west bank of the river and Fort St. Philip opposite it. It was here that the Union Fleet under Admiral Farragut broke a chain boom and sailed up the river April 24, 1862, and captured New Orleans the next day. For six days fleet and forts had exchanged a heavy fire and on April 28 the two forts surrendered.

At a little settlement called Venice the pavement ends and the reason for the improved highway becomes apparent. It is oil. A number of the large companies have facilities here for loading petroleum products on barge and tanker, while out across the forbidding marshlands and the waters of the Gulf new wells are being drilled. Beyond Venice the road degenerates into an eroded shell highway which stops at a spot called Pilottown, where the New Orleans pilots take over to guide incoming ships up the river, or leave outbound vessels headed for the open waters of the Gulf. This is really the end of the line.

So far the motorist has been within shouting distance of the river for almost a hundred miles yet has not seen it. But leaving Venice to return he can take a narrow shell road northward for eight miles along the top of the levee and have a magnificent view of the great stream where it sweeps unimpeded for the last few miles of its long, long journey across the United States. Forty miles above Venice at a cluster of cottages called West Pointe a la Hache is a ferry landing where a small steam vessel, operated by the State Highway Department, makes a round trip to the village of Pointe a la Hache on the east bank of the river every hour. There is no charge and the ferry trip is almost worth the long drive down and back. North and south from the center of the river is a vista of the wide waters, restrained by willow-fringe levees, unmarred by docks or factories, rolling along for their rendezvous with the Gulf Stream and the world.

As the traveler returns to New Orleans along the east shore the scene is much like that on the west side, except that it is obviously an older road, with here and there a grove of spreading live oaks marking a homestead of the long ago. Where the river makes its last sharp bend on its southward journey and where the highway of necessity follows it, is a drab little village called English Turn. It commemorates an incident of early history that the French tell with gusto.

The young governor of the French province, Sieur Jean Baptiste Le Moyne de Bienville, was one day in a canoe at this point of the river when he met an English brig sailing upstream. He hailed the captain and ordered him back, declaring that the province was "a dependency of Canada and therefore a part of the dominions of France." The brig bowed to the canoe and sailed back down the river, and the spot has since been called English Turn.

A few miles farther on, following the curve of the river, the road enters the busy, uninviting suburbs of New Orleans. Here at the town of Chalmette is the site of one of the most important events in American history, the Battle of New Orleans, January 8, 1815, where General Andrew Jackson defeated the British under General Edward M. Pakenham, who was mortally wounded. In the center of the roadway, enclosed by an iron fence, is an ivy-covered angle of a brick wall, all that is left of an imposing colonial residence, "Versailles," erected in 1805 by Pierre Denis de La Ronde, a wealthy planter. The mansion faced the river, less than half a mile to the south, and a double line of live oaks show where a wide avenue once ran from the house to the river landing. A Louisiana State historical marker of stone just inside the wire fence that separates the field from the highway reads: "These Versailles Oaks were planted in 1783 by Pierre Denis de La Ronde, born in New Orleans, April 20, 1762, died December 2, 1824. Here he also built a French colonial residence."

Despite this the magnificent trees are universally known as the "Pakenham Oaks," for it was from this point that the British forces launched their final assault against the Americans. A near-by sign-board modestly proclaims: "Pakenham Oaks. Property of the Southern Railway System. Visitors welcome." The site is now a cow pasture, and the neighborhood is one of concrete highways, railroad tracks, filling stations, and large and small industrial plants. Only a few historically minded tourists visit the place.

"The Pakenham Oaks" at Chalmette

XII. *Jean Laffite and the Battle of New Orleans*

I T is a disquieting thought that in the story of nations as in that of individuals, we can never know what the alternative would have been. If Blucher had not come to the aid of Wellington at Waterloo, if Booth had missed, if the British had captured

New Orleans that January day in 1815—there is no end to speculation. School histories tell us that the Battle of New Orleans was fought fifteen days after the Treaty of Ghent had been signed and the war had ended. Had it? The commissioners, who had been arguing for six months in that neutral city, had at last put their names to a treaty but it still required the ratification of their respective governments to implement it.

The war, which began in June, 1812, was far from universally popular in the United States, and among the New England Federalists was referred to as "President Madison's War," although he had been reluctant to see war declared. It had been brought on largely by England's insistence on the principle of "Once an Englishman, always an Englishman," and her actions on stopping American vessels on the high seas and "impressing" into British service any member of its crew the officers might assume to be a former British seaman. In fact some captains held that any English-speaking sailorman was an Englishman unless he could prove otherwise. By 1810 there were more than four thousand such cases listed by the Federal government. These and other grievances eventually led to a declaration of war.

On land the war went badly for the new republic. General William Hull started out to invade Canada but soon surrendered without firing a shot. For this he was court-martialed and sentenced to death, but was pardoned by President Madison. In 1814, after the Battle of Bladensburg in which only eight American soldiers died in defense of their capital, Sir Alexander Cochrane, an English naval officer who had marched his men across the country from the Patuxent River, entered Washington where he burned the President's mansion, the Capitol and the Congressional Library. It should be said parenthetically that this vandalism was much criticized in England. On the sea where Great Britain was supposed to be the strongest she fared the worst. Young Captain Stephen Decatur commanding the war vessel *United States* captured H.M.S. *Macedonia*. Commodore Isaac Hull in the *Constitution* ("Old Ironsides") defeated the British frigate *Guerriere*; and Captain Oliver Hazard Perry sent his famous report from Lake Erie: "We have met the enemy and they are ours!"

In the meantime Napoleon Bonaparte was keeping England and the rest of Europe very busy, and early in 1814 England signified its willingness to discuss peace. President Madison accepted, but it was not until midsummer that three Englishmen and five Americans, including John Quincy Adams and Henry Clay, met in Ghent to discuss terms. By that time Napoleon's star had waned, he had abdicated in April and had been banished to Elba. This left England free to turn her attention to the war with her onetime colonies. Three expeditions were planned, even while the commissioners were talking of peace. One was to invade the country from Canada, another was to enter through Chesapeake Bay, and the third and most formidable of all was to strike at New Orleans, which the United States had held for only twelve years and which it could defend with difficulty.

While all these preparations were going on the English peace commissioners were dragging their feet. Weeks passed in the discussion of trivialities. August gave way to September and September to October. On October 24 Sir Edward M. Pakenham received orders to proceed to Louisiana to take command "of the forces operating there for the reduction of that province." The rendezvous for this great expedition was Negril Bay on the island of Jamaica. Here were assembled fifty ships and transports, ten thousand seamen, fifteen hundred Marines, and not less than nine thousand soldiers, many of whom were seasoned veterans of the campaigns against Napoleon. Not all of the personnel were fighting men. Included was a complete staff of civil government functionaries whose duty it would be to take over the administration of the "Crown Colony of Louisiana." In November while the eight commissioners were still haggling about peace terms the armada sailed for the Gulf Coast.

Now arises the unanswerable question: If this expedition had been successful; if, when the treaty came before the British government for ratification, General Pakenham had been in command of all the territory and commerce of the lower Mississippi, would England have accepted the work of its commissioners at Ghent and ordered him to pack up and come home? There can be little doubt that under such circumstances England could have reopened negotiations with war-weary America and won substantial concessions in the newly acquired Louisiana Territory.

Granted this, another disturbing question arises: If Jean Laffite and his fighting Baratarians had been on the side of the enemy at the Battle of New Orleans, could General Jackson and five thousand troops, consisting of regulars, militia, inexperienced recruits and "free men of color" have withstood the fierce assaults of the English? "Old Hickory" himself would have been slow to answer that one.

For a century and a half Jean Laffite has been one of the most enigmatic figures that ever crossed the American scene. Fact and fancy are all scrambled together in the legends that have grown up around him and his fellow buccaneers of Barataria Bay. Not all of the mystery has yet been cleared up but most of the story was made available a few years ago when his great-grandson came to Stanley Clisby Arthur, then executive director of the Louisiana State Museum in the old Cabildo, and placed at his disposal photostatic copies of family records, correspondence and other data concerning the remarkable Laffite. These and the old records of New Orleans enabled Mr. Arthur to compile a biography that throws a new light on the character of his subject, and heightens rather than dulls the aura of romance that long has enveloped this historic figure. The book was published in 1952 by Harmanson, of 333 Royal Street in New Orleans.

Jean Laffite was a true Creole of French-Spanish ancestry, and never in his exciting career did he step out of the character of Creole gentleman—courageous, commanding, suave, courteous and as ruthless as fate when the situation called for it. He was born at

Port-au-Prince, on the island of Haiti (then called Santo Domingo) April 22, 1782, and died (this will surprise you) at Alton, Illinois, May 5, 1854. He was the youngest of five brothers and three sisters, children of a French father and a Spanish Jewess mother. His mother died soon after his birth and he was raised by his maternal grandmother, for whom he always had great love and admiration.

The great motivation in the life of Jean Laffite was hatred for Spain, a fact that throws a revealing light on his career. For this he had ample reason. While still a young man he had become a prosperous merchant, and had married a well-to-do young woman when he was eighteen years old. In 1803 he decided to visit Europe with his family and to that end closed out his business, bought a ship, loaded it with cargo and sailed. A week later he was overhauled by a Spanish man-of-war. A U.S. naval officer to whom he told the story quoted him as saying:

"The Spaniards captured us. They took everything—goods, specie, even my wife's jewels. They set us on shore upon a barren sand key, with just enough provisions to keep us alive a few days until an American schooner took us off and landed us in New Orleans. I did not care what became of me. I was a beggar. My wife took the fever from exposure and hardship and died in three weeks after my arrival.

"I met some daring fellows who were as poor as I was. We bought a schooner and declared against Spain eternal war. Fifteen years I have carried on a war against Spain. So long as I live I am at war with Spain, but no other nation."

Coupled with this experience was the fact that his beloved Jewess grandmother had been summoned as a witness before the Spanish Inquisition and her husband, Laffite's grandfather, had died in 1760 in the Zaragoza prison, having been charged with heresy.

The name Laffite first appears in the annals of New Orleans soon after the flag of the United States was raised over that city on December 20, 1803. A French privateer, the *La Soeur Chérie*, (not "sour cherry" but "beloved sister") put into New Orleans from

Santo Domingo, ostensibly to repair damage its captain, Pierre Laffite, said it had suffered in a storm. Pierre was three years older than his brother Jean, and throughout their long association acted as the business manager of the partnership. William C. C. Claiborne was the territorial governor of Louisiana, and was also the first governor after the territory became a state in 1812. He was to have various contacts with the Laffite brothers, of which this was the first. Suspicious of *La Soeur Chérie* he ordered the authorities to observe the actions of her commander carefully to make sure none of the neutrality laws were violated. Eventually the vessel was allowed to sail, but there were suspicions that a number of her Negro "crew" who had "deserted" while in port were really slaves that had been illegally smuggled into the city.

At that time France was at war with Spain and the seas were crawling with privateers preying on the rich Spanish commerce of the Americas. To become a privateer the owner of a vessel applied to the French authorities at Martinique or Guadaloupe and, for a price, was given "letters of marque and reprisal" that licensed him to attack and loot the ships of the enemy. It was a form of legalized piracy and was long hallowed by custom. Many a New England bank account was swelled by merchandise captured in this manner. Not until the signatories of the Declaration of Paris in 1856 agreed to abolish the practice did it decline. When the English captured Martinique and Guadaloupe in 1806 the privateers flocked to Cartagena, capital of Colombia which had just declared its independence of Spain, and there obtained new letters of marque and continued their legalized looting. The Laffites always operated as privateersmen and none of their ships ever raised the "Jolly Roger" of piracy.

Closely tied in with privateering was the universal practice of smuggling, by which the captured merchandise could be returned to the channels of trade. Continued successful operation required a haven where the ships could take refuge from expeditions sent against them, where the goods could be assembled and held for disposal, and from where they could be delivered to market with minimum risk. The island of Grande Terre, six miles long and half as wide and not more than fifty miles west of the Mississippi Delta, was ideal for such a purpose. It lies between Barataria Bay and the Gulf, and from there light craft, such as bateaus, can be rowed or poled almost to within sight of New Orleans. Not far from the city was a large shell mound that had been a sacred place for the Chawasha Indians. It was called "The Temple" and was a perfect spot for the sellers from the sea and the buyers from the city to meet and transact their shady business.

The haven at Grande Terre rapidly attracted privateersmen, "buccaneers," "freebooters," and no doubt a number of true pirates who needed no official paper to slit a throat and steal a cargo. But some of them were smart businessmen as well and saw the need for organization. The situation was to have its parallel more than a century later when prohibition in the United States turned the bootlegging of whisky into Big Business that clever and ruthless men soon brought to a high degree of efficiency. Early in its development the group at Grande Terre came to be known as "The Baratarians."

To dispose of their cargoes of merchandise the raiders maintained "agents" at New Orleans whose business it was to contact friendly merchants and acquaint them with what goods were on hand and how and where they could be delivered. Much of the traffic was in "black ivory," as the slave trade was euphemistically termed. Two of the leading agents were Pierre and Jean Laffite, both well regarded in the city although their business was no secret. Jean, with dark hair, flashing eyes, a suavity that covered a relentless will, and a fluent command of English, French, Spanish and Italian, was the beau ideal of a Creole gentleman and was welcome in the city's best homes. Business was growing at Grande Terre, from where the Laffites and their captains had a number of ships operating. A stronger hand was needed there, and in 1811 Jean Laffite, by common consent of the leading captains, moved down to take command as *patron*, or as the Baratarians called him, "the *bos*." He was only twenty-nine years old but his word was the law of Grande Terre.

He saw to the equitable distribution of proceeds from captured goods, and at his nod a recalcitrant bad man might be banished or hanged.

Business boomed. Merchandise of all sorts piled up at "The Temple" and leading merchants went there to purchase it at auction or private sale. Several respectable New Orleans fortunes are said to have had their beginnings there. Of course the goods were smuggled into the city (the Laffites never denied that they were smugglers) and the merchants taking them were able to undersell their more scrupulous competitors. That spelled trouble. Louisiana became a state in 1812 and the Federal government began to take notice of the situation. Governor Claiborne was importuned by the honest merchants to do something to protect them, and he asked the state legislature for funds for such a purpose. But the Baratarians had many friends there and nothing came of it.

A new U.S. Customs Inspector, Captain Andrew H. Holmes, with a small force attempted to make a capture on Barataria Bay, but the Laffites, forewarned, evaded him and smuggled their cargo into New Orleans, much to the discomfiture of the law. In November of 1812 Captain Holmes tried again with more subtlety and haled twenty-four prisoners into the Federal court. Among them were Jean and Pierre Laffite. All were soon admitted to bail and were never brought to trial. It was a humiliating blow, but business at Grande Terre went on pretty much as usual.

The following October a party of revenue agents intercepted a sailboat loaded with smuggled goods and in the ensuing struggle one of the agents was wounded and the Baratarians escaped. This led Governor Claiborne to issue a proclamation dated November 24, 1813, urging all law enforcement officers to be vigilant in their duties, cautioning all citizens "against giving any kind of succor or support to the John Lafitte [sic] and all others in like manner offending," and offering five hundred dollars to anyone delivering Laffite to any sheriff in the state. To this the fugitive replied by offering five thousand dollars to anyone who would deliver the governor at Cat

Island, an outpost of the Baratarians near Grande Terre. That was good for many a chuckle along the river front.

Notwithstanding that several indictments against the Laffites and some of their captains were on record in New Orleans, charging them with violation of the revenue and neutrality laws, the year 1813 was the high point of prosperity at Grande Terre. Not less than five hundred hard-bitten men manned the fleet of swift, armed sailing vessels that swept out across the Gulf of Mexico and the Caribbean Sea and returned with their holds full of rich loot. Profits were honestly divided between captain and crew according to an accepted code, with Jean Laffite umpiring any differences. And then Pierre had to get careless and show himself on the streets of New Orleans, where he was promptly arrested and held in irons without bail.

Such was the situation as America's second war with England drew to a close. So far the Gulf Coast had hardly been affected, but the English press had been loud in its demands for a defeat and recapture of its sometime colonies, and England had looked with disfavor on the acquisition of the Louisiana Territory by France from Spain and its transfer to the United States in less than three weeks. Once in possession of its key city she could dictate the disposition of much of the heart of North America. So ships, men and munitions were assembled at Jamaica, and the armada sailed for Pensacola, Florida, then Spanish territory. Colonel Edward Nicolls, its commander, had asked the captain general of the Spanish government in Havana for permission to establish British headquarters in Pensacola Bay and had been refused. It made no difference. Decadent Spain was too weak to resist and Pensacola was occupied.

Now destiny reached out and touched Jean Laffite on the shoulder. Colonel Nicolls did not underestimate the difficulty of taking a city surrounded by marshes, uncharted waterways and shallow lakes as was New Orleans. So he sought the services of the one man who could help him more than any other. On September 2, 1814, the *Sophia*, a brig flying the British colors, appeared off the pass at

Grande Terre, fired a gun at a privateer about to enter, forcing it to run aground, and then entered the pass herself and dropped anchor. Jean Laffite immediately put off in a small boat to see what the stranger was about, and was met by a pinnace from the brig flying the British colors and a flag of truce. In it were Captain Lockyer of the Royal Navy, and Captain McWilliams of the infantry.

To their question, "Where is Mr. Laffite?" he replied that the man they sought was on shore, and received a packet directed to "Monsieur Lafit or the Commandant at Barataria." He persuaded the two officers to come ashore with him and when they had landed he disclosed his identity. Some two hundred Baratarians gathered along the shore did not conceal their hostility, hating the English almost as much as the Spanish, but Laffite silenced them and escorted the officers to his house where he showed them every courtesy.

The principal document in the packet was a letter from Colonel Nicolls addressed to Laffite, which began:

Sir:

I have arrived in the Floridas for the purpose of annoying the only enemy Great Britain has in the world, as France and England are now friends. I call on you with your brave followers to enter into the service of Great Britain in which you shall have the rank of Captain, lands will be given to you all in proportion to your respective ranks on a peace taking place, and I invite you on the following terms. . . .

The letter went on to state their property would be guaranteed them and their persons protected. Their vessels were to be surrendered but they would be paid for at a fair value. (They were soon to lose every ship without receiving a penny.) In addition Captain Lockyer said he was authorized to promise Jean Laffite the sum of thirty thousand dollars (six thousand pounds sterling), payable either in New Orleans or Pensacola. The captain also pointed out that as a captain in the Royal Navy he would have every opportunity to advance because of his familiarity with the Gulf and Caribbean waters.

Here was a tempting offer. His brother was in irons in New Orleans and Jean himself was under indictment there and dare not be seen on the streets. Now he could balance the score. Furthermore, should he refuse to aid Colonel Nicolls and should the British take New Orleans the Baratarians would soon be driven from their refuge. After due hesitation Laffite asked for a fortnight to consider the matter and consult his captains. Parting from Captain Lockyer he next morning he hinted he might accept, but the wily Creole was only seeking to gain time.

Hardly was the *Sophia* hull down on the horizon before Rancher, Laffite's most trusted aide, was en route to New Orleans carrying a letter setting forth all that had occurred, as well as the papers received from Colonel Nicolls. They included a copy of a bombastic "proclamation" addressed to "Natives of Louisiana" who were to be liberated from "a faithless, imbecile government." After a long disquisition it concluded: "After the experience of twenty-one years can you any longer support those brawlers for liberty who call it freedom when they themselves are free; be no longer their dupes." It was dated "Headquarters, Pensacola, August 29, 1814." The packet was delivered to Jean Blanque, a leading merchant and banker and a close friend of the Laffites. (He also was the second husband of Delphine Lalaurie of "Haunted House" fame.) Blanque took it at once to the governor and in a short time Rancher was summoned to the state house and told to hurry back to Jean and ask him to take no steps until it was determined what the government should do. When Rancher got back to Grande Terre, Pierre Laffite was with him, and in New Orleans a disconsolate jailer was offering a thousand dollars for his return!

The communication from Jean Laffite was the first word to reach New Orleans of the impending attack. At first there was a disposition to disregard it, but other sources soon confirmed the news. Realizing the urgency Jean wrote a second letter, this one addressed directly to Governor Claiborne, again offering the services of himself and his followers, and adding: "I have never sailed under any flag but that of the Republic of Carthagena, and my vessels are perfectly regular in that respect. If I could have brought my lawful prizes into the ports of this state I should not have employed the illicit means that have caused me to be proscribed." The day this letter was dispatched, September 10, 1814, Governor Claiborne was in conference with Major General Jacques Villère, commanding the Louisiana militia; Commodore Daniel T. Patterson of the U.S. Navy; Colonel George T. Ross, of the 44th U.S. Infantry; and Pierre F. Dubourg, collector of customs. Ross, Patterson and Dubourg insisted that Laffite's information was wrong and that the Baratarians' stronghold at Grande Terre should be attacked and destroyed at once. To this Governor Claiborne reluctantly gave his consent.

Rumors of how things were going reached the Laffites and alarmed them. The British brig, *Sophia*, appeared off the coast after two weeks and cruised up and down waiting for an answer to Colonel Nicoll's offer. It was not too late to accept it, but the brig received no signal and returned to Pensacola. Many of the Baratarians declared they would defend their island with their lives, but Jean dissuaded them. On September 16 the American schooner-of-war, *Carolina*, accompanied by a number of gunboats, appeared off the Grande Terre stronghold. They met with no opposition. Commodore Patterson said in his report he "perceived the pirates were abandoning their vessels and fleeing in all directions. I have captured all their vessels in port, dispersed their band, without one of my brave fellows being hurt."

Not all escaped, nor tried to, but the destruction was complete. Jean and Pierre Laffite fled in a pirogue up a bayou to a friendly plantation, but Dominique You, almost as famous as Jean Laffite, surrendered, as did a number of others, and was taken to New Orleans and locked up in the Cabildo. The forty palm-thatched houses on the island were burned and twenty-five vessels captured.

It may be unkind to question the patriotic motives of Colonel Ross, Commodore Patterson and their "brave fellows," but the fact remains that if the vessels and merchandise were taken and condemned as a "prize," the Army and Navy personnel would be entitled to a very substantial part of it. Judge Alexander Walker, in his *Jackson and New Orleans*, written more than a century ago, says: "The rich plunder of the 'Pirates' Retreat,' the valuable fleet of small coasting vessels that rode in the Bay of Barataria, the exaggerated stories of a vast amount of treasure, heaped up in glittering piles, in dark, mysterious caves, of chests of Spanish dobloons buried in the sand, continued to inflame the imagination and avarice of some of the individuals who were active in getting up the expedition." In his biography of Jean Laffite, Stanley C. Arthur says: "Both of them [Patterson and Ross] were more interested in the sale of the contraband taken from Grande Terre than in anything else."

Four days were spent by the soldiers and sailors in loading their own and the captured vessels with everything of value on the island. Then they returned to New Orleans and on October 17 there was filed in the Federal court a libel action of "D. T. Patterson & G. T. Ross & others vs. Certain vessels, goods & merchandise." The action was opposed by John R. Grymes, U.S. District Attorney, who asked that the goods be turned over to the collector of customs. (After the Laffites were restored to favor they instituted action to recover the property they alleged had been illegally seized. They retained Grymes as counsel and he wounded the opposing lawyer in a duel. The case dragged through the courts for years but neither the Laffites nor the raiders ever received any return.)

Time was running out. In Pensacola the British forces were preparing for the assault. The Laffite brothers were lying low at the plantation home of Alexander Labranche in St. Charles Parish. Dominique You and the ablest of the Baratarians were locked up in the Cabildo. At Mobile, 150 miles up the coast, was General Andrew Jackson, commander of the Seventh Military District, who, with a force of regulars and Tennessee militia, had been chasing the Creek Indians. Governor Claiborne hastened to acquaint him with the activities of the enemy and of the attempt they had made to enlist the aid of the Baratarians. Jackson issued a proclamation to match that put out by Colonel Nicolls, one paragraph of which read:

"I ask you, Louisianians, can we place any confidence in the honor of men who have courted an alliance with pirates and robbers?"

Tension in New Orleans increased. The young Creoles organized five companies of the *Bataillon d'Orléans* that was soon to prove itself in battle. On November 30 Jackson arrived, weary and sick with dysentery but not lacking in energy. He found a city without defenses, guarded only by a few light gunboats (five of which were soon to be captured), and Colonel Ross with a regiment of infantry. The general moved fast. Among the first presented to him was Major A. Lacarrière Latour, a native of France and an accomplished engineer. Actually he was not in the military service but Jackson made him a sort of "major-pro-tem" and principal engineer. His services were of the highest importance but the War Department records do not show his name. Immediately after the battle he wrote a history of it that is still the most authentic record of that event.

While the city was girding for the attack it received disastrous news. Five American gunboats lying off Lake Borgne, actually a bay to the east of the city, had been captured by the British on December 14 after a fierce resistance. The situation was becoming desperate and a committee of state legislators and others tried to persuade Jackson to accept the services of the Laffites and their Baratarians, but he refused. Finally Governor Claiborne added his influence to the same end, and Jackson reluctantly agreed to receive the "hellish banditti." It is to Old Hickory's credit that having made this decision he accepted the Baratarians with good grace, and was loud in their praise when they distinguished themselves. Governor Claiborne on December 17 issued an order extending a free and full pardon to all Baratarians whose conduct on the field would meet with the approval of General Jackson.

So the doors of the Cabildo were opened and the Laffites hurried to New Orleans where Jean and Pierre immediately presented themselves to the commanding general. Says Latour: "Mr. (J.) Laffite solicited for himself and for all the Baratarians the honor of serving under our banners, that they might have an opportunity of proving that, if they had ever infringed the revenue laws, yet none was more ready than they to defend the country and combat its enemies. Persauded that the assistance of these men could not fail of being very useful, the General accepted their offers."

The great problem for Jackson now was at what point would the enemy attack? Past Grande Terre and up through Barataria Bay? Up the Mississippi after subduing the forts at Plaquemines Bend? From Lake Pontchartrain and up St. John's Bayou? Or overland along the Chef Menteur Road east of the city? Each of these approaches was scouted and a small force left on guard. Pierre Laffite remained at Jackson's elbow, giving him information as to every pass and waterway in the region. Jean and Captain Dominique were occupied with organizing their fellows into three artillery units, a trade in which they were expert and a department in which the defense was woefully weak.

Despite all precaution the enemy found a soft spot in the ring of defense. A sluggish stream, the Bayou Bienvenue, flows eastward across the marshes and empties into Lake Borgne. This point was supposed to have been watched by the gunboats, but they had been captured. The British reconnaissance had been excellent and on the night of December 22 they began landing their troops from small boats ascending the bayou. The following day General Keane with some two thousand soldiers captured the Villière Plantation, ten miles from New Orleans, and took the son of its owner prisoner. But Major Villière soon escaped and hurried to Jackson with the news of the invasion.

History says the Battle of New Orleans was fought January 8, 1815. Actually there were four land engagements, any one of which might have been decisive, the first of which was fought the night of December 23. (The commissioners at Ghent had not yet signed the draft of the peace treaty.) When Jackson learned the enemy had landed he determined to attack immediately. Every fighting man available was summoned "at once" to Fort St. Charles in the heart of the city. The *Bataillon d'Orléans,* stationed on the Bayou St.

John, ran all the way, seven miles, but Captain Dominique You could not move his artillery that fast and so missed the first fight. It was a mixed array of regulars, militia, aristocrats and volunteer "free men of color" that Jackson led down the levee as darkness was falling. At half-past seven the schooner-of-war, *Carolina*, opened fire on the British from the river, and the "Battle in the Dark" was on. For several hours friend and foe mingled in confusion. Pierre Laffite guided General Coffee and his Tennessee riflemen around the flank of the invaders from where they swept back through the British camp spreading chaos and taking a number of prisoners. For this he was later officially commended by Jackson. When British reinforcements began arriving from their ships the Americans retired toward the city. Their losses were 213 killed and wounded to the enemy's 277.

As a military action the battle of December 23 might be called a draw, but in his history of the campaign Major Latour wrote: "The result of the affair of the 23d was the saving of Louisiana, for it cannot be doubted that the enemy, had he not been attacked with such impetuosity when he had hardly effected his debarkation, would that very night or early next morning have marched against the city, which was not defended by any fortification." Jackson withdrew to the Chalmette Plantation where an abandoned drainage ditch stretched from the levee on the right to the marshes on his left, and with that in his front threw up an earthwork of heavy "gumbo" mud where the issue would eventually be decided. Today the site is a small National Historical Park where the grass-covered ridge that protected the defenders is still visible. Markers show where the several military units served, and a hundred-foot obelisk rises above the scene.

On Christmas Day there arrived in the British camp Lieutenant General Sir Edward Michael Pakenham, only thirty-six years old but a twenty-year veteran of campaigns in Ireland, the West Indies and Spain. With him was his second-in-command, Sir Samuel Gibbs.

They found their way to victory barred by the resourceful Jackson, who still bore the scar inflicted by a British officer's saber, when, as a fourteen-year-old prisoner late in the Revolutionary War, he had refused to shine the officer's boots. The newly arrived commander immediately went into action. On December 28 he ordered a "Grand Reconnaissance." Soon after sunrise two columns of red-coated soldiers advanced in the best European tradition toward the American line, supported by artillery fire. Only five cannon replied, two of them being twenty-four-pounders served by the Baratarians. As the attackers fanned out for the assault they were swept by a holocaust of rifle and artillery fire. The gun served by Dominique You knocked out two British field pieces. The engagement was soon over and the British fell back to the Villière Plantation. The American casualties were one officer wounded.

Three days passed and on Sunday, January 1, 1815, a heavy fog blanketed everything along the Mississippi. The young Creoles, weary with fighting and digging, asked that they be allowed to celebrate the holiday, so Jackson ordered a grand review of the whole army in front of his headquarters. Hardly had the marching started when the fog lifted and thirty enemy guns opened up on the American ramparts, where the defenders now had ten guns mounted. This was to be an artillery action, with the British infantry ready to advance when a breach had been made in Jackson's line. Vincent Nolte, a New Orleans cotton merchant, took part in the battle and has left us an account of how the Baratarians fought. (A century and a quarter later Nolte was to serve as the model for Anthony Adverse in Hervey Allen's masterful novel of that title.)

"The largest British battery had directed its fire against the battery of the pirates, Dominique You and Beluche," wrote Nolte. "Once, as Dominique was examining the enemy through a glass, a cannon shot wounded his arm. He bound it up, saying, 'I will make them pay for that!' and resumed his glass. He then directed a 24-

pounder, gave the order to fire, and the ball knocked an English gun carriage to pieces and killed six or seven men."

After two hours Jackson ordered a cease-fire to allow the smoke to clear and the guns to cool, and it was soon seen that the British position was quite thoroughly shot up. There was no attempt to advance.

The preliminaries were now over. The next fight would be for the championship. From Sunday to Sunday there were no grand reviews as Jackson's polyglot army strengthened its defenses, and Pakenham prepared to storm the mud walls, beyond which lay New Orleans and, perhaps, a seat in the House of Lords. At three o'clock, Sunday morning, the eighth, Jackson and General William O. Butler made a tour of their line, the outposts having reported unusual activity along the enemy front. At Captain Dominique's battery they smelled coffee, and Old Hickory must have his little joke.

"Where did you get such fine coffee?" he asked the doughty captain. "Maybe you smuggled it?"

"Mebbe so, *zeneral*," said the grinning Dominique, serving him a tin cupful from the pot.

As they walked away Jackson said to Butler: "I wish I had fifty guns in line with five hundred such devils as those fellows are, at the butts."

Dawn was breaking, the last that General Pakenham and General Gibbs would ever see, when two rockets from the British line signaled the attack. Jackson, standing on the parapet, ordered word passed to the riflemen not to fire until ordered, and then to aim just above the cross-belt plates of the redcoats. As the enemy advanced across the cane stubble the artillery began to cut them down. Still they came on. Finally Jackson turned to his aides in command of the infantry and said, "They are near enough now, gentlemen," and the staccato of rifle fire was added to the deeper note of the cannon. The Tennessee and Kentucky riflemen stood behind the parapet in files of four. As the first man fired he stepped aside and the second

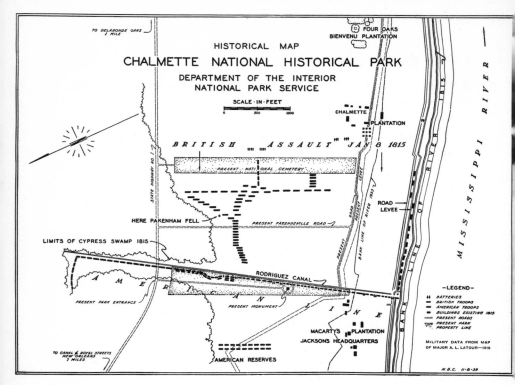

(*National Park Service*)

took his place. The third followed the second, and by the time the
fourth man had fired the first had reloaded his piece and the routine was repeated.

The British infantry tried valiantly to return the fire, but it was
too galling. When General Gibbs fell his men began to turn back.
Pakenham tried to rally them and received a mortal wound. General Keane was struck and had to be carried from the field. British
batteries became silent and the American artillerists outshot them.
A few redcoats got as far as the American defenses but died in the
attempt to breach them. Across the river, where a small American
force was pushed back by General Thornton, the attack was mo-
mentarily successful, but the disaster at Chalmette more than can-
celed it. By eight-thirty, before the day had well begun, the battle

was over. Official reports gave the British casualties as 291 killed, 1,262 wounded, 484 missing. American casualities were 13 killed, 39 wounded, and 19 missing.

The battles left no question as to the courage and patriotism of the Laffites and their Baratarians, however they may have played fast-and-loose with the revenue laws. President Madison on February 6 issued a proclamation of praise and pardon for all of them who had aided in the defense of the city. Jackson gave Pierre Laffite a letter which began: "Before I leave this city I do an act of justice, and at the same time one very agreeable to my feelings, to state the services you have rendered during the late invasion of your country."

Once again the Laffites were free and popular. But now they were broke. The ships, which Colonel Nicolls had offered to buy, and the fruits of privateering at Grande Terre had been confiscated. In spite of their services at Chalmette they had never been on the rolls of Jackson's paymaster. Jean was to remark that he had received *"pas une decoration en bois!"* ("Not even a wooden medal!"). He and Pierre recouped their fortunes in part in the Galveston adventure, which ended March 3, 1821, as we have seen in the Galveston chapter, when the Federal government ordered them to move on.

Thus ended the career of the enigmatic but always romantic Laffites on the curving shore of the Gulf of Mexico. They were to live longer and die far from its sparkling waters, Pierre in Creve Coeur ("Broken Heart"!) just outside of St. Louis, March 9, 1844; and Jean in Alton, Illinois, May 5, 1854. What happened in the meantime is another story.

Dominique You, or Frederic Youx as he gave his name in court, lived out his life in his beloved New Orleans, most of the time in bitter poverty, but when he died in November, 1830, the funeral service was held in the cathedral and the whole city turned out to do him honor. Shortly before his death a tall, awkward youth who had come down the river as a flatboat hand, called on him with a letter of introduction from a riverman friend in St. Louis. Dominique took the young man around the city where he saw the slave market auctions, and paid two fortunetellers to read his future. They cannot have read it aright, for that would have caused a riot. The youth was Abraham Lincoln, and the truth of this tale is set forth in a letter written by Lincoln and now in the possession of the Laffite family. But one thing more remains to be said about Dominique You. Records of the Laffite family recently brought to light show that he was the eldest of the five Laffite brothers, having been born in Santo Domingo (Haiti) on April 14, 1771, and christened Alexandre Frederic Laffite. Why the relationship was concealed and why the name "You" or "Youx" was adopted remains a mystery.

There is a curious footnote to Jackson's stay in New Orleans after the defeat of the British. No word had yet been received as to peace negotiations, and Jackson feared the attack might be renewed. Consequently he kept the city under martial law, much to the distress of some of its citizens. Served with a writ of habeas corpus from Judge Dominic A. Hall for delivery of a citizen he had arrested, Jackson tore up the writ and expelled the judge from the city. Two days later word was received that the treaty had been ratified, whereupon Judge Hall returned and summoned Jackson to appear and answer a charge of contempt of court. Jackson's friends, particularly the Baratarians, were ready to take the court apart, but the general quieted them with a look. Facing the court Jackson awaited sentence, with the comment that "it is expected that censure will form no part of the punishment which your honor may imagine it is your duty to perform."

Judge Hall referred to the great services Jackson had rendered the country and fined him a thousand dollars, for which the general immediately wrote a check. A popular subscription was immediately taken up to reimburse him, but he directed that it be distributed among the familes of those who had died in the recent battles. Thirty years later Congress voted him $2,700 to cover the cost of the fine and accrued interest.

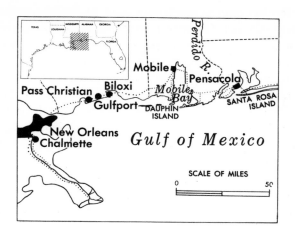

XIII. *East from New Orleans*

U.s. Route 90, the principal highway between New Orleans and Jacksonville, Florida, 570 miles due east, is known as "The Old Spanish Trail," but its eastern terminus in the day of the Spaniard was St. Augustine, thirty miles south of Jacksonville. Driving over it today one may well wonder how the Spaniards ever negotiated it before the days of modern roadmaking machinery and steel bridges. The fact is the present highway only approximates the route of two centuries ago, following a ribbon of concrete over marsh and stream that were avoided by the early explorers or crossed by cumbersome log-raft ferries.

Crossing over the Mississippi River via the Huey Long Bridge, the highway enters the suburbs of New Orleans from the west, winds through the downtown section, and then runs for almost thirty miles a little north of west before it leaves the municipal confines. But the last twenty miles have none of the characteristics of the usual city suburbs. The road runs through marshlands typical of the Louisiana coast, "trembling prairies," half land and two-thirds water, with tall, feather-topped marsh grass or stunted oaks stretching away to Lake Pontchartrain on the north and Lake Borgne (which is really an arm of the Gulf) on the south. Here the road is marked as "Chef Menteur Highway" and eventually it crosses a long steel drawbridge over Chef Menteur Pass, the first waterway connecting Lake Pontchartrain with the Gulf. Just south of the bridge approach are the ruins of old Fort Macomb, an early fortification and officially a state monument, but completely overgrown with weeds and brambles. On the other side of the roadway is the village of Chef Menteur, consisting of two gasoline pumps, a tavern and a few weather-beaten shanties.

"But we are still in the city of New Orleans," said the amiable barmaid, "and a liquor license for this place costs just as much as it does on Canal Street."

Beyond Chef Menteur Pass the road runs the length of an irregular island ten miles long, and at its eastern end is another large bridge over "The Rigolets," also a channel into Pontchartrain. In the haze to the southward can be seen the nine steel spans of the bridge where the Louisville & Nashville Railroad, after following another chain of islets, crosses the same channel. This waterway marks the end of the city of New Orleans, which is now so far behind none of its buildings break the distant skyline.

Thus far the route has shown little to attract the eye, but it has one great asset—it is a Land of Promise for fishermen. Along the shores of Lake Pontchartrain, Lake Borgne, and little channels leading to them, are clusters of fishermen's shanties perched high on stilts and surrounded by a clutter of boats and gear. Most of them are privately owned, some are owned by groups of fishing enthusiasts, and some stand ready to furnish boats, bait and guide to anyone who has the price. The passing motorist can tell by the smell that there is good fishing in these parts.

Once across the Rigolets the traveler is out of New Orleans Parish and into the southern tip of St. Tammany Parish. Farther north the parish contains rich farm and pasture lands, but here it is a waste of marsh grass, stunted pine and willows, crossed by sluggish bayous. Ten miles of this and a bridge carries the highway across the Pearl River and into the state of Mississippi.

Immediately on crossing the Pearl the landscape changes. Marsh and stunted trees are succeeded by tall pines and solid grasslands. The highway is as straight as a string with only one bend in fifteen miles. It is a lonesome road but the temptation to speed calls for caution as Mississippi allows "open range" and a cow ambling across the road can result in complete wreckage of cow and car.

This is Hancock County and Bay St. Louis, the county seat, is the first settlement on U.S. 90 after entering Mississippi from the west. The center of a cattle and lumber industry and a growing rice cultivation, Bay St. Louis is renowned through this part of the South for its amateur theatrical organization that has its own theater and puts on five plays a year with professional aplomb. It is also the home of the oldest druggist in Mississippi, M. René DeMontluzin, who celebrated his ninetieth birthday in December, 1955, and is able to recall a forgotten footnote to American sports. In 1885 word circulated in Mississippi that two exponents of the disreputable art of prize fighting were going to battle for the championship, one being the accredited champion Jake Kilrain, and the other a Johnny-come-lately named John L. Sullivan. Governor J. J. McRae ordered out the state militia, of which young DeMontluzin was a member, to stop the disgraceful affair but before the law could catch up with them the contestants and their followers foregathered at the little village of Richburg, Mississippi. There on July 8 was fought the last championship bout with bare knuckles, and Sullivan overcame Kilrain in seventy-five rounds. M. René says that all he got out of it was a train ride.

A fine four-lane toll bridge spans the two-mile entrance to the bay, replacing an earlier wooden structure that seemed to catch fire

periodically. Across the bridge the road swings south to the beach and the town of Pass Christian (accent on the last syllable).

From "The Pass," as it is called locally, through Long Beach, Gulfport and Biloxi, a distance of twenty-seven miles, runs the most beautiful shore drive to be found on the Gulf or South Atlantic Coast. Above a wide, gently sloping beach of white sand is a four-lane divided highway of ample width. Back of the highway are stately old homes shaded by majestic live oaks and surrounded by well-kept lawns. Sometimes the big houses give way to hotels. motels or cottages, but throughout the whole distance there is no rubbish and no suggestion of the "honky-tonk" that too often characterizes a popular playground. Sanitary crews keep the beaches as clean as the private lawns. Fishing piers built on pilings, many of them privately owned, extend out into the Gulf but they do not interfere with the public's enjoyment of the long shoreline—a striking contrast to the "gold coast" of Miami Beach where the swank hotels have been allowed to shut off all but a few puny stretches of the ocean front from the general public.

Pass Christian "still proudly wears crinoline," looks askance at the modern craze for neon lights, and thus far has successfully retained much of the atmosphere of the Old South, as represented by columned porticoes, moss-hung oaks and magnolias. Here Presidents Theodore Roosevelt and Woodrow Wilson vacationed during their terms of office, and several wealthy New Orleans families have long had manorial homes here. The town was incorporated in 1838 and now has a population of about four thousand. But as a settlement the town is older than New Orleans, and dates its beginnings from 1699. When D'Iberville was governor of the French province of Louisiana, which then embraced the central Gulf Coast and extended up the Mississippi Valley to Canada, the provincial capital was first established on the eastern shore of Biloxi Bay. The governor delegated two of his aides, Christian L'Adnier and his brother Marianne L'Adnier, to chart the offshore waters of this coast, now known as Mississippi Sound. Two passes were discovered and named for the two brothers, the outer one for Marianne and the inner one for Christian. The L'Adniers settled here giving the town the name of the inner pass, and many of their descendants are still to be found in the region under the name of Ladnier and Ladner.

Gulfport, twelve miles up the coast from Pass Christian, has an air of modernity about it as befits a county seat. Harrison County's shoreline extends from Bay St. Louis on the west to Biloxi Bay on the east and its principal business is lumber and pulpwood. The International Paper Company and the Gaylord Container Company have large holdings here and the De Soto National Forest occupies a large part of its acreage. Early in the present century the "tung nut boom" hit this part of the coast and wily promoters convinced hundreds of investors that a few acres of tung nut trees would make them independent. Tung nuts yield an oil that is widely used in the manufacture of paints and varnishes, and most of the world supply comes from Asia. Hundreds of acres of tung orchards were planted, many of which, due to inexperience or absentee ownership, never came to maturity. Those that did mature did not always produce a crop when weather conditions were unfavorable, and most of them have been cut out. One large planting still survives near Tallahassee, Florida.

Before the coming of tung nuts there was a boom in oranges. Thousands of acres were put out along the Gulf shore and for a time the citrus business flourished. But a heavy freeze killed practically all of the trees and millions of dollars were lost. On U.S. 90 in the southeastern corner of Mississippi is a neat little village named Orange Grove, but there is not an orange grove within a hundred miles of it. Later plantings were made of Satsumas, a hardy type of orange, and some of them are still grown in this region, but these, too, have been hurt by unseasonably cold winters and only a few groves are left.

The greatest cultivated tree crop today in southern Mississippi and Alabama is pecans, which are grown all the way from the Louisiana line to the coasts of Georgia and South Carolina. These trees are well adapted to the soil and climate of the region, for they are native to the south temperate zone of North America. Though late freezes may damage the crop it is seldom a total loss, and small yields are usually compensated for by higher prices. Most of the plantings are small, all the way from a few "dooryard" trees to groves covering from thirty to forty acres. As one tree may produce from one to two hundred pounds of nuts a few trees in a yard can be an appreciable source of income. A pecan tree is a graceful work of nature and has a characteristic and unmistakable structure. It does not have a large central trunk like a pine or maple tree, but five or six feet from the ground its branches begin to divide and subdivide until its outer parts are a pattern of slender, lacy twigs. Even in winter when the trees have lost their leaves a pecan grove is an attractive scene. In most mature groves the trees are thirty-five or forty feet tall, but here and there in some dooryard may be seen an old monarch that stretches its height up to at least seventy feet. The nuts develop in thin husks that begin to open early in October, when nuts and husks fall to the ground. Reluctant ones may be knocked loose with a long bamboo pole, and recently a tractor-operated "shaker" has been developed that vibrates the larger limbs and brings down their harvest.

More than two hundred varieties of pecans have been catalogued but only a fraction of that number have been developed commercially. The Mississippi Agricultural Service names eight varieties, five of which are recommended to meet different soil or market conditions, and three are not recommended because of susceptibility to "pecan scab" which damages the crop. Some groves are planted with seedling trees but most of the newer plantings are

A pecan grove in southern Alabama

"budded" trees, budding being a method of grafting a desired variety on a growing stock when the tree is very small. Seedlings may vary considerably in the fruit they produce but a budded tree can be depended on to develop the same characteristics that distinguished the tree from which the graft was taken. Pecans from budded trees bring a higher price than those from seedlings, but there are some who say the seedling nuts have a better flavor. Young pecan groves must be cultivated in summer, but after the trees begin to bear the land may be made to yield additional income by livestock pasturage.

A few minutes' drive eastward along the coastal boulevard from Gulfport brings the motorist to Biloxi, the third largest city in Mississippi. It is surrounded on three sides by water and looks to the sea for most of its sustenance. South of it lies the Gulf of Mexico, to the east is the Bay of Biloxi, and north is the long, narrow Back Bay of Biloxi. It is the home port of more than five hundred boats engaged in the shrimp and oyster industries, and these employ five thousand persons. Along the shore of Back Bay are thirty establishments which pack and ship seafood, a fortunate location for it keeps the inevitable odors from annoying the tourists who frolic along the Gulf-washed beaches on the other side of town. A feature of the Shrimp Festival, usually held in late summer, is the formal blessing of the shrimp fleet as it begins its season's work. The city lays claim to being the largest shrimp and oyster port in the world, a boast that may be challenged by Key West or Port Brownsville.

Not all of the fishing is of a commercial nature. Sportsmen come from all over the country to try their luck with everything from tarpon and crevalle in the Gulf to bass and crappie in the many streams and lakes of the region. The nautical atmosphere of the city is heightened by the glistening white lighthouse, more than a hundred years old, that stands between the north and south lanes of U.S. Route 90 along the beach and still casts its beams seaward every night. For sixty-two years it was attended by a mother and her daughter who lived in a cottage across the road. Now it is electrically operated under the direction of the U.S. Coast Guard and the cottage is occupied by the Biloxi Chamber of Commerce.

A short distance from the lighthouse is "Beauvoir," the last home of Jefferson Davis, where he wrote *The Rise and Fall of the Confederate Government*. It is a charming place, well preserved by the Sons of the Confederacy, and is open to the public. Along the north shore of the city on Back Bay is the National Soldiers' Home and Hospital that occupies five hundred acres of well-kept woodland to which the public is admitted. Adjoining it is Keesler Air Force Base, the largest technical station of the U.S. Air Force, with schools for radar, electronics and tower control.

It was on the eastern shore of the Bay of Biloxi that Pierre Le Moyne, Sieur d'Iberville, landed in 1699 and established the first capital of the Louisiana Territory. The site is across the bay from the present city and for a time was referred to as "Old Biloxi" but it is now occupied by a small settlement called Ocean Springs. A concrete bridge with a drawspan joins the new Biloxi with the old. The French gave names to a number of islands offshore, the largest being Ship Island, so called because their vessels were anchored there for a time. It has had a part in subsequent history, being the place where the English ships assembled just prior to the Battle of New Orleans. From here they raided the mainland for cattle and here they brought five gunboats captured in Lake Borgne just before the land engagement. During the Civil War the United States erected a fort on the western end of the island, calling it Fort Massachusetts after the battleship which was the first to land there. The old fortification is still intact and a lighthouse stands near by. An excursion boat takes vacationers to the spot from Biloxi every morning and afternoon.

A neighboring island is called Cat Island because when the French saw many raccoons there, an animal unknown in Europe, they mistook them for cats and called the place "Isle aux Chats." Two hundred years ago Cat Island was the scene of a bitter tragedy. It was the period of the French and Indian War, as American histories term it, and a detail of Marines and soldiers was stationed there to prevent its capture by the English. Their commanding officer was one Sieur Duroux and he immediately put his force at such nonmilitary duties as making lime from oyster shells, cutting lumber, burning charcoal, and any other activity that might bring in a few francs. The men were told they would share in the proceeds when the products were sold in New Orleans. When payments were not forthcoming a corporal was delegated to ask Duroux when they might expect a dividend. The officer flew into a rage, ordered the corporal flogged, and dropped all pretense of rewarding the men for their labors. There followed floggings and tortures for all who were suspected of malingering, and a number of deaths resulted. When one of the men succeeded in getting to New Orleans in hope of appealing to the commandant there he was intercepted by an aide who was sharing in the loot and sent back to Cat Island in chains. Eventually the situation became so unbearable that a conspiracy was formed and Duroux was killed as he returned from a fishing trip. The soldiers immediately fled the island and some of them escaped to join the English in the north. Others took refuge with the Indians but these were captured, taken to New Orleans, tried for mutiny, and condemned to death by torture. The executions took place in the Place d'Armes, now Jackson Square, before the old cathedral, some being broken on the wheel and one being nailed in a coffin which was then sawed in half. Today Cat Island is privately owned and but one family lives there.

Deer Island, named by the Indians, lies closer to the mainland and is occupied by a number of attractive homes. Biloxi is discussing the possibility of connecting it to the city by a causeway and developing it as a playground.

From the Bay of Biloxi the highway runs through young pine forests for twenty miles to the marshes at the mouth of the Pascagoula River. Crossing the causeway and the toll bridge one can see downstream on the farther shore the giant cranes of the Ingalls Shipbuilding Corporation, builders of small Navy vessels, barges, and more recently the weird seagoing oil rigs that are being used

in drilling oil wells along the Texas and Louisiana coasts. It is the
principal industry of Pascagoula, a small but thriving town that is
the seat of Jackson County. Other local plants are those of the
Animal Trap Company of Mississippi and the Pascagoula Decoy
Company, makers of decoys, paddles, oars and saw handles. A short
distance out of town is one of the larger plants of the International
Paper Company and its managed forests occupy most of the southern part of the county. Along the highway one is seldom out of
sight of a small grove of pecans.

Roadside signs make frequent reference to "The Singing River"
and a stranger may get the impression that the term is a translation
of the Indian word "Pascagoula." But the name comes from the
Pascagoula Indians who occupied this region before the arrival of
the white man, and the "singing river," if indeed it sings, is a
phenomenon that has never been explained. Residents say that the
singing sound, like a swarm of bees in flight, is best heard in the
late summer and autumn months in the stillness of the twilight.
Barely audible at first, the music grows nearer and louder until it
seems to surround the listener. William Baxter, writing in 1848, said
he heard it a number of times and that it resembled "the breathing
of an Aeolian harp." Indian legends, most of them dealing with the
theme of thwarted love, tell of the strange sounds but no ·authentic
scientific explanation has ever been established.*

Sixteen miles northeast of Pascagoula the highway crosses the
Mississippi-Alabama state line. This is the only state boundary on
any coast south of the Carolinas that is not marked by a river. The

---

* A similar tale is associated with ancient Egypt. Amenhotep III erected near
Thebes a number of colossal statues of Memnon, a figure in Greek mythology,
two of which still stand. In 27 B.C. an earthquake tumbled the upper part of
one of these to the ground. Says the *Encyclopaedia Britannica*: "A curious
phenomenon then occurred. Every morning, when the rays of the rising sun
touched the statue, it gave forth musical sounds, like the moaning noise or the
sharp twang of a harp string. . . . The sound, which has been heard by
modern travellers, is generally attributed to the passage of the air through the
pores of the stone, chiefly due to the change of temperature at sunrise. . . .
Strabo, the first to mention the sound, declares that he himself heard it, and
Pausanias says 'one would compare the sound most nearly to the broken chord
of a harp or lute.'"

(*William Lavendar*)
Mobile's beautiful Government Street

Rio Grande flows between Texas and Mexico, the Sabine between Texas and Louisiana, the Pearl between Louisiana and Mississippi, the Perdido between Alabama and Florida, the St. Marys between Florida and Georgia, and the Savannah between Georgia and South Carolina.

Soon after it enters Alabama, U.S. 90 spreads out into a fine four-lane divided highway, thickly dotted with motels, and rolls down Government Street, the main artery of Mobile.

The Gulf of Mexico reaches its northmost point at Mobile Bay. The latitude of the city of Mobile is 30 degrees, 41 minutes and 36 seconds. That places it 330 miles farther from the Equator than is Brownsville, Texas. A world port and an industrial center producing for national and international markets, it has nonetheless succeeded in holding much of the charm that characterized the more quiet days of a century ago.

Here the giant International Paper Company has just added a twenty-million-dollar newsprint mill to its already sizable Kraft paper plant. The Aluminum Company of America recently put into operation a twelve-million-dollar expansion of its local plant, making it the largest aluminum refinery in the world. The Mathieson Chemical Company has a plant near by for the manufacture of chlorine and caustic soda, matching its many million-dollar installation at Lake Charles, Louisiana. Courtaulds, Inc., recently completed a $25 million plant for the production of rayon fiber. But with all this industrial activity Mobile remains a city of beauty and fun. The venerable live oaks touch their finger tips over Government Street in a never-failing canopy of green, and on "Fat Tuesday," immediately before Lent, the city has a Mardi Gras Festival, not so pretentious as the Mardi Gras of New Orleans, but everybody has just as much fun. The Mobile celebrants insist their carnival had its beginning in 1830, several years before it was introduced into New Orleans by former Mobile residents, but the cautious visitor will not take sides in this family feud.

Every year early in spring the entire region makes a tour of "The Azalea Trail," which is seventeen miles of blooming beauty, punctuated by fine old antebellum homes. The tour is sponsored by the Historic Mobile Preservation Society and the old houses are open for public view. Bienville Square in the center of the city is a verdant spot among the tall buildings and fat squirrels beg for peanuts around a quaint summerhouse among the trees.

With a population approximating 150,000 Mobile is the second city in size in the state, being surpassed only by Birmingham. It ranks sixth in the nation in the volume of imports, and handles more bauxite (aluminum ore) than any other port in the world. The city stands at the mouth of the Mobile River where it flows into Mobile Bay, thirty-one miles from the Gulf of Mexico.

Famous throughout the horticultural world are the Bellingrath Gardens, twenty-one miles south of Mobile, on the banks of the Isle-aux-Oies River, unromantically translated by road signs as

"Fowl River." Here in a setting of natural lake and forest is a collection of azaleas, camellias, crepe myrtle, hydrangeas, allamandas—in all more than five hundred varieties of blossoming trees, shrubs, vines and perennials. Apart from the rest of the garden is one of the finest collections of roses to be found in the South. The camellias, introduced here from Japan more than a century ago, begin blooming in October. Before they have finished in early spring the showy azaleas are opening, and these are followed by summer-blooming species. The gardens are open the year 'round and there is always something blossoming along the woodland paths.

The gardens were developed by Walter Duncan Bellingrath, a native of Atlanta, who came to Mobile in 1904 and became one of the city's leading industrialists. He married Miss Betty Morse of Mobile and in 1917 they acquired a large tract of unspoiled woodland for a hunting preserve. Its beauty inspired them to make it a garden shrine and they toured America and Europe for plantings and ideas. In 1932 its sixty acres were opened to the public, an admission price being charged and the proceeds given to charities. Mrs. Bellingrath died in 1943 and Mr. Bellingrath in 1955, but prior to his death he conveyed the gardens in perpetuity to the Bellingrath-Morse Foundation for Religious and Educational Purposes.

The entrance to Mobile Bay from the Gulf is a narrow pass, guarded on the west by Dauphin Island, six miles off the mainland, and on the east by a long narrow peninsula known as Mobile Point. Here on August 5, 1864, was fought the heaviest naval engagement of the Civil War. It was not the first time that the roar of cannon and the acrid smoke of burned powder had drifted across these waters, but it was the last. Ask the man on the street who said, "Damn the torpedoes! Go ahead!" and two times out of three the answer will be, "Dewey at Manila Bay, wasn't it?" But it was Admiral David G. Farragut who made the phrase famous, and the scene was the entrance to Mobile Bay. (Dewey's immortal command at Manila Bay was: "You may fire when ready, Gridley.")

Early in the war the Confederate forces had occupied Fort Gaines on the eastern end of Dauphin Island. Opposite Fort Gaines and on the point of the peninsula was Fort Morgan, also held by the Confederates. The Union Navy had never been able to blockade these waters effectively and Admiral Farragut, in command of the West Gulf Blockading Squadron, which had successfully ascended the Mississippi River and captured New Orleans in 1862, was ordered to take Mobile. As a preliminary maneuver General Gordon Granger landed with fifteen hundred troops on Dauphin Island back of Fort Gaines and co-ordinated his attack with the naval engagement. The fort was commanded by Colonel C. D. Anderson whose force consisted of 46 officers and 818 enlisted men.

As a further defense of the bay five rows of pilings had been driven in the channel to which were attached sixty-seven explosive charges, called torpedoes at that period though they would now be called mines. This left two narrow passages open, one under the guns of Fort Gaines on Dauphin Island and the other near Fort Morgan on Mobile Point. Another fortification, Fort Powell, guarded the waters between Dauphin Island and the mainland, and the city's defenses had been pronounced by General Joseph E. Johnston to be the strongest in the Confederacy. In the bay was the Confederate ram, the *Tennessee,* commanded by Admiral Franklin Buchanan and supported by three small gunboats. To oppose this Farragut had his flagship the *Hartford,* another battleship the *Brooklyn,* four ironclad monitors and a fleet of smaller craft, mounting in all 199 guns and carrying 2,700 men. *The Photographic History of the Civil War* (Vol. 9, p. 107) says the Federal fleet carried more power for destruction than the combined English, French and Spanish fleets at Trafalgar.

Farragut elected to enter the eastern side of the bay near Fort Morgan. At five forty-five on the morning of August 5, 1864, the fleet began to move, the four monitors leading the line, and soon was within range of Fort Morgan's guns. Hardly had the battle been joined when the monitor *Tecumseh* struck a "torpedo" and was literally blown out of the water. As the monitor sank the *Brook-*

(Harper's Weekly)
The capture of the Rebel ram *Tennessee* in Mobile Bay

lyn recoiled. "What is the trouble?" signaled Farragut. "Torpedoes" was the answer. "Damn the torpedoes!" shouted Farragut who had climbed the *Hartford*'s rigging to see above the smoke, "Go ahead, Captain Drayton."

The *Hartford* led the way through the mines but they had been under salt water so long that they were corroded and no more exploded. Once past the forts the Union ships were attacked by the *Tennessee* but were able to avoid being struck by her ram and concentrated their fire on her. The engagement lasted for an hour and by that time the outgunned defensive vessels were shot to pieces and Admiral Buchanan was severely wounded. Four days later Fort Gaines surrendered and Farragut was in complete command of Mobile Bay.

The brownstone ramparts and two hundred granite gun mounts of Fort Gaines still look eastward across the entrance to Mobile

Bay but today they are a playground for children. Under the leadership of the Mobile Chamber of Commerce a five-mile bridge with a drawspan has been constructed between Dauphin Island and the mainland and the site is rapidly becoming an attractive residential district. Two thousand building lots have been laid out, along with provisions for parks, beaches and schools, and wide Bienville Boulevard runs the length of the island, much of which is covered with tall pines.

It is fitting that the boulevard should be so named, for the shadow of the great French seigneur lies across this coast from Mobile to New Orleans. From these shores he directed the destinies of the great Louisiana province for more than thirty years after succeeding his brother D'Iberville who died of yellow fever in Havana in 1706. Under D'Iberville the French had first settled on Biloxi Bay in 1699, but believing it to be unhealthy the government dispatched the young Bienville to establish a new base and in 1702 he built Fort Louis at a point on the Mobile River above the present site of the city. It was called "Mobile" after the tribe of Mabila Indians with whom De Soto had fought a stirring battle in October, 1540, when he explored this region. A fortification was built on Dauphin Island and Du Pratz, an early historian, called Mobile the birthplace and Dauphin the cradle of the colony of Louisiana. A heavy flood, and probably a desire to be within sound of the signal gun on Dauphin, led Bienville to move the settlement down to the present site of Mobile at the mouth of the river in 1709. A fort was built there which he called Fort Condé, but when the English took possession in 1763 the name was changed to Fort Charlotte in honor of the queen of George III. Eventually orders came from France to establish the capital of the province somewhere on the lower Mississippi River, and the government was moved to New Orleans in 1717.

What the Mobile of today needs more than anything else is a better gateway to the east. At present the only acceptable highway. to Florida and the east within eighty-five miles of the city is through the two-lane Bankhead Tunnel under the Mobile River, where the toll is twenty-five cents for passenger cars and up to a dollar for trucks. The city makes no secret of the fact that the tunnel, which was opened in 1940, cost $5,000,000 and nets $700,000 a year, thus knocking off a neat 14 per cent profit long after the original investment has been recovered. The only alternative is to follow a narrow, winding, crowded and poorly maintained route that finally crosses the river over an inadequate bridge and adds twelve miles to the east-west distance. The city's promotion literature fails to say whether the Bankhead Tunnel was named for the late Senator or Tallulah.

Thirty-five miles above the head of Mobile Bay the Tombigbee and Alabama rivers enter a wide marshland where they are connected by a series of natural channels. The streams writhe and turn, unite and divide, until on the map the valley looks like a long plate of spaghetti. To add to the confusion the Tombigbee becomes the Mobile River and the Alabama is rechristened the Tensas. Just below the marshy mouths of the rivers U.S. Routes 31, 90 and 98, after leaving the Bankhead Tunnel, cross to the eastern shore over a causeway six and a half miles long. There they divide, 31 going northeast to Montgomery and on to Canada, 90 heading for Tallahassee and Jacksonville but dropping a loop down to Pensacola, and 98 turning due south to follow the shoreline of the bay twenty miles before it cuts eastward to Pensacola.

The eastern shore of Mobile Bay is a high ridge heavily wooded with pines and beneath them the cottages of Daphne, Montrose, Fairhope and Point Clear look out across the water to the misty outline of the city on the other side. Two-thirds of the way down the bay shore the road turns east through pecan groves, potato and soybean fields, and cattle-dotted pasturelands. At the thriving village of Foley State Route No. 3 offers a road to the Gulf shore, ten miles south. Here is none of the "trembling prairie" characteristic of the Louisiana coast. Oak and pine trees firmly rooted in the clay and sand grow right down to the beach that stretches for thirty miles from the entrance to Mobile Bay on the west to the estuary of the Perdido River on the east. A mile from the beach and directly south of Foley a hard-surfaced road runs west for twenty-one miles along the peninsula, at the far end of which stand the frowning, heavy walls of old Fort Morgan. Here we re-enter history.

Eight historical markers have been placed along the road to Fort Morgan by the Alabama Historical Association. The first one reads:

MOBILE BAY AREA
HISTORY UNDER SIX FLAGS
1519–1699 SPANISH FLORIDA
by colonization, exploration and trade
1699–1763 FRENCH LOUISIANA
by colonization, exploration and trade
1763–1780 BRITISH WEST FLORIDA
by treaty, occupation and administration
1780–1813 SPANISH WEST FLORIDA
by invasion, seizure and treaty
1813–1861 UNITED STATES
by invasion, seizure and treaty
1861 INDEPENDENT STATE OF ALABAMA
1861–1865 CONFEDERATE STATES OF AMERICA
1865 UNITED STATES

To understand this hodgepodge of sovereignty it must be borne in mind that for more than two centuries this entire region was at the mercy of the intrigues of European courts, and events halfway around the world often determined what flag would fly over this or that little settlement as it struggled with Indians, hurricanes and threatened famine. The entire Gulf Coast was first seen by Spaniards, but in the main they were looking only for treasure such as they had found in Mexico and Peru, and many of them—Ponce de León, De Narváez, De Soto—lost their lives in this part of the world. Spain's sovereignty was challenged when La Salle came down the Mississippi from Canada and claimed the adjoining coastal lands for France. Just where the boundary between Spanish Florida and French Louisiana lay was long a matter of dispute.

Spain, busy with her development on the Atlantic Coast around St. Augustine, for many years showed little interest in anything between Pensacola and her rich holdings in Mexico.

In 1762 France secretly ceded Louisiana to Spain. A few months later at the close of the Seven Years' War (known in American History as the French and Indian War) Great Britain through the Treaty of Paris got into the act by acquiring "The Floridas" from Spain, and divided the province into East Florida and West Florida. The English established the northern boundary of West Florida along the thirty-first parallel of latitude, where it is today, but its western boundary reached to the Mississippi River, except for the city of New Orleans, and the southeastern parishes of Louisiana are still referred to as the "Florida parishes."

By another treaty negotiated in 1783 Spain regained possession of the Floridas and seemed in a fair way to recapture some of her former glory, but a new world power had come into being—the United States of America—soon to challenge her control of the Gulf of Mexico. An act of Congress, approved April 7, 1798, established the "Territory of Mississippi" which included the present states of Alabama and Mississippi but did not reach to the Gulf. It stopped at the thirty-first parallel, and the region between that line and the Gulf was occupied—and claimed—by Spain. During the next five years things happened rapidly. Spanish rule in Louisiana came to an end in 1800 when the province was returned to France, but the formal transfer did not take place until three years later. France held the title for twenty days and then sold it to the United States.

With the Louisiana Purchase in 1803 the question of the east-west boundary between Florida and Louisiana became acute. Spain still held Mobile and said the dividing line was west of that point. The United States insisted that its bargain with France took in everything to the Perdido River, a few miles from Pensacola. In the meantime the venturesome pioneers of the new country were pushing south and crowding along the thirty-first parallel between Mississippi Territory and the disputed ground of West Florida. Soon they began crossing it and Spain was not strong enough to stop them. In 1810 a group of these venturesome citizens raised the flag of "West Florida" in Baton Rouge, declaring it a free and independent state. President Madison refused to recognize the new government but issued a proclamation on October 27 of that year saying the lands in question belonged to the United States. There the matter rested for a time and Spain remained in possession of Mobile until war broke out between the United States and Great Britain in 1812 and British forces began using Mobile as a base of operations. That did it. President Madison with the authorization of Congress ordered General James Wilkinson to take the city. When he advanced on it with a superior force General Perez surrendered without making any resistance, and the Territory of Mississippi was extended to include the Gulf Coast from the Perdido River to the Pearl. That is why the historical marker states the territory was obtained "by invasion, seizure and treaty."

One more act remained before the boundaries were fixed as they are today. Settlers along the Tombigbee raised a loud outcry because, they insisted, the more thickly populated area along the Mississippi River controlled the affairs of the territory. A happy solution was reached when the territory was divided down the middle to make two states, giving Biloxi Bay to Mississippi and Mobile Bay to Alabama. Mississippi was admitted to the Union as a state in 1817 and Alabama in 1819.

Much of this story is set forth in the historical markers along the road that winds through heavy pine woods out to Fort Morgan. Along the last mile or two where the peninsula narrows to a point the trees give way to sculptured sand dunes and dwarfed shrubbery. There is something awe-inspiring about the old fort's massive walls of brick and stone looking sullenly out across the sparkling waters that almost completely surround them. The site is a state park and is kept in good repair. Entrance to the inner court is through two archways, the second one guarded by heavy oaken doors. Over it is the inscription: "Morgan. 1833." It was named for General Daniel

Looking west toward Dauphin Island from Fort Morgan

Morgan, a Revolutionary War officer. The old muzzle-loading cannon have long been removed but the gun emplacements seem
waiting for them to be restored. To the west across the bay can be
seen the outlines of Fort Gaines on Dauphin Island. It is easy for
the imagination to picture Farragut's fleet steaming between their
combined fire with his 199 guns thundering a reply.

The first fortification on this point was built by General Wilkinson in 1813 after he had driven the Spaniards from Mobile, and was
named Fort Bowyer in honor of Colonel John Bowyer. A marker at
the entrance to the grounds reads:

1833. This fort replaced Fort Bowyer. Built on the star shaped design
of Michaelangelo it is one of the finest examples of military architecture
in the New World.

A more arresting plaque is a bronze casting mounted on a granite boulder just outside the fort which bears the following legend:

In Memory of Prince Modoc, a Welsh explorer, who landed on the shores of Mobile Bay in 1170 and left behind, with Indians, the Welsh language. Authority is Encyclopedia Britannica, copyright 1918. Webster's Encyclopedia. Richard Hakluyt, 1552 to 1616, a Welsh historian and geographer. Ridpath's History of the World. Ancient Roman coins found in forts in Tennessee. These forts resemble the forts of Wales of the 9th and 10th centuries and of the White Indians of the Tennessee and Missouri Rivers. Erected by the Virginia Cavalier Chapter of the Daughters of the American Revolution.

Inside the fort and placed flat on the ground in the shade of a row of oleander bushes are fourteen memorial tablets of marble. Several were placed there only recently and all but two were presented by individuals. Some raise controversial points of history and spelling and some are quite naïve. A few are worth quoting:

In memory of Alonso Alvarez de Pineda who landed here in 1519, being 101 years before the Pilgrims landed at New Plymouth, who erected a huge cross to Christ and holding mass under this gave to Alabama the high honor of holding the first recorded worship of God in America, who also gave to Alabama the first battle between the white man and the Indians—20 years before De Soto fought the battle of Mobilia for which Mobile is named. Presented by the Society of the Daughters of Colonial Wars in the State of Alabama.

In memory of Cabeza de Vaca who was one of the four survivors of the massacre of Narvaez's colony, who took off from here in 1528, headed west and reached the Pacific coast, where Culcican is today, nine years later, thus was the first white man to cross the American Continent. Presented by Mr. and Mrs. Paschal P. Vaca.

In memory of Mothe Cadillac, for whom the Cadillac car is named, who was the governor of the Province of Louisiana, who founded the city of Detroit and who held headquarters here in the spring 1713 in a tent built of palmettos 63 years before the birth of our nation. Presented by Mr. and Mrs. Robart Summersell.

IN MEMORY OF LITTLE NUNO DE TOBAR, JR.
THE FIRST WHITE CHILD TO BE BORN IN AMERICA. BORN HERE ON ON
OF DE SOTO'S SHIPS IN 1540. 80 YEARS BEFORE THE PILGRIMS LANDI
AT NEW PLYMOUTH. HE WAS THE CHILD OF A "SHOT-GUN WEDDINC
THE FIRST WEDDING TO BE HELD IN THE U.S.A.
PRESENTED BY MR & MRS. CEPHUS HOLLIMAN

America's first shotgun wedding?

In memory of Panphilo da Narzaez [sic] who landed here in 1528 and whose whole colony was massacred by the Indians. Presented by Bill Lyerly.

In memory of little Nuno de Tobar, Jr., the first white child to be born in America. Born here in one of De Soto's ships in 1540, 80 years before the Pilgrims landed at New Plymouth. He was the child of a "shotgun wedding," the first wedding to be held in the U. S. A. Presented by Mr. and Mrs. Cephus Holliman.

Other tablets are in memory of Thomas Jefferson, James Madison, James Monroe, General Andrew Jackson, Sieur Bienville, the Rt. Rev. Juan Juarez and General Simon Bernard. A tourist wag suggested that someone should donate a slab to the memory of P. T. Barnum and that would make it unanimous. But the old fort needs no eloquence of sculptural phrase to impress the visitor with the glories of its past. Its deep arches and lonely, wind-swept ramparts tell its story more graphically than words.

Returning from Fort Morgan to Foley one sees little of the beach. But the crossroad where the route turns north is only a mile from a long stretch of sandy shore where there are several small villages of summer cottages, and a state-owned trailer park and picnic area. At Foley the eastbound motorist again picks up U.S. Route 98 and twenty miles farther on crosses a long bridge over the estuary of the Perdido River. When he reaches the farther shore he is in Florida, eight miles from the outskirts of Pensacola.

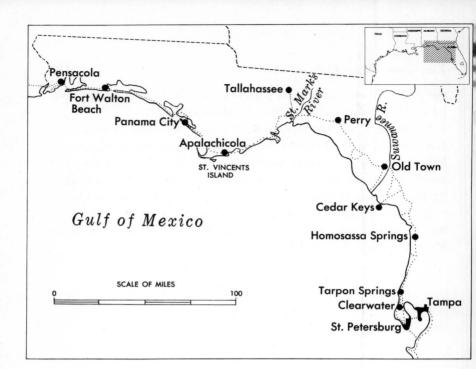

Gulf of Mexico

SCALE OF MILES

0   100

XIV. *From the Perdido to Tampa Bay*

Entrance to Pensacola from the west does not give a flattering view of the city. The route follows Cervantes Street which is lined with small shops, filling stations and small residences, some of which are neatly kept but many are in a state of careless disrepair. The city has done nothing to make the route attractive. The downtown section lies a few blocks south of the east-west axis.

Historically Pensacola has much in common with Mobile, fifty-nine miles up the coast, but the French influence stopped at Mobile Bay and the great Bienville did nothing for Pensacola except to attack it in 1719 and burn it to the ground. Here are no long avenues of old oak trees uniting their foliage above the street, and no azalea trails, although the city has some beautiful modern homes and its schools and newer business structures are worthy of attention. Invidious comparisons with Mobile are out of order, for Pensacola was for two hundred years the pawn of contending great powers, and has been captured, recaptured, besieged, burned, plundered and neglected more than any other city in the entire domain of the United States. All this now belongs to the past. No hostile foot has touched its shore for almost a century and the city has become one of the most thriving communities of the South.

Escambia County, of which Pensacola is the seat, includes the entire western end of Florida. Like the three counties to the east of it, Santa Rosa, Okaloosa and Walton, it extends all the way from the Gulf to the Alabama line. Three-fourths of its area is wooded and forest products are the most important crop. The St. Regis Paper Company controls much of this and has a large paper and bag manufacturing plant here. Corn, soybeans, potatoes and a little cotton are raised on the fifteen hundred small farms in the county, and its dairy farms gross a million dollars a year. The harbor in Pensacola Bay is one of the best on the coast and this has been a factor in bringing a number of industries to the city. The world's largest nylon plant, owned by the Chemstrand Corporation, is located just north of the municipal limits.

The biggest enterprise in all of western Florida, however, is the Naval Air Station adjoining Pensacola on the southwest. It is the Navy's largest shore-based command and it is charged with training new Naval aviators, developing a skilled aviation technical personnel, and maintaining a trained and ever-ready Naval Reserve. Until recently its principal function was to provide basic training for young flying cadets, who were usually sent to Corpus Christi for their advanced training. Recently the Pensacola station was enlarged so that every phase of the making of a pilot, from preflight training to landing the meteor-like jets on a "flattop" can now be completed here. Approximately 3,500 Navy personnel are located here and the

(*Naval Air Station, Pensacola*)

base employs more than 8,000 civilians who live in and around Pensacola, an important factor in the city's economy. Its payroll and local expenditures amount to $55 million annually.

Located just inside the pass to Pensacola Bay the Naval Air Station is on a site historically important in the annals of the country and of Naval aviation. On the five thousand acres now occupied by the station are the ruins of the old semicircular Fort San Carlos, built by the Spaniards in 1696, which changed hands a number of times before the United States purchased Florida from Spain in 1821. The Congress in 1824 authorized the construction of a Navy Yard and Station at Pensacola and construction was started two years later, but it did not include the site of the fort. In the early 1840's the Army built Fort Barrancas just behind and above the older fortification and made it one of the strongest points along the

U.S. coastline. On Santa Rosa Island across the narrow entrance to the bay was Fort Pickens, and between them they completely controlled the harbor.

Such was the situation when the Civil War broke out in 1861. The Confederates immediately took possession of the Navy Yard and Fort Barrancas, and the Union forces held on to Fort Pickens. Late in 1862 the Confederate forces were compelled to evacuate both sites. They burned the Navy Yard but did little damage to the fort. After the war ended the Navy Yard was restored, the large supply of pine and oak trees in the immediate vicinity making it an ideal place for construction of the ships of those days. By 1910 the day of the steel ship had dawned, Congress failed to make any appropriation for the Pensacola Yard, and it was closed.

But something else had dawned by 1910. It was the Age of Air, and in that year the first Naval officers were ordered to learn to fly under the direction of the Wright Brothers and Glenn Curtis. As the air service grew a training station became necessary, a board was appointed to select a site, and it unanimously recommended the one-time Pensacola Navy Yard. So in 1914 the first U.S. Naval Air Station was opened here and the first air mission of the service was the flight of Naval aviators from here to scout for the U.S. Fleet at Vera Cruz, Mexico.

The first fifteen weeks of the cadet's course at Pensacola is pre-flight training, during which he learns about navigation, engines, principles of flight, discipline, close order drill, and how to survive when he has to bail out over the North Pole or the Equator. Then he is ready to learn how to fly a plane. Large as it is, the Pensacola base does not have room for all the training planes, so there are a number of auxiliary fields near by where primary lessons in flight are given. The candidate for wings learns to handle ever faster and more powerful aircraft, until at last he sails out into the Gulf on one of the Navy's carriers that is always kept in service here, and demonstrates his ability to take off from and land on a six-hundred-foot flight deck. Some candidates go to Corpus Christi to complete their advanced training, and those who elect to handle the multi-engined planes are sent to Hutchinson, Kansas, for final training. During World War I the Pensacola station trained 999 Navy pilots, and for World War II the number exceeded 28,000.

In downtown Pensacola, across the street from the modest court-house and adjoining the shopping district, is Plaza Ferdinand, shaded by glossy-leaved magnolias, surrounded by a low stone wall and guarded at each corner by a rusty cannon. Here attached to a granite boulder is a bronze tablet which proclaims that "In this Plaza General Andrew Jackson received West Florida from Spain and raised the flag of the United States July 17, 1821." The marker was erected by the Pensacola Historical Society in 1935 "to recall the flags of five nations which have been raised in turn ten times over Pensacola."

The first date on the tablet, 1559, marks the arrival of Tristan de Luna, named by Philip II of Spain as captain general and governor of Florida, and ordered to found a colony on this shore. He sailed from Vera Cruz and landed with considerable pomp on August 14 at the head of fifteen hundred followers. One hundred and forty lots were staked out for a city that was to be called Santa Maria Filipina. Five weeks later a hurricane hit the colony and wrecked a number of ships from which the supplies had not been unloaded. Exploring parties could find no food in the surrounding forests, and after a series of misfortunes the venture was abandoned in 1569. Silence reigned over the bay until 1696, when Don Andreas de Arriola arrived and built Fort San Carlos.

A few years later the French settled at Mobile, just up the coast, and relations between the two colonies were amicable until 1719 when word drifted across the Atlantic that France and Spain were at war. The French heard of it first and the news reached the Spaniards when a French military force descended on them and demanded their surrender. There was nothing to do but submit, especially when the French agreed to send them to Havana. Two vessels were assigned to make the voyage, but when they reached Havana under a flag of truce the captain general there refused to recognize it. He seized the ships, armed them and manned them with Spaniards, and sent them back to Pensacola. This time it was the French who were taken by surprise and could offer no resistance.

When word of these goings on reached Bienville at Mobile he was much incensed. He organized a second expedition which sailed into Perdido Bay and attacked the town from the rear. This time there was considerable shooting, but the Spaniards were finally overcome and after allowing his Indian allies to plunder the place Bienville set fire to it. Here the French remained until word came from the old country that the war was over, and that by the terms of the peace treaty Pensacola had been returned to Spain. So in 1723 the French went back to Mobile and the Spanish returned to Pensacola.

For forty years all was peace along these shores, except for a hurricane in 1754 that killed a number of persons and wrecked most of the buildings. Then in 1763 Pensacola learned it had been traded to the British. Britain took more interest in the colony than Spain had done. The English laid out the city as it is today, made the Apalachicola River 150 miles to the east the dividing line between East Florida and West Florida, and opened the colony to settlement. Not all of the local Spaniards were pleased with the change and many of them moved to Havana. The period of British occupation was a prosperous one, but in 1783 the Floridas were returned to Spain.

In 1814 when General Andrew Jackson was campaigning against the Creek Indians in Georgia and Alabama he learned the Spaniards were co-operating with them and with the British. So he marched into Pensacola (without raising any flags in Plaza Ferdinand) but left it after warning the Spaniards to be neutral. The next hostile flag to enter the harbor came later in 1814 when the British fleet and convoy moving to the attack on New Orleans made this their base.

They had asked permission of the captain general in Havana for this action and he had refused it, but they moved in anyway and Spain was too weak to resist. When the Indians renewed their raids in the south in 1818 the Spaniards again gave them too much aid and comfort to suit Jackson so he entered Pensacola for the second time and set up a government that remained in operation for fourteen months. But the control of Spain along the Atlantic Coast was weakening, the frontiersmen from Georgia and Alabama were swarming across their southern borders, and four hundred years after Ponce de León's voyages along her coasts all of Florida was ceded to the United States by a treaty ratified in 1821.

Once more General Jackson rode into Pensacola, but this time there was a flag raising. Jackson was sick, as he was much of the time, and plagued by mosquitoes and fatigue, but still insistent on proper military punctilio. He invited the Spanish governor, Don José Callava, to breakfast with him but the governor declined. After an annoying delay a program for the ceremony was arranged, the Spanish flag came down from the much-used flagpole for the last time, and the Stars and Stripes went up, there to stay except for a two-year interval during the early Confederacy.

Such is a brief run-down of the flags of Pensacola, a record that any other American city will find it hard to match.

Starting from Pensacola U.S. Route 98, appropriately called "The Scenic Route," hugs the shore of the Gulf for two hundred miles, almost to St. Marks River below Tallahassee. It leaves Pensacola over a new cement bridge three miles long over Pensacola Bay. Signs on the bridge read: "Maximum speed 45 miles, minimum speed 35 miles." It is no place for crawlers. The causeway leading to the bridge has been made into an attractive free picnic and beach area. On both sides of the highway are concrete tables and benches covered with a substantial roof, and the place is a delight to hundreds of residents and visitors. A short distance beyond the western terminus of the bridge a side road leads south to another bridge, this one over Santa Rosa Sound to Pensacola Beach. There is a toll charge of twenty-five cents for the round trip.

Pensacola Beach on Santa Rosa Island is being developed as a vacation resort in an unusual manner. The island is more than forty miles long and the western half has by legislative enactment been placed under the jurisdiction of the Santa Rosa Island Authority, which must by law develop it for the public convenience. It cannot be commercialized except under lease by the commission. Only about three miles of the island near the bridgehead have been improved so far but this is to be considerably extended within a few years. On the Gulf side is a large casino with restaurant and bathhouses facing a beautiful beach of white sand. A hundred yards back of this, fronting on the bay, are picnic shelters, outdoor fireplaces and fishing piers. Hotels, motels and cottages are available for those who want to make an extended stay and the place has become a popular year-'round resort.

High on a dune near the bridge a white cross stands against the sky. At its base is the inscription: "This marker commemorates the first religious service in the Pensacola area, a Mass celebrated on August 15, 1559, the Feast of the Assumption, by the Dominican Friars who accompanied Tristan de Luna. Erected by the Knights of Columbus, Pensacola Council 778."

From this point to old Fort Pickens at the western end of the island is a distance of seven and a half miles, a lonesome strip of highway through snow-white sand dunes topped with gnarled shrubs, the nodding plumes of "beach oats," and stunted palmetto. As a spectacle Fort Pickens is disappointing, especially after one has climbed about Fort Morgan which occupies a similar position at the entrance to Mobile Bay. The entire fortification is covered with sand on which grow the shrubs and grasses common to the surrounding area, except at the corners where massive concrete entrances look darkly from beneath old gun positions. These points

A corner of Fort Pickens on Santa Rosa Island

had been allowed to fall into decay but were restored in 1942 when
the fort was reactivated during World War II. From a short distance away the fort resembles a very much oversize golf bunker.

Begun in 1829 and completed in 1834, it was named in honor of
General Andrew Pickens, a South Carolina officer in the Revolutionary War. With Fort Barrancas on the other side of the narrow
pass to Mobile and Escambia bays it guarded the entrance to Pensacola. Fort Pickens' chief claim to fame is the fact that it was one of
three forts on the Gulf of Mexico that was never captured by the
Confederate forces during the Civil War, the other two being Fort
Zachary Taylor at Key West and Fort Jefferson on the Dry Tortugas.
The only time it was under fire was during the early part of the
war when the Confederates held Fort Barrancas and Pensacola.

As the crisis between the North and South developed in January,

1861, Lieutenant Slemmer commanding Barrancas and Commander James Armstrong commanding the adjoining Navy Yard agreed that in case of hostilities it would be best to abandon those two points and retire to Fort Pickens across the channel as it could be reinforced from the sea. Accordingly on January 10, the day Florida passed its ordinance of secession, Lieutenant Slemmer spiked the guns at Barrancas and taking his supply of ammunition crossed over to Fort Pickens, which was then in an advanced state of disrepair. Two days later Alabama troops demanded and received the surrender of the Navy Yard from Commander Armstrong. For several weeks no shots were fired by either side, due to an understanding called the "Fort Pickens Truce," but this was broken when the U.S. Battleship *Brooklyn* landed troops on Santa Rosa Island April 12. It is a coincidence that this occurred only a few hours after the Confederates had fired on Fort Sumter in Charleston Harbor. Fighting began in earnest the following September when the Southern troops attacked the fort from the land side but were repulsed. Following that the guns of Forts Pickens and Barrancas blazed away at one another with no advantage to either side. Finally on May 9, 1862, the Confederate forces abandoned Pensacola and peace has reigned there ever since.

Fort Pickens came briefly into the limelight again when the famous Apache chief, Geronimo, and his band were imprisoned there from October 25, 1886, until May 13, 1888. It was modernized and strengthened during the 1890's, but eventually new methods of attack and defense made it obsolete and in November, 1949, it was turned over to the Florida Board of Parks and Historic Memorials.

It is forty miles from Pensacola to Fort Walton Beach, which is at the entrance to a sizable body of water called Choctawhatchee Bay. There, too, is the eastern end of Santa Rosa Island and Santa Rosa Sound which lies between the island and the mainland. The Intracoastal Waterway runs the length of the sound and continues through the bay. Most of the road is through an area of small pines—

long-leaf, slash and loblolly—interspersed with oak and palmetto. There are no farms, no pastures and only a few small houses and motels to relieve the monotonous scene, but after some twenty-five miles signs begin to appear at the roadside: "Eglin Air Force. Do not leave paved highway." A few more miles and the road comes in sight of Santa Rosa Sound and passes through a waterside village with the intriguing name of Mary Esther. Fort Walton Beach is just beyond.

The casual motorist will pass through Fort Walton Beach and never give it a thought unless he decides he hasn't enough gas to get him to Panama City in one direction or Pensacola in the other, but this is a sort of "believe-it-or-not" town. For one thing, there is no "Fort Walton" and never was. George Walton of Georgia was one of the signers of the Declaration of Independence. He later moved to Florida where the family became prominent among the early settlers. A little settlement on Choctawhatchee Bay during the last century was first known as "Walton's Camp" and later "Camp Walton." The place had less than a hundred population but they were ambitious for their town and thought it would be more impressive as "Fort Walton," so they changed the name. A few years ago when its very remarkable beach area began to develop they agreed "Fort Walton Beach" was still better, and that is the name of the town today. The 1900 census gave the town 90 residents, in 1950 the number was 2,385, and today it has at least 8,000.

In the files of the Smithsonian Institution can be found the statement that the "Camp Walton" area contains some of the largest Indian mounds and ancient village sites in the South. The town itself is on an old Indian mound and a number of ancient artifacts were found when the water and gas pipes were laid. This would indicate that a thousand years ago, as today, the region was one of the best hunting and fishing grounds on the Gulf Coast.

All along this part of the coast the sand, of which there is plenty, is noted for its whiteness. Homer Davis of the Massachusetts Institute of Technology, who is a "collector" of sands from everywhere, has written that this is the whitest sand he has ever seen and perhaps the whitest in the world. There is a credible story that in the days of sugar rationing during the last war an enterprising black marketer took a truckload of it in to Alabama and sold it for sugar. Recently it has been proved that this sand contains small amounts of the rare metal, titanium, and two chemical companies have leased a large tract of land and developed a method of extracting the titanium by a flotation process. Geologists say the bits of metal were washed down from the Appalachian Mountains eons ago, and though much of it remains there it is contained in the rocks and cannot be recovered economically. Combined with carbon it can be used in jet planes where it will withstand the tremendous heat developed better than any other metal or alloy.

Fort Walton Beach has no railroad and has small prospects of getting one as it is entirely surrounded by Eglin Field which occupies more than two-thirds of Okaloosa County. If the great Air Force Base constricts the town it also goes far toward supporting it, for most of the residents are in the employ of the government and most of the retail trade comes from the Air Force personnel. The Eglin Air Force Base stretches over approximately 465,000 acres, which is a little more than 725 square miles, and reaches out several hundred miles into the Gulf. It is a giant laboratory where the Air Proving Ground Command and the Air Force Armament Center test everything (and that means *every*thing) that enters into aerial warfare. Because of its ideal location and extraordinary facilities the field is sometimes used by other branches of the service for training or testing purposes. A statement of the mission of the Air Proving Ground Command says in part:

An error in selecting modern aerial weapons can cost human lives, billions of dollars, and even jeopardize our survival as a free nation. Two types of testing are done: 1) operational suitability testing to determine whether new equipment is capable of performing the mission for which it was designated under all foreseeable conditions, and 2) testing of new tactics and operational procedures so that the personnel who eventually use the new equipment can do so with knowing, capable hands.

After an aircraft of new or improved design has been thoroughly tested in actual flight it is taken to Eglin's "Climatic Hangar." The main chamber of this building is 200 by 250 feet, large enough to accommodate a B-36 intercontinental bomber and several smaller planes at the same time. Here the temperature can be lowered to 65 degrees below zero in less than forty-eight hours, then raised to 165 above. It contains bomb pits, landing gear actuator stands, ports for running jet engines, and firing guns. There is also a "desert room," a "tropic-marine room," and a special stratochamber capable of simulating conditions found eighty thousand feet above the earth. In fact any climatic condition anywhere in the world can be duplicated here. Obviously most of the projects at APGC have a high security classification.

The Air Proving Ground Command occupies most of the southern part of Okaloosa and Walton counties, but the greater part of this is pine woodland and of little use for agriculture. It is well stocked with game including an estimated eight thousand deer in addition to wild turkey, quail, bobcats and a number of beaver. These latter were imported but have thrived in their new environment. Those holding hunting licenses can, in season, obtain permits that will allow them to hunt on the Air Force grounds.

Although the southern part of the counties that reach from the Gulf to Alabama is given over largely to pinelands, the northern sections are excellent farming country. Walton County has more than 1,250 farms and has 18,000 acres in corn, most of which is fed to Hereford or Angus beef stock. This is sometimes called the "hog and hominy" section of Florida. Peanuts are a popular crop and make good hog feed. They are economical as the hogs are allowed to root for their food and this saves harvesting costs. Cotton, corn and pecans flourish, but the Satsuma orange and tung nut trees have mostly been killed by freezes. Economically these counties belong to Alabama, for most of their trade is with near-by Alabama markets, but anyone advocating such a change in state sovereignty would be very unpopular in northwest Florida.

Just east of Fort Walton Beach the highway crosses a bridge over East Pass, a comparatively narrow inlet to Choctawhatchee Bay, a body of water thirty miles long and a third as wide. It extends east from the pass and is separated from the Gulf by a long finger of land. For several miles east of the bridge the highway runs literally within a stone's throw of a fine beach, with cottages and motels along the shore. Then it enters a forest of tall, southern long-leaf pine, a beautiful drive, especially in late afternoon when the shadows make patterns of pencil lines across the pavement. Twenty miles outside of Panama City the pines are left behind and again the road skirts the water's edge. The white sand supports no trees but cottages and motels are on either hand. Although a part of the Florida coastline, this is a summer playground. June, July and August are the busy months. After Labor Day many of the motels put out signs announcing "winter rates," and a number of stores and places of amusement close for the season. At the southern end of the state the "summer rates" signs are being taken down in preparation for the winter rush.

Situated on St. Andrews Bay, one of the finest natural harbors of the Gulf, Panama City is a town that never quite realized its early ambition. The towns of St. Andrews and Millville were much elated when a railroad was constructed from their port to Dothan, Alabama, in the early 1900's. The United States was then engaged in digging the Panama Canal and it was generally believed that its completion would create a great boom in ocean transportation between the Isthmus and southern U.S. ports. What with the new railroad and the new canal, St. Andrews Bay would soon be filled with shipping from all over the world, so they renamed the place Panama City. Somehow the world never beat a path to Panama City's mousetrap, but the town cannot be blamed for trying.

St. Andrews Bay is a sprawling body of water with one long arm called West Bay, another called North Bay, and the longest of all, meandering near the coastline, called East Bay. The town is the seat of Bay County, most of which is covered by the forests of the International Paper Company which has a mill just outside Panama City. There it employs fifteen hundred of the local citizenry in manufacturing Kraft papers. The Du Pont Bridge, a nine-span structure, carries the highway across East Bay, and soon beside the road running through the pine barrens there appears a large sign: "Entering Military Reservation. Do not leave paved highway. Taking of photographs prohibited."

This is Tyndall Field, an Air Force Base established in 1941. Here are highly restricted grounds extending for eighteen miles along the highway where Air Force personnel are trained in jet interception, aircraft control, mechanics and all the intracacies of aerial warfare. Cottages and barracks for the base personnel constitute a small city and many others live in Mexico Beach and Beacon Hill just east of the airfield, one of the most attractive stretches of the entire coast. Beacon Hill is but a short distance east of the line dividing Eastern and Central Time zones. Those traveling east lose an hour here (they must turn their watches forward) and those westwardbound gain an hour.

Port St. Joe, nine miles inside the Eastern Time zone, might be called the birthplace of Florida statehood, for here in 1838 the convention met to draft the state's first constitution. The place was important economically and politically in those days. A railroad reached the town the next year and fifty thousand bales of cotton were shipped from its port. Then in July, 1841, a ship came in with yellow fever on board and the town was doomed. The dead piled up faster than the living could bury them and in a few weeks the place was deserted. So it remained for more than three-quarters of a century, until Alfred I. Du Pont, one of the first industrialists to realize the value of Florida's pine forests as a source of pulpwood, bought up a half-million acres of pinewood in the region. Now the mill of the St. Joe Paper Company is one of the largest in the country, its tall chimneys rising beyond mountains of "bolts" ready to be processed and long strings of flatcars from the woods waiting to be unloaded.

Originally U.S. 98 followed the beaches due south from St. Joe for ten miles and then made a sharp turn eastward toward Apalachicola, twenty miles farther on. Recently a new road has been cut through the pine swamps making a hypotenuse to the right angle and saving ten miles. This entire area is wooded swamplands and the nearest agricultural development is twenty-five or more miles to the north. But the highway is well maintained, the right-of-way is wide, and the drive is not unattractive.

Apalachicola, seat of Franklin County, is on Apalachicola Bay but this bay is not an indent in the shoreline. It is formed by three large offshore islands, St. Vincent, St. George and Dog Island, which stretch along the coast for fifty miles. St. Vincent is triangular with its western apex separated from the mainland by Indian Pass, so narrow that deer sometimes swim across it. Privately owned by A. L. Loomis, Jr., and his brother Henry Loomis, of New York, it is well stocked with many kinds of game. St. George is more than twenty miles long and not more than half a mile wide in most places. With Dog Island, also narrow and long, it is being developed as a resort with motels and private cottages. Each is about six miles from the mainland and is served by ferries. The town is located at the mouth of the Apalachicola River and looks out across East Bay, an inlet from the much larger Apalachicola Bay.

The Apalachicola River is formed by the junction of the Chattahoochee and Flint rivers at the Florida-Georgia state line, seventy-five miles due north of its mouth. In the days of side-wheel river boats it was a water highway from tidewater to northern Florida, Georgia and Alabama. As this is written three large dams with navigation locks are being constructed on the upper reaches of these streams and a revival of the old trade is confidently predicted. In the swampy lands along the lower stretches of the river are thousands of tupelo, or "gum," trees that in spring are covered with

nectar-filled blossoms. Several apiaries are located around the town's
suburbs and it is noted for its production of "tupelo honey," a honey
that never becomes granular and is the only form of this sweet that
can be eaten by diabetics.

Apalachicola's greatest claim to fame is its reputation as the birthplace of artificial ice and refrigeration. More than a century ago it
was the home of Dr. John Gorrie, physician and onetime mayor.
In treating malarial patients he found they were helped when the
temperature of the room was lowered, which he accomplished by
suspending a bag of ice from the ceiling. This was an expensive
process especially in summer. When ice could be obtained at all it
cost from $0.75 to $1.25 a pound. Being of an inventive mind the
doctor sought a better solution and by 1844 he was artificially cool-
ing two rooms in his house that were used as a hospital. On March
16, 1849, he applied for a U.S. patent on his ice-making machine
and it was given him May 6, 1851. In the meantime he had received
a British patent in 1850. His statue is one of two which Florida is
permitted to place in the Hall of Fame in the national capitol at
Washington. A model of his first machine may be seen in the foyer
of the courthouse in Apalachicola. It is an unwieldy-looking contraption standing five feet high on a brick base, but it is the father of
all modern refrigerators. The bridge that spans East Bay where the
highway leaves Apalachicola is named the Gorrie Bridge.

After it crosses the Gorrie Bridge the highway sticks close to the
water's edge, but from here on there is no beach. For twelve miles,
as far as Carrabelle, the sea has encroached on the land and the
surf breaks against the pine stumps that once stood on dry ground.
Beyond Carrabelle the land appears to have advanced against the
sea, the waters are shallow and sprinkled with marsh grass, making
it an ideal hunting ground for waterfowl. Carrabelle is on Crooked
River, an odd stream that breaks off from the Ochlockonee (accent
on the "LOCK") River and wanders twenty miles across the marshes
before entering the Gulf. Carrabelle grew, but not very much, from
a lumber mill established at the mouth of Crooked River in 1875,

and by 1891 the settlement was large enough to support a post office and a name. Miss Carrie Hall, a member of one of the older families, was the belle of the village and it was christened "Rio Carrabelle."

Twenty miles east of Carrabelle a T-shaped side road branches off from Route 98 to a small peninsula. The stem of the T is four miles long as is each of its arms. The right hand is Alligator Point and the other is Bald Point. This isolated road is traveled mostly by hunters looking for ducks and geese which congregate here in large numbers in the winter to feed in the surrounding marshes. But it was a busy place during World War II when it was used as a firing range and practice ground by the Army in training soldiers for amphibious warfare. So littered were the beaches on the seaward side with shell cases, cables and other military debris after the war that the Army spent weeks cleaning it up. Just beyond this point the shoreline of the Gulf turns southward around Apalachee Bay. Passing through the village of Panacea, so called because there was once a locally popular mineral spring there, one can see through the trees an arm of the Gulf. This is the last glimpse of its waters from a main highway until the Tampa Bay region is reached, 250 miles down the coast. Between these points the only access to tidewater is by way of secondary roads that lead to isolated beaches or fishing villages.

The Apalachicola National Forest, the Wild Life Refuge of the U.S. Department of the Interior, and the holdings of the St. Joe Paper Company take up 85 per cent of Wakulla County at the head of Apalachee Bay and a similar portion of Liberty County which joins it on the west. These forests are not being destroyed, as the timber is cut selectively and new trees allowed to grow. Fifty years from now it will be the source of more marketable timber than it is today. A short distance beyond Crawfordsville, the seat of Wakulla County, is Wakulla Springs and Wakulla Springs Lodge, set in a grove of giant, moss-draped oaks. Here over an area of four and a half acres a great crystal-clear spring rises from a depth of 185 feet and forms the Wakulla River which flows into the St. Marks River a few miles away. Originally a private retreat, the springs and lodge were opened to the public thirty years ago. The motion picture companies of Hollywood (California) have found the place ideal for romantic settings and have filmed twenty-two movies here, among them a number from the "Tarzan" series. Excavations in the region of the springs have disclosed the bones of a number of prehistoric animals and the complete skeletons of two mammoths have been unearthed, one being mounted in the Smithsonian Institution in Washington and the other at the Florida State University in Tallahassee.

U.S. Route 98, which follows Florida's Gulf coastline for more than four hundred miles, passes thirteen miles south of Tallahassee,

The State Capitol Building, Tallahassee

(Florida State News Bureau)

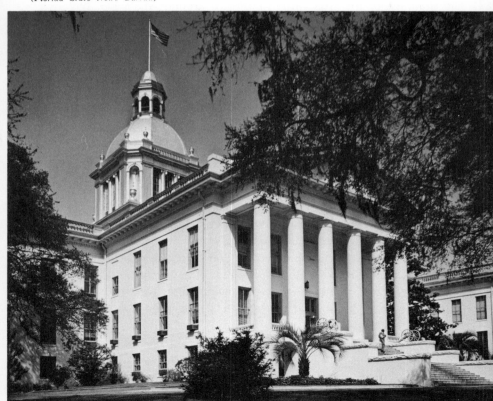

the state capital. In this region where the long Florida peninsula merges into the mainland there is little commercial activity along the coast and Tallahassee can be classified as an inland city, although before the coming of the railroads it was the center of considerable traffic that touched tidewater at St. Marks, twenty miles south.

When Tallahassee was selected by the Federal government in 1824 to be the capital of the newly acquired territory of Florida there was no settlement of consequence at the site. But it was strategically situated where the road from Thomasville, Georgia, to the port at St. Marks crossed the old Spanish Trail between Jacksonville and Pensacola. The first Florida land boom got under way soon after the new government was established and cotton plantations soon extended from the Georgia line to the coast. By the late 1830's the boom was at its height and like so many booms it soon burst. Banking facilities had been limited and the leading citizens had organized the Union Bank of Tallahassee. The bank collapsed and the weeds grew in the cotton fields.

One of the new citizens remained and he brought the little capital city a fame of sorts. He was Prince Charles Louis Napoleon Achille Murat, born in France in 1801. His mother was a sister of Napoleon Bonaparte and his father, Joachim Murat, was the son of an innkeeper who became one of Napoleon's most inspired cavalry leaders and was later installed by the little Corsican as "King of Naples." Arrogant and ambitious, Joachim quarreled with everyone, including Napoleon who refused his aid prior to Waterloo, only to admit later that his presence there might have made the difference between defeat and victory. Eventually he died before a firing squad on a charge of disturbing the peace. The older of his two sons, Charles, came to Florida in 1821, became a naturalized citizen, and was successively alderman, mayor and postmaster in Tallahassee. He married Catherine Grey, née Willis, a young widow who was a grandniece of George Washington, and the two lie side by side in the Episcopal Cemetery.

Florida State University was established in Tallahassee in 1857,

Looking down the historic St. Marks River

being first called the West Florida Seminary. In March, 1865, when Union troops were marching to attack the town, cadets from the seminary joined with the regular Confederate forces to defend it. The engagement took place a few miles southeast of the capital where the St. Marks River flows for a short distance underground, and is recorded in history as the Battle of Natural Bridge. So successful were the Confederates and their schoolboy allies that Tallahassee was the only Southern state capital east of the Mississippi that did not fall to the Union forces during the Civil War. The battleground is now a state park and a favorite picnic rendezvous.

The quaint village of St. Marks near the mouth of the St. Marks River is but three miles south of the speeding traffic of U.S. 98 yet only a few tourists ever see it. Here in 1527 Pánfilo de Narváez with his second-in-command, Cabeza de Vaca, arrived with the tattered survivors of the three hundred soldiers that had started out from Tampa Bay several months previously. They had missed their rendezvous with the ships that had brought them to the coast, had marched up to what is now southern Georgia looking for gold, and had eaten the last of their forty horses to keep from starving. Where the Wakulla River joins the St. Marks they beat their swords and armor into crude tools and constructed five small "ships," actually no more than barges, in which they hoped to sail to Mexico. Contrary winds carried them along the coast and one craft after another was wrecked. Cabeza's vessel got as far as Galveston Island where it, too, was broken up. He and three companions who reached Mexico City eight years later after journeying to the Pacific, were the only survivors of the expedition.

The bleached bones of De Narváez' horses were found on the banks of the St. Marks by De Soto when he established a winter camp here in 1539–40 before he began his two-year trek to the north and west. In 1673 a small fortification was built here and in 1718 the Spanish captain, Primo de Ribera, built Fort St. Marks at the confluence of the two rivers. Then the English manned it when they held Florida from 1763 to 1783. It was here in the 1780's that the renegade British officer, William Augustus Bowles, married a Creek squaw and set himself up as "King of Florida." Captured by the Spanish, he escaped and returned to the St. Marks River to organize a band of Indians and runaway Negro slaves and operate as a pirate until he was finally caught and put in jail to die.

Today historic old Fort Marks is buried beneath a tangle of jungle growth. The site can be reached only by boat although it can be seen from the fishing wharf at the village. Plans are afoot to clear away the litter that surrounds it and restore its outline at least in part. After the close of the Civil War the town of St. Marks flourished for a while as a port but a fire in 1868 destroyed its six large warehouses, a four-hundred-foot wharf and a cotton press. Now it drowses in the sun, content to be the fishing capital of Apalachee Bay.

From the village of Wakulla to the Suwannee River is more than a hundred miles, and except for the town of Perry about midway, and Cross City, twelve miles from the Suwannee, there is hardly a house to be seen. Even filling stations and motels are scarce, but the road is a pleasant one. The right-of-way has been cleared of all trees and shrubbery so that it is a broad avenue between forests of pine, oaks of several species, cypress, sabal palms, sweetgum, hickory and an occasional *Magnolia grandiflora.* There are no sharp turns and the curves are wide. So most of the tourists coming from the North or going home stomp the accelerator pedal to the floor and pass the sixty-mile-an-hour driver as though he were in a wheelchair. Perry is the seat of Taylor County and Cross City the seat of Dixie County. Ask the agricultural agents about farming and they smile and say "Not much," although the sections farthest from the Gulf produce considerable tobacco and corn.

The land through here is given over to the production of pulpwood which is source material for many products. In Perry the big plant of the Buckeye Cellulose Corporation takes the wood and turns out a product that is shipped to other plants as a base for textile yarns, nylon, tire cording and similar fabrics. It has 570,000 acres of forest from which to draw its supply. Much of the Dixie County pulpwood is shipped to the plant of the Hudson Pulp & Paper Company's plant at Palatka where it is converted into coarse paper products.

Between Perry and Cross City a side road winds down to Adams Beach, eighteen miles off the main highway, and follows the shore eight miles farther to Keaton's Beach and Fish Creek. These are fishing points with a few cottages for those who like solitude. The only place to go from there is back. Farther on another road runs down to Steinhatchee at the mouth of the Steinhatchee River, which in Texas or Louisiana would be called a bayou. Here, in addition to fishing as a sport and a business, are several Greek-owned sponge boats that bring their harvest from the Gulf and send it to the Sponge Exchange at Tarpon Springs farther down the coast. From Oldtown, four miles from the bridge across the Suwannee, is a road down to the village of Suwannee at the mouth of the river, twenty-three miles below the bridge. Here the famous stream empties into the Gulf amid a welter of marsh grass and sand, having none of the beauty to be found a few miles upstream. Hog Island at the mouth of the river divides its waters into East Pass and West Pass as they flow into the Gulf.

Even if Stephen Foster had never lived or had never written his haunting melody the Suwannee River would be one of the best-known streams along the Southern coasts. Rising amid the dark jungles of the great Okefenokee Swamp in southwest Georgia it meanders erratically south and west, accepting the waters of tributary streams and innumerable springs. Its source is only a few miles from the Atlantic Coast watershed, but after twisting across Florida for more than two hundred miles it eventually spills its waters into the Gulf of Mexico. Wide and deep along its lower stretches, with

The Suwannee River

tall, moss-bedecked cypress trees, eternally green pines and live oaks growing right down to its clear waters, it is indeed a stream to inspire a song. Pity it is that Foster, who sent its name around the world, never saw it. Writing "Old Folks at Home," a sentimental ballad about the Deep South a century ago, he searched for the name of a river with the desired lilt and accent to be the scene of his nostalgic theme. When someone suggested "Suwannee" he seized on it as ideal. Had the pronunciation and accent suited him he would just have soon as used the Apalachicola or the Caloosahatchee. But he chose the Suwannee and the river is deserving of the immortality he bestowed on it.

Somewhere near the place where U.S. Routes 98, 19 and 27A unite to cross the stream, De Narváez and De Soto with their weary helmeted followers crossed over centuries ago, covertly watched by the wondering Indians. General Andrew Jackson was familiar with the river during his Indian campaigns and here Colonel J. W. Fannin built a fort shortly after the United States acquired Florida from Spain. From here he wandered out to Texas where he was captured by the Mexicans while fighting for Texas' independence and died at Goliad in 1836 when the prisoners were massacred by their captors. A beautiful spring near the bridge is still called Fannin's Spring, and a few yards away is the site of Fannin's Fort. Unfortunately careless tourist-pamphlet writers often spell it "Fanning."

Just south of Oldtown is the home of Tom Chaires, a cattle raiser, who was born on the banks of the Suwannee in 1873. His great-grandfather, Benjamin Chaires, came to this part of Florida from Alabama in the early 1800's, and the family was prominent in the development that followed the purchase of the province from Spain. Oldtown was an old Indian village at that time and the name of the modern settlement is a translation of the Indian term.

When the settlement of this part of Florida began there were heavy stands of red cedar in the region and the Eagle Pencil Company and the Eberhard Faber Company built mills on Cedar Key, twelve miles below the mouth of the Suwannee, to manufacture cedar pencils. For years there was a wooden trestle bridge over the river near its mouth and a road to Cedar Key but by 1916 the cedars were gone and the factories abandoned. The bridge was dismantled and reconstructed twenty miles upstream where a steel bridge replaced it ten years later. This bridge is now the first one above the mouth of the stream.

Following the Civil War a heavy steamboat traffic developed on the Suwannee between the railroad point at Branford, fifty miles upstream, and Cedar Key which had become a busy seaport. Seven turpentine stills and a number of sawmills flourished along the banks, thousands of crossties for the rapidly expanding railroads were piled up at the landings, and these with the cargoes of general merchandise furnished considerable tonnage for the fifteen stern-wheel steamboats that sent their smoke over the virgin forests. These vessels were among the finest of their day. The *Belle of the Suwannee*, the *Eagle Pencil* and the *C. D. Owens* were among those equipped with mahogany-paneled passenger quarters and famed for their cuisine. As the big timber disappeared and the railroads were extended the river traffic declined and the old boats disappeared. The sunken wreckage of one of them may be seen on the west bank of the river a few miles from Oldtown.

Cedar Key, a few miles down the coast from the mouth of the Suwannee, like St. Marks is a town that has known better days. It is situated on one of a group of small islands that stand offshore from the mainland, separated by a waste of tidal flats and salt marshes. It is twenty-two miles from the main highway running down the west coast. The town is more of the sea than of the land. Fish nets drape its barnacle-covered piers, to which commercial and sports craft of all sorts are moored, and there is good fishing right on the wharf. On the high land a few blocks in extent, which is locally called "The Hill," are weather-beaten cottages surrounded by chinaberry trees and a few cedars, reminiscent of the forest of cedar that once covered this part of the coast. Down by the beach is an attractive state park equipped with sheltered picnic tables, fireplaces and all the facilities for the family to enjoy a day at the seashore.

Time was when the only railroad across Florida reached the Key, ships from New Orleans, Havana and more distant points called there regularly, river boats brought down cargoes of cotton and forest products, and it was a busy, brawling seaport. Captured by the Yankees during the Civil War and pretty well smashed up by the Southerners before they retreated, it was rebuilt and continued as a busy place until near the end of the century. By that time progress had bypassed it, the railroad was discontinued, and it was left to the fishermen and sportsmen. The worst blow was a fire that swept the town simultaneously with a tidal wave in 1896. Most of the buildings were burned or swept away and twenty-eight persons were killed.

There are those who say it was the town's own fault that it did not continue to grow. When Henry B. Plant, who did a great deal to develop southwestern Florida, offered to make Cedar Key the terminus of his railroad the town refused to make any kind of deal with him. He is reported to have declared that he would "live to see the day when owls would roost in every attic in Cedar Key." Eventually he built his railroad into Tampa and Cedar Key began to regress.

The next approach to the Gulf after leaving Cedar Key is twenty-four miles down the highway, where a side road from Inglis leads to Yankeetown, three miles to the west on the banks of the Withlacoochee River, one of the most charming unspoiled spots along the Florida coast. The clear waters, their banks overhung with semi-tropical foliage, wind past the town and out to the Gulf by way of a channel cut through the shallows. This was to be the western terminus of the proposed trans-Florida canal that has been a subject of state and national controversy since 1933. Promoted as a "made work" project during the early "New Deal" era, it was planned to connect the Gulf of Mexico with the Atlantic Ocean by way of a ship canal across the state, ending in the St. Johns River that flows into the ocean below Jacksonville. The estimated cost was $142,700,-000, and more than $5,000,000 was spent in the central part of the state before the work was discontinued. The Florida Ship Canal Authority still functions and makes periodic reports to the governor, and under an act of Congress passed more than thirty years ago the work could be completed if appropriations were made for it.

Proponents of the canal say it would shorten the distance for intracoastal shipping that now has to go around Key West and would result in increased shipment of oil by barge from Texas and Louisiana fields to terminals in New York and New Jersey. Another argument is that such a route would be a great protection to American shipping in time of war. Opponents of the plan say it would lower the water table of the rich farming lands and orange groves through which it would pass and would result in the intrusion of salt water to the detriment of wells and agriculture, as has happened in other parts of the state. Some say that covert opposition to the plan has come from Tampa and other seaports south of the proposed canal, where commerce might be adversely affected by such a route. Geologists, shipping interests and politicians can be found to testify for either side.

The channel at the mouth of the Withlacoochee, however, was dredged out long before the days of the New Deal. Phosphate deposits were discovered in central Florida in 1882 and today the state produces twelve million tons a year, most of which is used in the manufacture of fertilizers. In the 1890's a Belgian firm established a port on an island just below the mouth of the Withlacoochee where phosphate brought down the river on barges was transferred to ships bound for Europe. A considerable settlement developed there, including a customshouse, a school, a church and a comfortable clubhouse. When World War I broke out in 1914 business ceased abruptly, the place was abandoned, and jungle vegetation covered the ruins within a few years. No road leads to the site but curious persons visiting the place by boat found the clubhouse still equipped with furniture, dishes and hangings, much of which was salvaged as there was no one left to claim it.

Along the northern shore of the Gulf it is the summer tourist who seeks the beaches and good fishing grounds, but halfway down its eastern coast the winter resort area begins, although there is considerable year-round travel all over the state. Crystal River is expanding its facilities for attracting vacationers, and seven miles down the road is Homosassa Springs, one of the several places along this shore where a great volume of clear water boils out of the ground to flow as a small river to the sea. Like Weeki Wachee Springs a few miles farther on, it has been commercialized and made a "show place" that is interesting to many, but lacks the natural beauty that characterized the spot before a fee was charged to see it.

From the village of Homosassa Springs there is a road down to Old Homosassa on the Homosassa River, an attractive retreat where the road winds between great trees and small cottages. At the edge of the town is an old square stone chimney on which is a bronze plaque that reads: "1810—David Levy Yulee—1886. This tablet marks the ruin of the sugar mill constructed by David Levy Yulee in 1851. The plantation covered approximately 100 acres. It is the property of the Citrus County Federation of Women's Clubs by presentation from the owner, Mr. Claude Root, in 1923."

The "100 acres" is a "typographical error" for according to Mrs. Mary MacRae who has written a history of the Yulee family, the plantation included 35,000 acres, of which 5,000 were in sugar cane. This was only one of several large sugar cane plantations along the Florida coast, all of which vanished when the Civil War freed the slaves and disrupted the entire economy. Old Homosassa was incorporated in 1880 and shared the prosperity of the pencil-producing cedar forests until they were gone. Below Homosassa Springs U.S. Highway 98 turns off to the southeast toward the central part of the state, and Route 19 continues down the coast to St. Petersburg. Six miles east and a little south of Homosassa is the geographical center of the state of Florida. It seems out of place so close to the coastline, but the odd shape of the state with a long peninsula to the south and the West Florida counties to the west determines the point. In 1930 the center of population in the state was fifteen miles north of Homosassa.

At Weeki Wachee Springs, complete with mermaids and other attractions, a side road leaves the main highway to end at Pine Island and Bayport State Park on the coast, seven miles east. Clumps of cabbage palms stand amid acres of sawgrass between the mainland and two small islands. Here are a few permanent residents, but the road is used mostly by those bent on a picnic at the park or a day's fishing in the prolific waters. Palmettos are often seen along the northern coast of the Gulf but it is through this region that they become an integral part of the landscape. The palmetto thickets are never more than waist-high, although the palmetto is a fully developed tree with stiff, fan-shaped leaves. Its peculiarity is that it is a recumbent or "prostrate" tree, its trunk, four or five inches in diameter, running along the ground like an overgrown vine. It will not grow in damp ground and flourishes best in pine woodlands. There is a saying that where pine and palmetto grow, fruit trees do well. That may be, but fertilization is also necessary.

New Port Richey on the Pithlachascotee River, locally abbreviated to "the Cotee," along with its older neighbor, Port Richey, did not begin to grow until after World War II, but since then it has developed into one of the popular vacation spots of the west Florida coast. The river is spring-fed and winds three miles through the palms and pines before it enters the Gulf, although the distance by road is only one mile. Five miles below New Port Richey Highway 19 divides, the main road leading to St. Petersburg thirty-five miles south, and Alternate 19, the old route, winding through a number of suburban towns along the beaches, the principal ones being Tarpon Springs and Clearwater.

Tarpon Springs is the "sponge capital" of the Gulf Coast and until about 1940 there were more than 150 "sponge boats" operating from its piers at the mouth of the Anclote River. In 1938 a mysterious

(*Joan Wyeth Griggs*)

Grading sponges for auction in the sponge market at Tarpon Springs

malady usually called "the red tide," began to deplete the sponge beds and ten years later so few marketable sponges were found in the nine thousand square miles of sponge-producing waters of the Gulf that business almost ceased. Within the last five years it has revived and today there are about twenty boats operating out of the harbor. These are augmented by other boats from small harbors all the way from Key West to St. Marks, all of which send their cargoes to be sold at the Sponge Exchange in Tarpon Springs. The Florida sponge industry began in a small way when Grecian-born spongers started working from Key West about 1890. When the Spanish-American War broke out in 1898 they moved up to Tarpon Springs. Until 1925 all sponges recovered from the sea were "hooked" by means of long poles, but these could not reach to a depth of more than thirty feet. In that year expert divers were brought from Greece, along with their equipment, and beds as deep as 130 feet could be worked. There are plenty of marketable sponges in the Gulf today, but when business fell off in the last decade the crews sought other work and now most of the younger men prefer the assured income of a payroll to the uncertainties of winning a livelihood from the sea.

Greeks make up a large part of the town's population and St. Nicholas' Cathedral of the Greek Orthodox Church is one of its most beautiful buildings. At the Feast of the Epiphany on January 6 of each year the Archbishop and his attendants go to the waterside where he blesses the sponge fleet and releases a white dove. He then casts a golden cross into the waters of the harbor and the younger divers plunge in to recover it. The lucky finder returns it to the Archbishop who gives him a special blessing which portends a lucrative season for him. Tarpon Springs is growing industrially, its largest plant being the Victor Chemical Works where phosphate products are refined. This and several textile mills and machinery companies employ many who formerly sailed with the sponge fleet.

Clearwater with a population of thirty thousand is primarily a town for vacationists, winter or summer, a role for which it is well fitted. It is situated on the highest point along the Florida coast, most of the town being seventy-five feet above high tide—almost a mountain in southern Florida. Two miles offshore across Clearwater Bay is Clearwater Beach, a part of the municipality, with wide beaches, hotels from the modest to the luxurious, and an elaborate municipally owned "marina" for the accommodation of noncommercial fishing craft. Connecting the island with the mainland is a wide, double-lane causeway, well landscaped and bordered by palms.

Tampa Bay looks like two enormous fingers thrust at an angle into the side of Florida, pushing a part of the land out into the Gulf. This irregular piece of land between the bay and the Gulf is Pinellas Peninsula, about thirty miles long and from five to twelve miles wide. It has been generally assumed that the name came from the Spaniards for "Point of Pines" (*pinta pinal*) but it was recently noted that there is a small village on the coast of Spain called "Pinellas" and the name may have been brought to Florida by some homesick Spaniard. Along the coast on the Gulf side is a chain of long, narrow islands with hard sand beaches, all highly developed as vacation resorts, some quite exclusive and some "honky-tonk." All can be reached by roads over short causeways and in despair of naming each small village the road signs pointing west along U.S. Route 19 say simply, "Gulf Beaches." The southern tip of these islands is Pass-a-Grille, two miles long and one block wide, the site of many attractive homes. Beyond Pass-a-Grille and reached by ferry is Mullet Key, a V-shaped island owned by the park department of Pinellas County. Here Fort De Soto was built at the beginning of the Spanish-American War and here a defensive force was stationed during World War I. Having seen no hostile action during those two wars it was subjected to heavy bombardment during World War II when it was a practice ground for bombing planes. Now it is famous as a recreation park and fishing ground.

The city of St. Petersburg occupies the southern end of the Pinellas Peninsula. Although it has a population of 135,000 and is still growing it is a newcomer among Florida cities, having been incorporated in 1892 when its population was only three hundred. In the ensuing years it has won a reputation for its five thousand green benches along the wide downtown streets where residents and visitors relax in the sun, for its magnificent municipal pier of steel and concrete reaching more than a half-mile out into the bay, and for its "Most Unusual Drug Store," Webb's City.

The early Spanish explorers left the names of their saints scat-

The famous green benches of St. Petersburg

tered all along the Gulf Coast but they did not name St. Petersburg. The city had its beginning when one John C. Williams of Detroit, Michigan (his whiskers reached below his belt), bought up most of Pinellas Peninsula and began to clear it. He made a deal with a wealthy Russian exile of noble birth, named Pietr Dementieff, later shortened to Peter Demens, whereby the Russian would build a railroad to the place in return for a half-interest in it. The road, a narrow-gauge line from the eastern part of the state, was completed in 1888. The community numbered thirty souls and was large enough to have a name. Legend is that William and Demens could not agree on a moniker and tossed a coin for the privilege of naming the place. Demens won and in a moment of nostalgia named it St. Petersburg, then the capital of Russia. The Russian city was later christened "Petrograd" and then "Leningrad" but there has been no disposition to change the name of the Florida metropolis. Balked in his desire to name the city, Williams erected a large hotel and named it the Detroit for his home town. It was well built and is still doing business.

St. Petersburg was among the first Florida vacation centers to make a bid for the swelling tourist trade and those retiring on modest incomes. Illinois and Indiana each claim to have the oldest "State Society" in the city, both having been organized in 1902. Now there are twenty-two such organizations that hold their meetings in the Tourist Center adjoining the Chamber of Commerce Building, coming from states as far west as Iowa and as far north as Minnesota, Maine and Canada. The Pennsylvania Society has 2,700 members.

Although far from the big-league ball parks, baseball fans in this area get an opportunity to see most of the famous stars in action. Twelve of the sixteen major baseball teams have training grounds in Florida. The New York Yankees and the St. Louis Cardinals have their base in St. Petersburg; the Chicago White Sox and the Cincinnati Red Legs are twenty miles distant in Tampa; the Philadelphia Phillies at Clearwater, the Milwaukee Braves at Bradenton; the Boston Red Sox at Sarasota, and the Pittsburgh Pirates at Fort Myers can all be reached by a drive of two hours or less from St. Petersburg. The Detroit Tigers train at Lakeland, the Washington Senators at Orlando, the Kansas City Athletics at West Palm Beach, and the Brooklyn Dodgers at Vero Beach and Miami.

Shuffleboard, the game that finally came ashore after growing up on ocean liners, is, however, the most popular sport in St. Petersburg. The city has four large outdoor shuffleboard clubs, one of them with more than six thousand members. In all there are three hundred courts, and club memberships exceed fifteen thousand persons. The larger courts have grandstands for spectators and shuffleboard tournaments are a regular winter feature. The St. Petersburg *Inde-*

pendent, an afternoon newspaper, carries the following box at its masthead: "The Sunshine Newspaper will give away its Sunshine (11:30 A.M.) Edition every day the sun fails to shine on the Independent building in the previous 24 hours."

It was a great boon to the city when, in 1924, the Gandy Bridge across Tampa Bay was completed, uniting St. Petersburg with Tampa and the highways to the east. The bridge was the dream of George S. Gandy, a Philadelphia utility operator who had moved to this area. The outbreak of World War I stymied the earlier plans for a bridge, but in 1922 Gandy and his associates sold two million dollars' worth of preferred stock to the public, and then confounded their critics by building the bridge in two years. For twenty years it operated as a toll bridge amid mounting demands for a freeway, and in 1944 the Federal government took it over as a war measure. The bridge itself is two and a half miles long in addition to a long filled causeway at its western end. Originally a two-lane bridge it eventually became so congested that a second two-lane span was built alongside it and put in operation late in 1955 with eastbound traffic using the old span and westbound traffic the new. The new span has three features not found in the old: it is wider, it has a high-level span over the ship channel instead of a drawbridge, and it has a thousand-foot catwalk at each end for the accommodation of fishermen—and women.

Completion of the Gandy Bridge put an end to the St. Petersburg—Tampa Airboat Line, which in 1914 inaugurated the first scheduled passenger and cargo-carrying air service in the world. The aircraft of this line were of the bailing-wire-and-canvas type and no hostesses were required. The trip across the bay was made in eighteen minutes. From Clearwater on the upper Pinellas Peninsula the Courtney Campbell Parkway crosses the bay over a nine-mile-long fill lined with picnic tables and barbecue pits, giving the upper Gulf beaches quick access to the heart of Tampa.

The Gandy Bridge gave St. Petersburg an outlet to the east and in part relieved its isolation from the region's main highways, but

The "Sunshine Skyway" across Tampa Bay

until 1954 all southbound traffic that did not want to go through Tampa and run up considerable extra mileage was compelled to use the ferries across the entries to Tampa Bay, a distance of twelve miles that often delayed the motorist an hour or more, especially when traffic was heavy. To remedy this serious bottleneck in Florida's west coast travel the "Sunshine Skyway" was built by the state at a cost of $22,000,000 and opened on Labor Day, 1954. In spite of a toll rate of $1.75 for a passenger car the Skyway took in $1,827,-942 during its first year of operation, which was 63 per cent more than had been estimated. Fifty weeks after its opening a million cars had used it. Eleven and a half miles long, the Skyway consists of four short bridges and a main span connected by six and a half miles of embankments. These causeways have sheltered picnic tables and afford excellent opportunity for fishing. No drawspan is needed for the central arch of the main section carries the motorist 160 feet above the waters of the bay.

Seven hundred and fifty miles from St. Petersburg, especially up Tennessee way, one may see signboards advertising "Webb's City in St. Petersburg, the World's Most Unusual Drug Store." The title has never been challenged. James Earle ("Doc") Webb and his over-size drug store are as much a part of St. Petersburg as the city hall. Born in Tennessee in 1899, Doc landed in the town in 1925 with five thousand dollars, an unlimited supply of self-confidence, and seven years' experience in various drug stores. He had quit school while in the seventh grade and never attempted to qualify as a registered pharmacist. With a partner he opened a 17 x 28 drug store a little way out from downtown and hired four employees. The first year's receipts were $38,990.45, gross. Came the "depression" and the partner cried quits, so Doc Webb bought him out.

Today Webb's City has fifty-seven departments, five restaurants, thirty registered pharmacists who put up seven hundred prescriptions every day, a barbershop with twenty-one chairs where haircuts are fifty-five cents, eight parking lots that will accommodate fifteen hundred cars, a "trading post" that carries a line of hardware and paints, a gas station where attendants are usually filling two lines of cars standing bumper to bumper, a supermarket, a beauty shop, and 45,000 customers a day. This large and varied business has been built up not by bargain merchandise alone, but also by a policy of showmanship and advertising that would have made the late Phineas T. Barnum sick with envy. Doc Webb has at various times sold a carload of canned peaches in one day, a carload of cantaloupes at two cents each, a carload of stale cigars and the world's largest cheese—2,480 pounds of Wisconsin Cheddar. When he opened his cafeteria he served a breakfast consisting of an egg, two strips of bacon, three slices of toast, grits and ham gravy for three cents. When the place was well advertised, as it soon was, he raised the price to fourteen cents but later reduced it to nine cents. Once he sold two thousand one-dollar bills at $0.95 each and bought them back the next day at $1.35 each. The place was mobbed. He cashes checks totaling $25 million a year, more than his gross business. Losses through bad checks are negligible, for Doc will chase a bad check passer from St. Petersburg to Timbuktu. This service has no banking hours and checks can be cashed whenever the store is open.

Doc insists that he has the right to sell at any price the goods he has bought and paid for and this has frequently brought him in conflict with the so-called "fair trade" laws. At one time he had six law firms defending his various dealings. In 1940, pressed for ready cash, he needed $200,000 which the local banks did not have, and the underwriters wanted a 10 per cent commission to handle a sale of preferred stock. So Doc got a broker's license and advertised that the following Monday the public could buy the stock at one hundred dollars a share. Thursday an official of the Securities Exchange Commission came bustling in to tell Doc he couldn't sell stock that way, but the Thursday morning papers had carried a big ad saying: "Thank you! Stock all sold." Webb's City is not the accepted type of department store. It is an aggregate of fifty departments, each under the direction of a manager who buys stock, hires his help many of whom are elderly persons, and runs his own show. That gives Doc time to stand around the store in the afternoons and chat with the customers, which he frequently does.

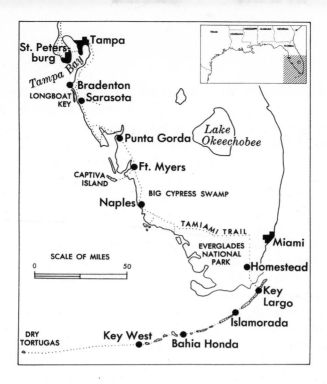

XV. *Along the Tamiami Trail*

T AMPA, chief port and industrial center of Florida's west coast, ranking only below Miami and Jacksonville in size, has an outline shaped like a piece of a jigsaw puzzle. This is fitting, because bits of its erratic past involving Spaniards, Cubans, Indians, railroad tycoons, soldiers and politicians, somehow have been pieced together over a long period of years to make up a picturesque, prosperous and highly versatile metropolis. It has what Miami has not, a wide, productive hinterland that comes right up to its door. Two-thirds of the state's citrus- and vegetable-processing plants are in Hillsborough County of which Tampa is the seat. Its docks are loading points for phosphates mined in Hillsborough and adjoining counties and shipped all over the world. Plant City, fifteen miles to the east, is "the winter strawberry capital of the world" with twenty million pints a year. All this despite the fact that more than 60 per cent of the county's acreage is in commercial forest lands, producing lumber, pulpwood and "naval stores," the old name for rosin and turpentine in the days of sailing ships. And Tampa has tourists swarming all over the place.

Tradition says that the name of the city sprang from the Seminole language and means "plenty of split wood for quick fires," which, if true, would indicate the Indians had a very concise language. The older part of the city occupies a peninsula that sticks southward into the waters of Tampa Bay, a very sizable body of water. That part of the bay lying between Tampa and the Pinellas Peninsula to the west is Old Tampa Bay and the smaller inlet to the east is Hillsborough Bay. The Hillsborough River, a stream of modest proportions, bisects the city and empties into the bay of the same name. At the extreme southern point of the peninsula is MacDill Air Field. Starting near the mouth of the river the city has grown until its boundaries are seven miles north and four miles east and west of that point.

Ybor City, immediately northeast of downtown Tampa, is a city within a city, where 167 factories turn out 632 million cigars annually, give or take a few hundred million. It is populated chiefly by Cubans, augmented by other Latin Americans and Italians, numbering in all about 45,000. Most of the tobacco used in the city is grown in Cuba, though some of the "shade-grown" wrapper leaves come from Connecticut. Two daily newspapers printed in Spanish are published there and its restaurants are frequented by tourists and others who enjoy exotic foods.

The cigar-making business came to Florida in 1869 when Señor V. Martinez Ybor transferred his factory from Cuba to Key West because the recurring revolutions of the Cubans against their Spanish overlords were a frequent source of interruption. The business prospered there but in 1886 labor troubles were still plaguing the industry and Ybor and his partner, Eduardo Manrara, moved to a site adjoining the small town of Tampa. Other factories followed and soon Ybor City was larger than Tampa. In time Tampa outgrew its neighbor and absorbed it, but Ybor City has kept its individuality and remains a Latin community. As the Cuban revolution gathered momentum during the 1890's, the Cubans of Ybor City were busy with intrigues, plots and counterplots, and considerable gun-running to the revolutionists. When the United States got into the war after the *Maine* blew up in Havana Harbor, more than five thousand Ybor City citizens joined the Cuban Army and were fighting under General Gomez months before the Americans got into action.

Occupying the southern tip of the Tampa peninsula, which places it right in the center of Tampa Bay, is MacDill Field, a base of the Strategic Air Command, similar to that near Lake Charles, Louisiana, and the control center for the Caribbean area. Home of the Sixth Air Division, which is composed of the 305th and 306th Bombardment Wings, this force is ready at any hour to launch a retaliatory blow "against any aggressor anywhere in the world." The base was established in 1931 and occupies more than ten thousand acres, almost surrounded by water. With eight thousand military personnel and a large number of civilian employees its monthly payroll in excess of $2,500,000 is an important factor in Tampa's economy.

What the Mardi Gras Festival is to New Orleans the "Gasparilla Pirate Festival" is to Tampa, a week-long celebration tied in with the Florida State Fair during the early days of February. The festival begins when the *José Gasparilla*, "a famed pirate ship," sails up the bay with colorful pennants flying from her three hundred-foot masts, and the 375 members of "Ye Mystic Krewe" take possession of the city amid the booming of cannon and the flashing of cutlasses. There follows a street parade of decorated floats and marching bands, during which miles of color film are used up and high carnival prevails. There is a children's parade and a torchlight parade through Ybor City, and on the final night amid a blaze of fireworks

(*Tampa News Bureau*)
The pirate ship, *José Gasparilla,* approaches the city of Tampa

the *José Gasparilla* sails away. It is an open secret that the steel-hulled vessel was built in the Tampa shipyard in 1933 for this very purpose and for eleven months of the year it lies at anchor off Bayshore Boulevard where it is much visited and photographed.

The whole thing started back in 1904 when a group of the city's well-to-do young bloods organized "Ye Mystic Krewe of Gasparilla" and put on the first coronation ball and street parade. The festival gained in popularity and in 1911 the feature of an "invasion" by water was added. At first some local vessel was used as the pirate craft but in 1953 funds were raised to build a replica of the beau ideal of pirate craft, complete with gunports, cannon that actually function, and a "Jolly Roger" at the masthead.

For its theme the festival takes the alleged career of one José Gaspar, who, according to the oft-repeated story told in the promotion literature, was a mutinous lieutenant in the Spanish Royal Navy who turned pirate in 1783. This "last of the buccaneers to sail the Spanish Main, the infamous Gaspar," is supposed to have captured gold and beautiful women from various ships and scourged the shipping of the Florida coast until 1821 when, attacking what he thought was a merchantman, it turned out to be a U.S. Navy war vessel, none other than the *Enterprise* commanded by Lieutenant Lawrence Kearny. Seeing the end was near Gaspar wrapped himself in an anchor chain and leaped into the sea, waving his cutlass in a final gesture of defiance.

All this makes very fine reading unless one picks up *The Mangrove Coast,* a most interesting book by Karl A. Bickel, former president of the United Press, and published in 1942. There can be no doubt about Lieutenant Kearny and the *Enterprise,* for it was he who warned Jean Laffite to cease operations on Galveston Island in 1821 and returned in March of that year to see that he was obeyed. Mr. Bickel, who did a lot of research along the Florida coast and in the old files of the U.S. Department of the Navy, finds that on the date of his alleged encounter with Gaspar, Lieutenant Kearny and the *Enterprise* were 250 miles away on the west coast of Cuba breaking up a gang of pirates whose place in history is much more stable. Furthermore, although the Navy records of pirate chasing in the Gulf and Caribbean are very complete there is to be found there not a word about José Gaspar. But if there was no Pirate Gaspar, or Gasparilla, what about Gasparilla Key and Little Gasparilla Key off Charlotte Harbor farther down the coast? For one thing, the name appeared on early maps long before José is alleged to have turned to evil ways. There is a record of Spanish missions in that area back in the late 1500's and references to a "Friar Gaspar." As for Johnny Gomez, the old beachcomber, and how it all started, that is for Mr. Bickel to tell.

Whether Juan Ponce de León was the first European to see Tampa

Bay and whether the date was early in June of 1513, is still something for historians to discuss, and perhaps it does not matter very much. The adventurous Spaniard had left Puerto Rico on March 3 with three small vessels, had sailed up the east coast of Florida almost to the mouth of the St. Johns River, and had given "Florida" its name. Then he turned back down the coast, stopped for a few days in Biscayne Bay where Miami now stands, and then continued south and west around the mainland, along the Keys, and finally rounded the Dry Tortugas. His journal has been lost and for the meager accounts of that voyage the historians must turn to later records of those who had an opportunity to study it. But from the Tortugas he sailed west and northwest and found a beautiful sheltered harbor where he careened his ship, the *San Cristoval*, to scrape the seaweed and barnacles from her bottom, fought off the hostile Indians, lost one sailor, and found a little gold. Then he sailed back to Puerto Rico.

The bay that Juan Ponce found was either Tampa Bay or Charlotte Harbor, seventy-five miles down the coast. The evidence points strongly to the former. If so this was the first of many early expeditions that were to disturb the quiet of these waters. Diego Miruelo showed up here in 1516, Francisco Córdoba touched here on his way back to Spain from Mexico in 1517. There were others recorded and very likely some unrecorded. Juan Ponce de León returned here in 1521 with the object of founding a colony, but an Indian's well-aimed arrow struck him in the side, the wound festered, and he returned to Havana to die. Pánfilo de Narváez sailed for Tampa Bay but missed it by a few miles and landed down the coast. But the most impressive cavalcade the watching Indians ever saw was that of Hernando de Soto who, with six hundred foot and horse landed just inside the bay in 1539 and in July of that year began his incredible march through four thousand miles of unmapped wilderness. On the campus of the University of Tampa is the "De Soto Oak," a venerable tree that might well be more than four hundred years old, under which the conquistador is said to have traded with the Indians.

Soon after the United States obtained Florida from Spain in 1821 the Army established Fort Brooke at the mouth of the Hillsborough River in what is now downtown Tampa. It was from here that Major Francis L. Dade with his force of 110 officers and men marched out on December 24, 1835, bound for Fort King, one hundred miles inland. Four days later the detachment was ambushed by the Indians and only three escaped. A stockade surrounded the fort and the settlers were allowed to build cabins inside it for protection. A post office was opened in 1831, and in 1848, after the Seminoles had been pretty well pushed back into the Everglades, the 160 acres of the military reservation were given to Hillsborough County, forming the basis for the present city. It was a frontier settlement with plenty of rough-and-ready characters, and was given its first charter by the legislature in 1855.

When the Civil War broke out the Confederates garrisoned old Fort Brooke and the Union gunboats patrolled the bay in an attempt to forestall blockade runners. Neither side had enough force to do much harm to the other. As the war progressed the region around the bay became an important source of supply for the Southern armies, some going by land and some by blockade-running craft, manned by captains who knew every bay, bayou, pass and cove along the coast. A cargo of food, drugs, cloth—almost anything—from Cuba commanded fantastic prices. With the coming of peace and the freeing of the Negroes the economy of the region collapsed, not to be revived for two decades.

The story of modern Tampa begins with the arrival of Henry Bradly Plant, wealthy and ambitious, whose dream was to outdo what Henry M. Flagler was accomplishing on Florida's Atlantic Coast. In 1884 he brought the railroad to the town, organized steamship lines and sparked the region's drooping industry. His most spectacular accomplishment was the erection in 1889 of "the most

magnificent hotel in the world," a giant, rambling structure patterned after the Alhambra in Granada, crowned with thirteen swelling minarets—one for each month in the Islamic calendar. It cost
more than three million dollars to erect, but the city bought it for
$140,000 in 1905. The University of Tampa was founded in 1931,
and in 1933 the city gave the University a ninety-nine-year lease
on the building.

The Spanish-American War period represents another piece in the
jigsaw history of Tampa. A circulation battle in New York City
between Joseph Pulitzer, publisher of the New York *World*, and
William Randolph Hearst and his New York *Journal*, was largely
responsible for this country's interest in Cuba's revolt against Spain.
Hearst, a newcomer to the East, elected to play up the conflict from
the standpoint of the rebels, and Pulitzer would not be outdone.
It was a poor day that did not furnish some new "atrocity." Once
headlines screamed that a woman U.S. citizen had been brutally
stripped and searched by the Spaniards. Frederick Remington was
retained to draw a picture of a nude female surrounded by rough-
looking men. When the lady got back to the States she denied she
had ever been stripped, searched or insulted, but her denial was
heard by few. Then, as now, editors throughout the country took
their news cues from New York, and soon the whole country was
in a stew over Cuba.

An understanding of this is necessary to appreciate the war fever
that swept over the country when news flashes announced that the
U.S. Battleship *Maine* had blown up in Havana Harbor the night
of February 15, 1898. Just what caused the explosion has never been
determined, or at least never made public, and it is doubtful that a
responsible person could be found today who would name Spain
as the culprit. Indeed it is doubtful that Spain had in Havana Harbor
the means for causing such an explosion, but as the weeks went by
the demand for war grew louder. On the walls of a thousand old-
fashioned water closets could be read the popular slogan:

Remember the Maine!
To Hell with Spain;
And don't forget to pull the chain!

Tampa's part in the tragicomic conflict began when it was decided to use that port as the embarkation point for the Cuba-bound Army. It was almost two months after the *Maine* disaster that war was declared but the War Department was totally unprepared to mobilize, transport, house, clothe or feed the Army of regulars, volunteers and National Guardsmen that began to converge on Tampa. A camp was constructed on 250 acres just outside the city and fifty thousand soldiers were soon milling about the place. Segregation raised its ugly head when a Negro regiment, commanded by white officers, hit the town and the difficulty was settled by hustling them off to the war. The big Plant Hotel was occupied by the "high brass" (a World War I term), and a scintillating contingent of "war correspondents" who had never seen a war. Outstanding among the stars on the hotel's broad verandas were Lieutenant Colonel Theodore Roosevelt who had arrived with his volunteer "Rough Riders," and the impeccable and unapproachable correspondent, Richard Harding Davis.

The big snarl-up was over the matter of transports to carry the soldiers across the Florida Straits to Cuba and the mystery of the location of the Spanish Fleet, which the Navy was long unable to find. Many writers have told of the situation and all have agreed that chaos settled over the city like a cloud. The soldiers sweated and suffered, the officers sweated and swore, but the restaurant keepers, the sandwich peddlers and the cab drivers reaped a harvest. The fact that the port of Tampa was ten miles from the camp and had only one pier from which transports could be loaded added considerably to the confusion. Roosevelt and his colonel, Leonard Wood, commandeered a coal train to get their troops to the docks and managed to get them on a crowded transport, which then waited out in the bay a week before it sailed with the convoy.

Finally on June 13 the fleet of thirty-six transports and escorting
vessels steamed past little Fort De Soto on Mullet Key at the mouth
of Tampa Bay, and headed for Santiago and the theater of war.
Tampa gave them a parting cheer and began to pick itself up out of
the dust.

The famous Tamiami (Tampa-Miami) Trail begins at Tampa,
skirts the eastern shore of Tampa Bay for thirty-five miles, follows
the coastline down to Naples, and there swings eastward through
Big Cypress Swamp and the Everglades to Miami, a total distance
of 270 miles. On the road map it is a part of U.S. Highway 41 from
Miami to Atlanta and the North. Completed in 1928 it is noted for
being the only highway across the 'Glades, although not more than
a hundred miles traverse that wilderness. For the most part it runs
through a well-settled region, much of it well suited to agriculture.

Fifty miles out of Tampa the road crosses the broad and beautiful Manatee River, a mile wide at this point, and enters Bradenton,
seat of Manatee County. Bradenton is a thriving city with a year-
'round population of eighteen thousand, entirely surrounded by
trailers. To this figure should be added the population of Palmetto,
which is at the other end of the bridge. With Sarasota, eleven miles
south in Sarasota County, it occupies the richest and most popular
portion of Florida's west coast. When house trailers first began to
roll south in early winter they were often given the "brush-off" by
communities which feared they would be a liability, but Bradenton
and Sarasota established trailer parks, and as they came in increasing numbers provided utilities, built roads to the beaches, and otherwise made them welcome. There was some rivalry but now there is
plenty of business for all. Bradenton claims to have the world's
largest trailer park and Sarasota the finest, but it is difficult to
choose. The Bradenton Trailer Park was started by the local
Kiwanis Club in 1936 with room for one hundred trailers. Now it
has eleven hundred well-equipped lots and nineteen shuffleboard

courts. All profits go to the support of underprivileged children in the community.

Most of the trailer folk today have a comfortable amount of money to spend and they leave a lot of it in this region. They come south in trailers because papa likes mama's cooking and the family can live as a unit, especially where there are small children. Hotels and motels, too, are all along this coast, where the transient visitor can stay a day or a season, but the trailers are most in evidence.

The state of Florida measures five hundred miles from north to south and falls naturally into three zones. The regions near its northern borders are south-temperate, as are Georgia and the Gulf states to the west. The central portion is semitropic, and it is this band across the peninsula that includes the great citrus groves. The southmost eighteen of the state's sixty-seven counties are in a sub-tropic zone and along the west coast this begins with Manatee County. From here south a killing frost is a rarity. Locally grown fruits and vegetables are for sale at roadside stands when Northern roads are being cleared by snowplows. Manatee County grows seven thousand acres of vegetables and three thousand acres of flowers, mostly gladiolas and chrysanthemums. The harvest season lasts from November through May. Oranges also are extensively grown but this is near the southern limit for the big groves. In door-yards and small groves are mangos, avocados, papayas, limes and lychee nuts, the latter an import from southern China that is becoming popular. Although the region has fifty-four inches of rainfall annually, most of it comes down in the summer months and the winters are dry. This is remedied by flowing wells which are extensively used for irrigation.

The botanist driving south along this route will notice new species of vegetation as he progresses. In the northern part of the state the fan-leafed "cabbage palm" (which is found throughout most of the South) is the only palm seen. In St. Petersburg and Tampa the most popular decorative palm is the graceful queen palm, or *cocos plumosa* (Liberty Hyde Bailey says it should be called *arecastrum romanzoffianum*), which is a hardy type of fronded palm. South of the Manatee long rows of the more tender royal palm appear, a tree native to the Everglades. More than one visitor from the North, seeing for the first time the tall gray columns of the royal palms in Fort Myers or Miami, has taken them for rows of concrete pillars crowned with some kind of tropical planting. Mango trees, which can be killed when small by a light freeze, are seen in many yards, and in the brackish swamps and along the beaches are the twisted branches and stubby, leathery leaves of the sea grape. The thorny vines or trimmed shrubbery of bougainvillaea covered with purple bracts or rarer varieties of lighter shades brighten the lawns, as do the yellow allamandas, that quick-growing stand-by of the suburbanite. These are but a few of the sun-loving, frost-hating trees and shrubs that greet the eye of the observing motorist.

Another stranger to the northern region is the tall, spire-shape Australian pine, sometimes called the "beefsteak tree" because of the color of its wood and known to botanists as a casuarina. Its long, feathery needles resemble those of the southern long-leaf pine, but the shape of the tree is quite different. Botanists insist it does not belong to the conifer family. This tree, introduced into Florida more than half a century ago, has spread all over the southern part of the state and unlike many prolific immigrants has proved of considerable benefit. Planted along roadsides by the highway department, especially where the roadbed has been formed by excavating a canal alongside, it soon becomes a decorative row of sentinels serving as a barrier between the highway and the ditch. Fruit growers use it as a windbreak for their groves. It makes an excellent hedge when kept trimmed, especially where a high screen is desired. It does not mind salt or brackish water and its seeds, which are borne in small cones, often wash up on the shore of coastal islands or beaches, take root, and in a few years a forest of green holds the land against the erosion of the sea. Unfortunately the wood is of little value.

Being so near the south entrance to Tampa Bay Bradenton shares

Shaw Point near the mouth of the Manatee River

in its historic associations. A well-paved highway leads from the town westward to Shaw Point where an act of Congress has established the De Soto National Monument embracing twenty-five acres.

"No other point of land within the boundaries of the United States, in the first sixty years following the Columbian discovery," says Karl Bickel, "has greater claims to historic interest than the narrow beach at Shaw Point and the shallow reaches that prevail in front of the high mounds that now mark all that is left of the old Indian town of Terra Ceia Beach, on McGill Bay." Only after four years' research did a commission, headed by Dr. John R. Swanton of the Smithsonian Institution, fix on Shaw Point as De Soto's landing place. Here on May 30, 1539, the veteran explorer unloaded the nine vessels of his fleet with their cargoes of horses, dogs, arms, armor, tools, and even seeds and grains suitable for establishing a colony. From the shores of Tampa Bay he began his long journey through Georgia, Alabama, Mississippi and Arkansas, finally to keep his rendezvous with death in 1542.

It was at or near this point that Pánfilo de Narváez landed in 1528 to begin his fatal trek up the coast, having tried to find the entrance to Tampa Bay which he missed. It was also here that Juan Ortiz, a young Spaniard sent by Señora de Narváez to search for her husband, was captured by the Indians, condemned to be burned to death, and was saved by the daughter of the chief of the Timucuans after the flames had begun to sear his skin. This was fifty years before the alleged rescue of Captain John Smith by Pocahontas in Virginia and some say it is the basis for that story. When De Soto came along in 1539, Ortiz, who had been living with the Indians for eight years, managed to rejoin the Spaniards and marched with them until he died beside the Mississippi in 1542.

The most tragic event on these shores was the martyrdom of Father Luís Cancer, a devout and trusting Dominican friar who believed that if he approached the Indians in all humility and peace they would receive him kindly. Accompanied only by three fellow priests he sailed from Vera Cruz to the Florida coast, but at their first landing the Indians, after a show of friendliness, seized two of the brothers and vanished with them into the forest. Father Cancer sailed slowly up the coast, trying to get some word of his companions. Near the mouth of the Manatee, Indians appeared begging presents. The ship was leaking, supplies were low, and the captain insisted on returning to Vera Cruz. But Father Cancer refused. He was rowed ashore in a small boat, and although the Indians at the edge of the woods showed every evidence of hostility he advanced slowly toward them, kneeling now and then to pray. Two Indians ran forward and seized the advancing priest, a third struck him down with a war club, and while his red blood ran into the yellow sand others belabored the cassock-clad body. A flight of arrows drove the little boat back to the ship and it returned to Mexico with only one priest aboard.

A graphic account of this incident is given in Marjory Stoneman Douglas' excellent volume, *The Everglades: River of Grass.* Says Mrs. Douglas: "He [Father Cancer] died, truly a martyr, but not more by the savagery of the Indians than by their inability to understand how a Spaniard could be anything but dangerous to them. Father Cancer fell also at the hands of all those other Spaniards who had shed the blood of so many thousands of Indians, in wanton defiance of his own belief that all men are brothers."

The death of Father Cancer marks the end of the early era of Tampa Bay and the adjoining coasts. The Indians had been almost unceasingly hostile. It has been estimated that the Spaniards killed or enslaved not less than a million Indians in the Caribbean during the first few years of their occupancy, and these facts were not unknown to the Timucuans around Tampa Bay. Though the Indians did not win a victory over the white race they at least won a truce on the west coast of Florida, and for two centuries were left in comparative peace.

The land on each side of the lower valley of the Manatee is very fertile and here in the 1840's there developed a sugar-growing aristocracy that rose, flourished and fell within a period of twenty-five years. Following the purchase of Florida by the United States in 1821, a number of wealthy adventurers came to the new territory and settled in and around Tallahassee. The region boomed, and as so often happens, speculation got out of hand and the boom "busted." Some.went back north and some stayed, not having lost faith in the new country. Among the latter were Major Robert Gamble and Dr. Joe Braden. Major Gamble took up land on the north side of the Manatee River, planted it to sugar cane, and built the "Gamble Mansion" where the village of Ellenton now stands. On the opposite side of the river Dr. Braden constructed "Braden Castle," surrounded on three sides by cane fields. Other planters followed them and within a few years hundreds of slaves were working amid thousands of acres of sugar cane fields and manufacturing sugar in the largest sugar mills in the South. Steamboats landed at the docks and took the sweet cargo to New Orleans, and the planters prospered exceedingly.

But up along the Mason-Dixon line the North and South were preparing for battle, Fort Sumter was fired on, and the Civil War began. The Union hastened to blockade the Southern ports, and in 1861 a Navy vessel steamed up the Manatee and destroyed the Gamble sugar mills, but did not harm the houses. Most of the other mills escaped, but at the end of the war the slaves were freed, the planters were impoverished, and sugar cane grows no more along the Manatee.

The Gamble mansion still stands, its white columns looking toward the river, and it is now a museum of the Confederacy operated by the U.D.C. Shortly after the end of the war it played a peculiar role in history. Judah P. Benjamin, secretary of state in Jefferson Davis' cabinet, had fled Richmond in company with his fellow cabinet officers and using various disguises had reached Tampa. Federal officers were on his trail and he was spirited away one night to the Gamble home where he was concealed for two weeks. Once the place was searched by soldiers but Benjamin eluded them by hiding in a swamp. Eventually, disguised as a cook on a fishing boat, he reached Nassau and finally arrived safely in London.

The years have not been so kind to Braden Castle and today it stands a picturesque ruin amid a clutter of cottages on the outskirts of Bradenton. Like most buildings of the period its thick walls were made of shells, burnt shell lime and marl, a combination called "tabby," which gives the ruins the appearance of a medieval castle. The walls proved a strong defense when the place was attacked by Indians early in 1856, the last uprising of the Seminoles. Fire destroyed the interior in 1900 and in 1924 the Camping Tourists of America bought the grounds and built their cottages around it. The Braden Castle Post Office is near by.

At the south end of Bradenton a road turns off the Trail to Anna Maria Island, six miles east and a mile offshore. A rickety bridge over Sarasota Bay connects the island and mainland but work has been started on a new bridge that is badly needed. The island is seven miles long and is pretty well covered with modest cottages and motels. It is a popular fishing spot and from the little park at the upper end one gets an inspiring view of lower Tampa Bay and the graceful outline of the Sunshine Skyway connecting St. Petersburg with the Tamiami Trail. Along the shore south of Anna Maria is another and longer island, Longboat Key, the southern end of which is opposite Sarasota. It is reached by a bridge at Sarasota and is traversed by a highway.

It is only eleven miles from downtown Bradentown to downtown Sarasota and the route is more like a city street than a highway. Motels, trailer parks, trailer sales displays and new real estate devel-

The ruins of "Braden Castle"

opments line both sides of the road. The maximum speed is forty-five mph and the minimum thirty-five. But there is nothing "junky" about the highway. The lawns are neat, the houses painted, and even the business premises are well kept. This entire coast is bidding for new visitors and new residents and seems to be getting them.

Just inside the north limits of Sarasota and three miles from the heart of the city is the John and Mabel Ringling Museum of Art, one of the most valuable and best-displayed collections of medieval paintings, tapestries and sculptures to be found in America. Ringling, who died December 2, 1936, bequeathed his entire Sarasota estate to the state of Florida, including his magnificent home adjoining the museum. It embraces thirty-seven acres and reaches from the Trail highway to Sarasota Bay. Only the Art Museum can be seen from the road at the end of a royal palm bordered plaza, but it commands the attention of the most casual motorist. The entire property is under the authority of the Florida State Board of Control, which also has jurisdiction over the state's institutions of higher learning.

It is difficult to say which deserves the higher praise, the great collection of paintings and other works of art, valued at forty million dollars and which could not be duplicated at any price, or the arresting example of Florentine architecture in which they are displayed. The façade of the building which faces the highway is 250 feet long, and the three arches of the entrance are reached by marble steps. The two wings that extend to the rear from either end of the façade enclose a formal garden court 350 feet long and 150 feet wide. Columns, fountains, statues and mosaics were brought over from Italy by the shipload and incorporated in the building by the architect, John H. Phillips. In the southeast corner a small but elaborately designed theater, constructed in Asolo, Italy, in 1798, has been installed in what was originally an auditorium. Italy was not robbed to furnish this treasure, for it had been dismantled in 1930 to make room for a movie theater and was acquired by the state of Florida in 1950. It was formally opened February

26, 1952, and plays and musical programs are frequently given there. The museum building cost Mr. and Mrs. Ringling no less than a million and a half dollars in addition to many of its decorative features purchased during their trips to Europe. Construction was started in June, 1927, and was finished early in 1930. From the inception of the idea to build a museum to house the Ringling art treasures Mrs. Mabel Ringling had enthusiastically worked with her husband and the architect to make it outstanding, and it was a tragedy when she died June 8, 1929, and never saw it finished.

Mr. and Mrs. Ringling were both admirers of Italian art and architecture and had acquired a small but carefully chosen collection before they considered equipping a museum. The idea began to take shape in 1925 and by 1930 their collection included five hundred "old masters" in addition to tapestries, ceramics, medallions, etc. The late Lord Duveen offered Ringling $300,000 for a painting by Frans Hals shortly after it had been acquired for the museum but the offer was refused. With the Ringling treasurehouse as a focal point, art colonies and local museums have sprung up all along the west Florida coast.

Back of the Art Museum and facing the bay is the John Ringling home, a tower-topped structure of colored brick and tile, suggestive of a doge's palace in old Venice. Its architect was Dwight James Baum but the ideas were mostly those of Mrs. Ringling. Including the sea wall and swimming pool the cost exceeded $1,250,000, and another $400,000 was spent for the furnishings, which are still there. The home was completed in 1926 and was christened "Ca' d'Zan," the Venetian dialect for "John's House."

Between the museum and the residence in what was once a warehouse is another museum, not built or endowed by John Ringling but installed in his memory in 1948 by the state of Florida. It is the "Museum of the American Circus" and for many it has more appeal than either the Art Museum or the Ringling palace. Recently it has been so increased by gifts and purchases that a special building is being constructed to display the collection adequately. Here is to be seen everything connected with the circus from its earliest days to the present—ornate wagons; chariots and cages that cost as much as a modern motorcar; flamboyant lithographs that blossomed on barns and fences in the 1880's and '90's to the awe of hayseed and city slicker alike; costumes of Dan Rice, America's greatest clown; Buffalo Bill's gauntlets; Alfredo Codona's trapeze; and the suspension hook from which Lillian Leitzel fell to her death. A woodcut of Phineas T. Barnum gazes smudgily from the top of a poster announcing "100,000 Curiosities!" And of course there is the "steam piano" (calliope) that always brought up the rear of the parade. So extensive has the collection become that it now illustrates the entire history of the circus from the days of the Circus Maximus built by Tarquin I in Rome 2,500 years ago, and its development in England and France in the eighteenth century.

The admission fee to the Art Museum and the Ringling home is one dollar each and the fee for the Circus Museum is fifty cents, but all three can be seen for two dollars. Even with this income the state is obliged to contribute to the support of the buildings and grounds. The enterprise has no connection at all with the present circus.

Born in McGregor, Iowa, May 30, 1866, John Ringling was one of five sons whose parents came from Germany and settled in Baraboo, Wisconsin. A sister, Ida, was the youngest child and became Mrs. John North. John Ringling was a boy when the family moved back to Baraboo and he and his three older brothers soon showed a natural aptitude for showmanship. When he was sixteen they organized the "Ringling Brothers' Classic and Comic Concert Company" and later called their show the "Grand Carnival of Fun." In two years they had enough money to buy an interest in a circus company and soon began to prosper. They bought the rival Barnum & Bailey Circus in 1907 and combined it with their own in 1919. By that time Ringling was quite wealthy with extensive oil and mine investments in addition to the circus business. He had first visited Florida in 1911 and had bought considerable acreage around Sarasota, then only a small town. He did not build at once, and his palatial home there was not completed until 1926. In 1927 he moved the winter quarters of the circus from Baraboo to Sarasota.

The Ringling fortune continued to increase until 1929 when he overreached himself. He had helped to build Madison Square Garden in New York (the "old" Garden where Harry K. Thaw would one night shoot Stanford White) and was shocked when its management announced they were leasing it to the Sells-Floto Circus in March and April the following year, instead of to Ringling who had formerly showed there. With characteristic impulse he immediately bought the American Circus Company, which owned Sells-Floto, for $1,900,000. Although heavily involved he might have weathered the storm but for the financial crisis that followed the stock market crash in October, 1929. From that time until his death in 1936 he was beset by difficulty and at the end the Great Show was his in little more than name.

On the other side of Sarasota from the Ringling home and Art Museum are the winter quarters of the circus that John Ringling developed. Here the big installation that covers 168 acres is almost deserted from the last week in March, when the colorful circus trains depart for the north and west, until the first of December when they return. Then the menagerie animals are loosed in their big steel barred cages, the horses are allowed to graze and romp in the winter pasture, the elephants are stabled in the big barns, and the acrobats resume housekeeping in their winter homes. Yet it is still a circus. The public, including winter vacationists from all Florida, flock to the place to see the animals fed in the big menagerie house; to see the trainers teaching old lions and tigers new tricks, or teaching new ones old tricks, in the big training cages; to see the equestrians training their horses and working out new acts; to see the elephants, the zebras, the giraffes and the unpredictable monkeys. Every winter 150,000 of them pay ninety cents (children fifty cents) for this privilege and they get their money's worth. On Sunday afternoons there is a special show when the acrobats go through their gyrations on bars and swings, and the new acts are perfected before hitting the road. There are picnic grounds on the lot and a stand where sandwiches and circus lemonade can be bought.

Where does the new generation of acrobats come from? A lot of them come from Sarasota. Encouraged and supported by the circus management, pupils in grade and high school may take up acrobatics as a part of their athletic program and many become very proficient. Every February they put on a big "Sailor Circus" before an applauding crowd. Next time the show goes on the road some of them may go with it. While all this activity is going on, the work crews are repainting the cars and traveling cages, repairing the tents and replacing ropes that are beginning to fray. Every piece of equipment is inspected to make sure there is no failure during the show season. By early spring everything is in readiness, the cars are loaded, the trunks packed and the trains move out. Only a few brood mares and menagerie animals "in a delicate condition" are left behind. Then the home staff goes to work refurbishing the stables, painting the buildings, repairing the roads and getting ready for the Big Show's return.

This routine gradually evolved during the thirty years that the circus winter headquarters have been in Florida, but a crisis developed in 1956 when the Big Show cut its season short and returned to Sarasota in midsummer. Rising costs and labor difficulties were given as the reason for this action. The management said it would continue to show in cities where large amphitheaters, such as Madison Square Garden in New York, could contain it, but admitted the future of exhibitions under "the Big Top" of canvas was undecided. If indeed the flag-topped circus tent with the sideshows nestling in its shadow, with its tanbark, ticket wagons, hoarse-voiced barkers and its array of sights and smells passes from the American scene it will be a major sacrifice on the altar of "progress."

Sarasota would be one of the bright spots on Florida's west coast even without the advantages of the Ringling Museum and the circus quarters. A causeway across Sarasota Bay connects the mainland with Longboat Key and within the area are forty miles of white sand beaches. The Lido Beach Casino, constructed under municipal direction, has thirteen hundred feet of bathing beach along the Gulf and is a rallying point for thousands of winter tourists who account for about 30 per cent of the city's income. So many of these decide to make Sarasota their permanent home that its resident population has increased 50 per cent in the last fifteen years. The average annual temperature is 71 degrees and the January average is 61.5 degrees.

Seventeen miles southeast of Sarasota is Myakka River State Park on State Highway 72. Its 26,746 acres make it the largest of Florida's state parks and one of the largest in the country, but only a small part of it can be reached except by boat. The only overnight accommodations are five comfortable but rustic log cabins which can be reserved by writing the park superintendent at Sarasota. For others there are camping grounds, picnic tables and fireplaces under the live oak trees beside Upper Myakka Lake. There is plenty of good fishing in the lake but hunting or trapping is not allowed, and the palm and oak woods are full of wildlife. Here the stroller may see wild turkeys, of which there are hundreds in the park, besides deer, raccoons, squirrels and many species of waterfowl. It is an unspoiled bit of the Florida of bygone days.

The Tamiami Trail follows the coastline south from Sarasota for twenty-four miles and then bends to the east to get around Charlotte Harbor at the mouth of Peace River. A state road continues on down the coast to reach half a dozen villages on Lemon Bay which divides the mainland from the long, narrow Manasota Peninsula. After the Trail leaves the coast the towns become more scarce. Punta Gorda at the south end of the bridge across Charlotte Harbor is the only settlement of any size for twenty-five miles in either direction. This is cattle country, and has been for a hundred years. Today they are "smart" cattle—Black Angus, Santa Gertrudis, Herefords, Shorthorns, Brahmans and a variety of crosses that have re-

placed the "scrubs" that used to roam the unfenced palmetto
prairies. A century ago Charlotte Harbor was the loading point for
cattle shipments to Cuba, and in the blockade-running days of the
Civil War they were lucrative cargo. Following the war and the
freeing of the slaves the Cuban cattle trade was the principal factor
in restoring the region's shattered economy. Now the beef is of
better grade and is shipped by rail to domestic markets.

Charlotte Harbor is a sizable stretch of water, as long as Tampa
Bay but not so wide. Pine, Gasparilla, Captiva and Sanibel islands
shelter it from the Gulf, a fact of which the early Spanish explorers
were well aware. Local folklore holds that Captiva Island is so
called because Pirate José Gaspar kept his captives, mostly beautiful
women, there. This explanation will have to do until a better one
is found. Legends of pirates and buried treasure abound along this
part of the coast and there is reason to believe that a few doubloons
have been recovered. But Punta Gorda advertises itself as "Home
of the Silver Tarpon," which has more allure for visitors than tales
of Spanish gold.

There is not much exaggeration in the statement that most of the
tourists and half of the residents in this region are collectors of sea-
shells, and Sanibel Island at the mouth of the Caloosahatchee River
just below Charlotte Harbor is their Happy Hunting Ground. A
story in the *Saturday Evening Post* several years ago said there was
only one other beach in the world that had a greater variety of
shells, and it was in the Indian Ocean. It costs $1.50 for car and
driver to cross to the island by ferry from Punta Rassa, fifteen miles
from Fort Myers, and as much to get back, but shell fans pay that
willingly to walk the beaches or wade the shallow waters in search
of a specimen that will enhance their own collection and excite the
envy of their fellow enthusiasts. It is not necessary to go to Sanibel
or more accessible beaches, however, to get a collection of seashore
novelties. From Tampa down to Naples, where the Trail starts across
the Everglades, there are roadside "shell factories," some of them
quite pretentious, that advertise shells not only from Florida beaches

but from all over the world—big shells, little shells, cheap shells, dear shells, smooth shells and jagged shells. This stock is augmented by shell necklaces, bracelets, ash trays, lamps, imitation flowers, imitation birds and other dust-catching knickknacks. It is Big Business.

The Caloosahatchee rises very near Lake Okeechobee and flows almost due west. South of it lies Big Cypress Swamp which merges into the Everglades and has much in common with that mysterious region. Here the irreconcilable Seminoles made their last stand in what was until a few years ago an uncharted wilderness. It was near Fort Myers that an act of military stupidity a century ago led to the last bitter revolt of a long-suffering people. The story of the Seminole Wars is a long and unhappy one and much of it revolves around the tribesmen who refused to leave the land where they had lived so long and be transplanted to the West. Those who remained and survived had, by 1855, established themselves on "hammocks" deep in the sawgrass fastness and were living in peace with the whites who occupied the fertile lands along the coasts. At the end of the Second Seminole War, Chief Hotale Micco, whom the whites called "Billy Bowlegs," had a final meeting with Brigadier General W. J. Worth at which he agreed to be responsible for the good conduct of the Indians. He had kept that promise for thirteen years, sometimes under great provocation.

It was shortly before Christmas, 1855, that Lieutenant George Hartsuff of the U.S. Engineers, was ordered at the behest of the Land Office to assist in a survey of Big Cypress. He was proceeding through the jungle with a force of eight soldiers and two teamsters when they came on a hidden garden, rich with ripening bananas, pumpkins, squash and other vegetables, the winter food supply for Billy Bowlegs and his tribe. In a spirit of wanton destruction they broke down the banana stalks, shot and kicked the pumpkins to bits, and completely wrecked the place. When Billy went to their camp to protest he was further humiliated by taunts and buffetings. This was the end. It was evident the Indian had no rights the white man

was bound to respect. Returning to his village Billy sent runners
through the hidden waterways to summon the other braves.

Shortly before daylight while the military heroes were at breakfast there was a war cry followed by the roar of muskets. Lieutenant
Hartsuff was hit and hit again, and lay for five days in the swamp
before he was rescued. Four others got back to Fort Myers. Soon the
Indians were carrying the war all along the coast. Dr. Braden's
home on the Manatee was attacked but the occupants managed to
beat off their foes. The Whitaker home on Sarasota Bay was raided
and burned. Troops were ordered out and the Indians eventually
were driven back into the swamps where many were captured,
among them Billy Bowlegs. In a little less than three years after his
garden had been raided, Billy and more than a hundred of his
tribesmen were loaded on a transport and shipped out to Oklahoma.
From the still smaller group that remained hidden in the Everglades
have come all the Seminoles in Florida today.

Fort Myers, on the south bank of the Caloosahatchee fifteen miles
above its mouth, was one of the first winter vacation resorts to be
established on Florida's west coast and is still one of the most attractive and popular. Its miles-long avenues bordered by royal palms
are among the most frequently reproduced photographs of the state.
It is the seat of Lee County which has three thousand acres devoted
to raising gladioli. The blossoming spikes are cut during the winter
months and shipped to Northern cities by rail and air, a consignment
of an express car entirely filled with gladioli being not unusual.
Coconut palms, heavy with large clusters of nuts, are common in
Fort Myers. The late Professor Talcott Williams said that wherever
the coconut palm bore viable fruit might be considered within the
tropics.

As an outpost for defense against the Indians Fort Myers was
built in 1840 on the site of a fortified trading post and was named for
the state's chief quartermaster. It remained little more than a village
at the southern terminus of civilization until Thomas Alva Edison
discovered its attractions in 1885 and bought fourteen acres on the

river shore just below town for three thousand dollars. The following year he had a prefabricated two-story frame house shipped here
from Maine, probably the world's first prefab, and built a half-mile
pier out into the river where it could be unloaded. Here he brought
his bride, Mina Miller Edison, after their marriage in 1886 and this
remained their winter home until Edison's death, October 18, 1931,
at the age of eighty-four. Shortly before Mrs. Edison died in 1947
she gave the property to the city of Fort Myers as a memorial to her
husband. It is managed by a board of directors named by the local
Junior Chamber of Commerce, and house and grounds are maintained as they were during Edison's lifetime. It is a focal point for
visitors from everywhere who are shown through the buildings and
grounds by competent guides.

More than three hundred trees, representing every region of the
tropics, make the Edison estate an exciting place for botanists.
Some are from seeds or cuttings sent the inventor by his friends and
some he sought out himself. In the decades that have passed since
their planting many have grown to huge size in the rich soil of the
river bank, and some are colorful with their burden of orchids and
bromeliads. Adjoining the grounds is the onetime home of Henry
Ford, and through these paths wandered the three "cronies," Edison,
Ford and Harvey Firestone, the most famous trio of their generation.

As his fame and fortune increased Edison built an addition to his
home and constructed near by a well-equipped laboratory where he
and a staff of helpers and selected students worked to develop the
electric light, the phonograph, new sources for rubber and a multi-
tude of other innovations. All this equipment is intact as Edison left
it, including the little cot where he took short naps when engaged
in some demanding experiment. Around the grounds are various
species of bamboo from which he developed a fiber that when properly treated served as a filament for the earliest electric light bulbs.
Fort Myers' citizens admit rather ruefully that when Edison offered
to supply the town with an electric lighting system free of charge

in 1887 if it would provide the poles the city fathers turned the offer down because the poles would cost too much, and besides electricity was dangerous. Thus Fort Myers missed the opportunity to become the first electrically lighted community in the world.

Edison, Ford and Firestone were not real estate promoters but their presence and their praise did more to stimulate interest in the town than all the brightly colored pamphlets ever printed. It has never had a "boom" to be followed by weed-grown sidewalks in subdivisions that were never built, but has expanded quietly and remembers its Greatest Citizen with gratitude.

Dark with the waters of the Big Cypress Swamp the little Estero River flows between banks that are always green and empties into Estero Bay, sheltered behind Estero Island, sixteen miles below Fort Myers. Here where the Trail crosses the river is the village of Estero, which has a peculiar history. It is the home of "Koreshanity," a belief founded on the theory that the world is a hollow shell instead of a round globe, that the sun is in the center, and that the antipodes are straight up instead of straight down. This is "The Cellular Cosmogony."

Dr. Cyrus R. Teed was born in New York State in 1839, served as a surgeon in the Union Army during the Civil War, and resumed his private practice after Appomattox. But he was interested in more than medicine and in time developed some original ideas as to religion, economics and astronomy. Like all prophets, true or false, he attracted a following and during the 1890's the pamphlets of the new faith were widely circulated through the Mississippi Valley. While he was considering establishing a colony at some favored spot an acquaintance described the Charlotte Harbor area, and on a visit to Florida in 1893 the doctor obtained a large tract of land near the mouth of the Estero on the promise that he would found a colony there. This was not too difficult, as there was little market for land in that remote region. Early in 1894 the first group of dedicated followers began clearing the jungle and erecting buildings. There were no individual homes, the men being quartered in one building and the women in another. The sexes ate at different tables but the men helped wash the community dishes.

Holding that the ancient term for "Cyrus" was "Koresh," Dr. Cyrus Teed called his new faith "Koreshanity." Disciples who joined the colony were required to serve six months' probation and give all their worldly possessions to the cause. This with the separation of the sexes was a severe test, but everybody worked hard and the community prospered. The doctor was something of a botanist and collected trees and shrubs from distant tropics to grow along the Estero. There was consternation when he died in 1908 at the age of sixty-nine. Old residents of Fort Myers say that his disciples refused to accept the fact and that it was necessary for the sheriff to go down there and take charge. He was finally put in a tomb at the south end of Estero Island where a guard stood watch day and night until a hurricane tide washed that part of the island into the Gulf.

Dr. Teed was succeeded as leader by A. H. Andrews, who won considerable renown for his knowledge of tropical botany and received the Barbour Medal from the Fairchild Tropical Garden for his contributions in that field. Since the death of Andrews in 1951 the community has taken on a new look and the rigid rules as applied to married couples have been relaxed. A modern inn, cottages, a trailer court, a tropical nursery and an art colony are capturing a good share of the tourist trade.

The many springs along the coast from Wakulla to the Everglades pour forth a clear sweet water, but at Bonita Springs, twenty miles south of Fort Myers, is a mineral spring with a marked sulphur content. Indians are reported to have drunk its waters before the coming of the Spaniards but the place has never become a Saratoga, and at present a large hotel owns the spring which gives the little town its name.

Naples, thirty-six miles due south of Fort Myers, is the last town on the Tamiami Trail before it swings across Big Cypress Swamp and the Everglades to Miami, nearly a hundred miles away. Although it was first settled in 1885 and the first hotel was built there in 1889 it is one of the latest communities to share in the development of the west Florida coastline. It was supposed to have been named by the late "Marse Henry" Watterson, publisher of the Louisville *Courier-Journal*, who as an early visitor found its long beach resembled that of the famous Italian city. The place was accessible only by boat until 1919. When the Tamiami Trail was opened in 1929 it put the town on the map but it was not until 1950 that an expansion began that is still going on. A thousand-foot free fishing pier extending into the Gulf is its most popular attraction.

The Big Cypress Swamp comes right up to the coastal ridge on which Naples is located. Before the white man came to this region the cypress giants reached a hundred feet and more above the sawgrass where their roots had been drawing nourishment from the wet earth for more than a thousand years. But the "big" in the name of the region does not refer to the trees. It was the bigness of the swamp—not less than two million acres—that impressed the early settlers. The traveler along the Trail today will see thousands of cypress on both sides of the highway but he will look in vain for the big ones, the "river cypress" as the lumbermen call it. All of the marketable timber accessible from the highway was cut long ago. As the cypress became scarcer the prices went up, and the interior was opened when the Atlantic Coast Line extended its tracks to the one-time Indian village of Immokalee (accent on the "MOK") near the center of the region, following World War I.

Cutting out the big cypress meant more than the loss of the timber. It meant that the whole nature of the swamp, its wildlife, its plant life including many native orchids, its entire ecology would be changed and in part destroyed. Naturalists and lovers of wildlife everywhere rallied to the rescue. The company holding the lumber rights to the last stand of the big trees agreed to sell a portion at a greatly reduced price. As a result $170,000 was paid for 5,680 acres lying partly in Lee County and part in Collier County, comprising what is known as "Corkscrew Swamp" because of the wandering watercourse that runs through it. This is now a wildlife refuge and an Audubon warden is stationed there. An elevated boardwalk through the most interesting portion enables visitors, under the direction of Audubon guides, to see a bit of unravaged tropical forest.

The cypress that today stretches out on either side of the Trail is the small "pond cypress" that never gets large enough to furnish marketable timber. Clumps of it amid the sawgrass prairies indicate low spots where there is moisture in times of drought. It is below Naples that the gray "Spanish moss" which has been a characteristic of the Gulf Coast all the way from the Texas bayous begins to disappear, for it is not a tropical plant. It is not a true moss but an epiphyte, which means that it draws its nourishment and moisture from the air and not from the tree on which it grows. Botanists group it with the pineapple family. In the South Central states where it flourishes it provides a small but steady income for many rural families. Pulled from the trees with long poles it is piled in heaps and kept moist. In a few months the gray outer coating rots off leaving a fine black center very much like a hair from a horse tail. This when further treated makes an acceptable stuffing for upholstery, particularly automobile seats. Sponge rubber has replaced it in part but costs three or four times as much.

Conspicuous amid the thin foliage of the cypress trees and growing on other trees as well is another epiphyte that is not found very far north of the Everglades. Commonly called an "air plant" it looks much like bunches of mistletoe in some more northern forest, but it has no berries. It bears a small red blossom that never opens and has small decorative value but newcomers to the region gather plants or buy them for a few cents in the "five and dime" under the impression that they are orchids. They are not orchids but bromeliads of the genus *Tillandsia* and soon die after being taken from the tree.

That "Beauty is in the eye of the beholder" is particularly true of the hundred miles of the Tamiami Trail lying between Naples and Miami. To many it is only a highway through a marsh to be covered as quickly as possible, an unfortunate fact that the accident statistics for that stretch of road will support. To others it is a tour through a wonderland of bird and plant life that never loses its charm no matter how often it is traveled. Most conspicuous because of their snowy white color are the American and snowy egrets, members of the heron family. The American is the larger of the two with a long yellow bill, black legs and feet, and a length of from thirty-six to forty-two inches. The snowy is smaller with a length not exceeding twenty-eight inches, black bill and legs and bright yellow feet—"golden slippers." Sometimes a white heron the size of the snowy will be seen, showing no yellow, but with dull greenish legs and a bluish bill. That will be an immature little blue heron. Toward the eastern end of the Trail may sometimes be seen a still larger white bird, the great white heron with a length of fifty-four inches, largest of the heron family. Its greenish-yellow legs as well as its size distinguish it from the American egret, and it is seldom seen north of the Trail. Due to indiscriminate shooting and the destructive hurricane of 1935 this species was reduced to less than 150 birds, but with careful protection their number has increased to at least a thousand in the south Florida area. Wild creatures soon learn where they have sanctuary and herons and egrets will stand placidly in the canal alongside the highway while automobiles whizz past within fifty feet of them.

Fifty miles below Naples in the tall trees opposite Collier-Seminole State Park the late afternoon often finds the big wood ibis, America's only member of the stork family with a wingspread of almost four feet, seeking a roosting place in the treetops. Beautiful in flight despite its naked, wattled head, this great white bird with black wing primaries is easy to distinguish from members of the heron family, for it flies with its neck outstretched while herons carry theirs doubled back like a flat letter "S." High in the sunny sky flies the swallow-tailed kite, recognizable as far as it can be seen by its forked tail and looking like an overgrown barn swallow measuring two feet from wing tip to wing tip. Slate-gray coots with white bills, Louisiana herons, white ibis—the list is a long one, and sometimes a sharp eye will spot an alligator in the canal beside the road. No two trips ever yield identical sights.

Marjory Stoneman Douglas in her exciting book *The Everglades: River of Grass,* says: "The shores that surround the Everglades were the first on this continent known to white men. The interior was almost the last. They have not yet been entirely mapped." There is mystery even in the name which probably had its origin in the old Anglo-Saxon "glade," meaning an open space in a forest. The term was first used on a map in 1823. To say "Florida Everglades" is redundant. There are no others. Although the region is largely covered with water during the rainy season and the reeds and grasses grow tall and lush it is not a true swamp. It is a layer of peat, the accumulated debris of the centuries, on top of a soft, porous oölite rock that rests on a foundation of limestone. Only the Seminole Indians, driven into its fastnesses because the white men wanted their more productive lands, have understood the Everglades. Assuming that the black soil was synonymous with fertility the inexperienced "developers" started digging canals to drain it and make it "the garden spot of the world." Then the water table dropped, the peat dried out, the fires started and smoke hung like a curtain of doom over the southern part of the state. In some places the surface of the land sank as much as five feet. Worst of all, the fresh water that had flowed through subterranean channels into the sea and held back the salt water now began to recede. The salt water came in, ruining wells, threatening even the water supply of Miami and other municipalities, and low lands that had been productive had to be abandoned because of seepage. The Miami *Herald* in a series of articles in 1948 said that $250 million had been spent in an attempt to drain the Everglades and $250 million worth of damage had been done. So water gates were installed in the canals and rivers and the damage was in part repaired. Now, working with the U.S. Army Engineers, the state of Florida and the counties affected have developed a long-range plan whereby areas suitable for cultivation will be drained, and in lower areas miles of dikes will impound the rainfall so the water table will be maintained.

It was the Tamiami Trail that first opened some of the mystery of the Everglades to others than a few adventurous souls. Dade County, on the east, voted $125,000 for the project in 1916 and started to build from that end. Lee County, of which Fort Myers is the seat, voted $355,000 and started two dredges working from the west. It was to be a simple matter—dig a canal and pile the dirt on one side and there was your roadbed. But again the Everglades fooled them. In wet weather the material sank into the muck and in dry weather the muck burned out. The only solution was to clear the ground with dynamite down to the limestone and build from there up. It was slow work and expensive but the route was finally opened in 1928 after an expenditure of six million dollars. Since that time there has never been an hour, day or night, when it was not in use.

At first the Trail wound through lonely stretches of dwarf cypress, sawgrass and mangrove but year by year this isolation is becoming rarer. Seminoles build their palm-thatched "chi-kees" beside the highway, enclose them with a high screen of the same material, put out a sign "Indian Village," and take in many a tourist dollar for admissions and the sale of dolls and trinkets. Certainly a dollar will buy more along the Trail than it will in a Miami Beach night club. Where there are waterways the young braves will take you for a ride in an "air boat," a clever contraption made by mounting a small airplane engine and propeller on the stern of a flat-bottomed craft. Even where there is only an inch or two of water it will skim over the 'Glades at an exciting speed. But for the most part civilization extends for only a hundred feet or so on either side of the road. Beyond that are the grassy flats, the clumps of cabbage palm and cypress, the raccoons, herons, hawks and wheeling vultures, just as they have been for a thousand years.

Seventeen miles below Naples is Collier-Seminole State Park, named for the late Barron G. Collier, wealthy streetcar advertising magnate who came to Florida right after World War I and bought thousands of acres in the southwest section of the Florida peninsula where the Big Cypress Swamp and the Everglades meet the Gulf. This was all a part of Lee County but in 1923 Collier induced the legislature to create Collier County with an area of 1,300,480 acres, one of the largest in the state. Collier, a man with big ideas and big money to match them, was sure mankind could improve on Nature and make this country a tropical paradise. He contributed largely to the construction of the Tamiami Trail, built roads and advertised extensively. All went well until the south Florida "boom" collapsed by its own weight in 1926 and the stock market did the same thing three years later. The Collier interests were severely crippled but managed to retain their holdings until normal values could be restored, and the name "Collier" still carries weight in this region.

The Collier-Seminole park is on comparatively high ground, long a refuge for the harassed Indians. Here a bronze bust of Collier looks out across an oval pool from a knoll surmounted by six fluted columns supporting a Grecian entablature. All about are the stately native royal palms that saw the Indian go and the white man come. On either side are two bronze tablets, each surmounted by an eagle, one dedicated to the Indian leaders and the other to the white commanding officers who opposed them in the Seminole Wars. The one on the east reads: "To the memory of Arpeika (Sam Jones), Chekika, Holate Micco (Billy Bowlegs), Otulke Thlocklo (The Prophet), and Tustenugge (Tiger Tail), the great Seminole Chieftains who, convinced of the perfidy of the white race, directed from the deep recesses of the Big Cypress with masterly strategy, the valiant struggle of a few against overwhelming numbers, that their people might remain free and undisputed masters of the land they loved."

The other tablet names Brigadier General W. J. Worth, Major W. G. Belknap and Captain George Wright of the Second Seminole War; and Colonel St. George Rogers, Captain W. H. Cone and Captain L. A. Hardee of the Third Seminole War.

Barron Collier Memorial at Collier-Seminole Park

Near the entrance to the park a road from the Trail leads west to Marco Island and the little town of Marco, twelve miles distant. Marco is near the upper end of the Ten Thousand Islands that start just below Naples and scatter down the coast for fifty miles. No one knows whether there are ten thousand islands in the group but no one who has ever seen the region ever challenges the name. Inexperienced fishermen and fliers have been lost in this vast maze of mangrove and water and have never been found. The town of Marco that looks out over the waters toward Marco Pass and the Gulf has been famed for three-quarters of a century as one of the finest fishing spots along the Florida coasts. About 1880 a wharf and store were built there by "Captain Bill" Collier (no relation to Barron G. Collier who was to come forty years later) who brought down the lumber from Fort Myers by boat, and the settlement began to grow. Between 1896 and 1900 archaelogists, some from the University of Pennsylvania, exploring the old Indian mounds on the island found artifacts that told of a prehistoric 'Glades people about whom very little is known. Shell mounds and temple sites now buried under a tangle of trees and vines tell of tribes that dwelt here centuries before the coming of the Spaniard, getting most of their sustenance from the sea.

Barron Collier bought up a large part of Marco Island in 1920 but the waterside at the village was purchased by George Rupert, New York brewer and brother of "Jake" Rupert who was owner of the Yankee ball team. Here he built a handsome two-story lodge where until his death he spent his winters and entertained his sportsmen friends who liked to hunt and fish. The property was acquired by its present owners in 1946 and is now operated as an inn and headquarters for fishing expeditions. On the seaward side of Marco and adjoining islands are several beautiful stretches of beach that rival Sanibel Island as a hunting ground for shells. A side road leads down to Collier City, formerly called Caxambas, where the present Collier interests are developing a winter resort.

Back to the state park and the Tamiami Trail it is sixteen miles

The Tamiami Trail near the town of Everglades

to where State Highway 29 crosses, leading south to the town of Everglades, four miles distant. Along this sixteen-mile stretch are thirty-five short bridges or culverts and though the highway maps do not name it this is the lower end of the Fahkahatchee Slough that leads its sluggish waters for fifty miles through the wilderness of the Big Cypress.

Everglades (the town), seat of Collier County, sits on the east bank of Collier River which just below the wharf flows into Chocoloskee Bay in the heart of the Ten Thousand Islands. Here Collier in 1920 started a development that he hoped would rival Miami. He dredged in land, bulkheaded the river banks, constructed sewer and water systems, landscaped the area, and erected a spacious building for the Rod and Gun Club. When the lean years came later the town did not retrograde but it grew very little until after

World War II. The Rod and Gun Club became a hotel with a regular winter clientele, the Audubon Society made it headquarters for excursions to the famous rookery at Duck Rock, and guides take fishing parties through the prolific waterways of the many islands.

Recently the town has taken on a "new look" under the direction of the Collier enterprise. With a million acres in Collier and adjoining counties the organization has launched a program to develop cattle raising, vegetable growing and forestry, as well as revitalizing the town. With the establishment of Everglades National Park, which comes right up to its back door, Everglades has taken on a new importance as the western gateway to the park. This is a "water gateway" with visitors taking trips along the Turner River under the supervision of Park Rangers.

From Everglades it is sixty miles along the Trail to State Highway 27 that runs due south to the Florida Keys. This last stretch of the Trail is almost straight, past "Indian Villages" and a few small scattered settlements. For thirty years a stone arch over the road at the Collier-Dade County line informed travelers from the East that they were entering Collierland, but this was recently removed by the state highway department. At the Dade County line begins one of the most attractive man-made features of the Trail—a row of green-plumed Australian pines between the roadway and the canal that reaches to the limits of Miami. Just beyond the county line the highway makes a slight turn at what is locally called "forty-mile bend" and heads straight as an arrow for the Atlantic Coast. This stretch is the true Everglades, devoid of pine or cypress, a home only for waterfowl, fish and amphibians. Even the Indians avoided it. The roadside canal in Dade County is in most places wide and deep enough to support a healthy fish population, mostly bream, but with a smattering of other fresh water species, including bass. Here, in spite of advertising folders announcing the glories of angling in the Gulf Stream, is the most popular fishing ground in the Miami area. The Florida game laws require no license for fishing with a cane pole (that keeps most of the natives honest) and this is

cane pole territory. Especially on Saturdays and Sundays the automobiles are parked bumper to bumper and the fishing folk, men
and women, white and Negro, line the bank beneath the Australian
pines and patiently watch the bobber as it dances on the breeze-
rippled waters.

Miami is not in the curving shore of the Gulf and with calm
hauteur it looks the other way across the Atlantic. Nor is it necessary to go to Miami to follow the Gulf Coast to Key West. Ten
miles out of Miami's city limits State Highway 27 takes off from
Tamiami Trail and twenty miles south at the town of Homestead
it unites with U.S. Route No. 1, the highway along the Keys.

Miles of tomatoes

XVI. Redlands and the National Park

I T is still Everglades country where Route 27 leaves the Trail and for ten miles it follows a canal bordered with Australian pines and with sawgrass flats on either hand. Then the sawgrass disappears to give way to tomato fields where, in fall and winter, the rows are so long they seem to meet on the horizon. In some fields the plantings may be potatoes, beans or sweet corn, but the tomato is king and occupies 22,000 acres of the 40,000 acres planted to winter vegetables in this area.

This is a peculiar economy, confined to a strip along the east coast some twenty-five miles long and almost as wide. For six months the land is completely idle, most of it covered with water. The U.S. Weather Bureau records at Homestead show an annual rainfall of 61.88 inches, which is a lot of rain. The September precipitation is 9.18 inches and October has 9.14 inches. The total for the next *five* months is 9.16 inches, being 2.13, 1.20, 1.94, 1.72 and 2.17 respectively. As soon as the soil is dry enough to be worked in the fall fleets of tractors start to work and in a short time the seed bed is ready. Carloads of fertilizer are scattered, the crop is put in and soon the spray and dusting schedule begins. Everything possible is done by machinery. The rewards may be great but there are many hazards. The tail end of a northern blizzard may whip across the peninsula and threaten frost, calling for smudge pots or a stepped-up watering schedule which may or may not avert the danger. Drought is not feared so much, as water lies not far below the surface and powerful pumps raise it and spray it, covering as much as two acres from one point. The greatest hazard is "wilt" or late blight that can strike a field of healthy-looking plants and within two or three days leave it looking as though a fire had swept over it. The only insurance against this is to spray or dust every few days, a process that runs into a lot of money for labor and material.

Power machinery takes care of almost everything except harvesting. There is a large Negro population in southern Dade County and in late winter and early spring this is augmented by hundreds of Negroes brought over from the Bahaman Islands by special arrangement with the immigration authorities. Proper living quarters and sanitary arrangements must be provided for these workers, which sometimes leads to controversy. The tomatoes are picked green but have ripened by the time they reach the retail markets in the North. Packing sheds equipped with machinery for sorting, grading and packing various vegetables line the railroad tracks at Homestead and other shipping points between there and Miami. This is the most southern bit of railroad in the United States, but there is no passenger service south of Miami.

Vegetable growing in the extreme southern part of Florida is as impersonal as it can be made. Few growers live on their acres and most of the land is held under lease. In many instances the operation is controlled by a syndicate, or by farmers with large holdings in Michigan, Maine, New York or other Northern states who pursue their calling down here when their Northern acres are under snow. There are no fiestas, no gay parades at harvest time as there is in the lower Rio Grande Valley. For the most part it is a coldly efficient proceeding with little of the romance—or hardship—so often associated with tillage of the soil.

What has been said of vegetable growing will not hold for the fruit-growing district that is centered at Homestead, thirty miles south of Miami at the end of the ridge that extends for two hundred miles down the Atlantic Coast. The area is called "The Redland District," or "Redlands" because of the color of its soil. Trees will not grow on the land under vegetable cultivation as the water table is too high and most of it is flooded during the rainy season, but the pine and palmetto lands along the ridge are well drained. A heavy stand of pine timber grew here until it was lumbered off more than half a century ago.

Now the largest town between Miami and Key West, Homestead was only an obscure settlement until the Florida East Coast Railroad reached it in 1904. A number of orange groves were put out in the early days but neither the soil nor the climate was suitable for orange culture and most of them have disappeared. The present plantings, most of which are small, include avocados, mangos, Tahiti limes (usually called Persian limes), guavas and the newly introduced lychees. Avocados will flourish here and reach a size and succulence matched nowhere else in the United States. There are many varieties of this fruit and because some of them are pear-shaped and have a rough skin they came to be called "alligator pears." This term is seldom used now, though locally avocados are often referred to as "pears."

Mangos have probably been cultivated by mankind longer than any other tree fruit. The ancient Hindu scriptures make a number of references to mangos, which originated somewhere around the Indian Ocean and are cultivated in many tropical countries. The only place in the United States they will grow is in the frost-free tip of extreme southern Florida and here they are becoming increasingly popular. The fruit is covered with a smooth skin which takes on a yellowish hue as it ripens. The most popular of the several varieties in south Florida is the Haden, which may weigh a pound or more. The flesh is yellow with a sweet, spicy taste and encloses a single flat seed. This variety originated from a seed borne on a tree imported from India in 1869 and planted at the home of Professor Elbridge Gale in Lake Worth, Florida. Of several seeds from this tree planted near Miami by Captain John J. Haden, one developed an especially delicious fruit, and all of thousands of Haden mango trees in the region can trace their ancestry through grafts to this original tree, which is still standing. Unfortunately it is not a heavy bearer, which makes a Haden mango grove an uncertain revenue producer. Hybridizers, horticulturists and nurserymen are busy cross-pollinating in an effort to develop a heavy-producing variety without loss of quality and it is very probable they will succeed in time.

For a long time lemons could not be successfully grown for market in Florida, but a new variety has proved so adaptable that a number of groves have been put out. Limes are a very popular crop. For the Northern market the best variety is the so-called Persian lime, a fruit that is almost as large as an average lemon and usually has a greenish cast when it reaches the consumer. But the favorite of most residents of south Florida is the smaller bright yellow "Key lime" with less eye appeal than the Persian. Key limes were brought to Florida by Dr. Henry E. Perrine, onetime U.S. Consul in Yucatan, who was murdered by the Indians at his home on the Florida Keys in 1840. In the decades that followed the seeds were scattered along the Keys by birds, winds and other forces of nature, where they still flourish in potholes and crannies in the rocks to be gathered by Negroes and sold along the roadside. Small Key lime trees can be purchased from nurserymen and are found in many Southern dooryards. South Florida "crackers" insist that the smaller fruits have a better flavor and more juice than the Persians.

Adjoining Homestead on the south side is the village of Florida City. Only a few yards from the line between them State Route 27 from the north and U.S. Route 1 from the northeast come together at an acute angle and No. 1 continues on to Key West. Florida City is the last spot on the highway until the Keys are reached twenty-three miles south across the Everglades. It is a shipping point for fruit and vegetables, and here is the southmost railroad crossing in the United States. It has achieved a newer prominence as the main gateway to Everglades National Park, a position of increasing importance as the park is developed.

Everglades National Park embracing a million and a half acres is the second largest of twenty-six national parks in continental United States, being exceeded only by Yellowstone. But there is a joker in this figure—much of the area is covered with water and in the rainy season a full 80 per cent may be inundated. The park embraces the southern tip of the Florida peninsula, takes in much of Florida Bay and its islands between the Keys and the mainland, and its central and western portions reach north to the Tamiami Trail.

The Indians called this region "Pahayokee," meaning "grassy waters," and Marjory Stoneman Douglas called it "River of Grass" in her book of that title. The wide stretches of sawgrass through which the water flows slowly southward most of the year are broken by "hammocks" where the processes of nature over the centuries have built up a mound of soil that supports a growth of trees and vines. These hammocks vary in size from a few square yards to many acres. Their soil is rich and those along the east coast were long ago put under cultivation. Where the sawgrass prairies meet the tidal waters the mangroves appear. There are three distinct species of mangroves here, black, white and red. It is the red that has had the greater part in making this region what it is today.

Wherever along the innumerable tidewater inlets or low beaches in south Florida you see a solid mass of tangled branches with dark, shiny leaves and stilt roots that arch out from the main stem like so many fingers clutching the soil—that is the red mangrove. It covers the Ten Thousand Islands along the southwest coast and grows halfway up the peninsula, but it does not like frost. It lines the countless waterways in Everglades National Park and has played an important role in building up the Florida Keys. Its long, thin seeds mature and fall into the shallow water around the parent tree. Nature has so designed this seed that it floats in an upright position. If undisturbed for a few days it sends a rootlet into the soft marl and soon the great wall of green has moved another step against the sea. Or the seed may be swept away by tidal currents to find anchor on some shallow bar, there to take hold and send out its stilt roots that catch and hold the flotsam of the changing tide. The years pass. It drops its seeds and they grow up about it, and another islet is formed amid the shallow wastes. Sometimes, however, the ground so slowly gained is suddenly lost when a hurricane washes out the shallow footing, or so wracks and twists the roots and branches that the growth will be killed over a large area.

It is these hammocks, mangrove thickets and forests, wide beaches and tepid tropical waters that make the Everglades National Park a haven for wildlife unsurpassed anywhere in the world. Emphasis is often placed on the bird life in this region, but its animal species while not so evident is hardly less varied. Black bears, panthers, crocodiles, alligators, raccoons, deer—these are not often seen by the visitor but they are at home in the region. Alligators are common in the fresh water streams and lakes, but the crocodiles live in the salt water estuaries and are comparatively rare. Like some of the bird species these animals were threatened with extinction by hunters but under the park's protection are increasing in numbers.

Although the park is open all the year the best time to see it is from December until April, inclusive. This is the dry season when the wildlife tends to concentrate in the water areas, many of the larger birds are nesting in their rookeries, and migrant species from the North are spending the winter here. Summer is the rainy season and though all-day rains are rare the sudden squalls pour out a lot of water. In the summer the mosquitoes are more troublesome and the wildlife is scattered over a wider area. Fishing, which is permitted in most places in the park for those who have a state license, is better in the summer but is fairly good the year round. Hunting is never allowed.

The National Park Service is charged by law with "the conservation of America's scenic, scientific and historic heritage for the benefit and enjoyment of the people." This is sometimes a difficult assignment and especially so in the Everglades. To conserve this rich heritage of wilderness life it must be protected from anything that would destroy it or drive it from the region, and yet it must be developed "for the benefit and enjoyment of the people." The park management under the direction of Dan Beard is tackling this problem, fortified with a wide knowledge of the ecology of the park and the experience of other national parks.

An improved roadway runs from the park headquarters at Royal Palm Ranger Station to the onetime village of Flamingo on Florida Bay where there is a small restaurant and where boats may be hired. For the present there are no overnight accommodations in the park but these are available at Homestead and Florida City, nine miles from the entrance. By far the most satisfactory way to see the park is by boat, and work is now going forward to develop an inland channel through a maze of waterways that will unite the Flamingo area with the recently opened "water gateway" at Everglades city. Although the park naturalist at the Royal Palm Ranger Station conducts programs and walks during the winter season it is only as a member of a guided tour that a visitor can see what the park has to offer. Such tours are conducted by the National Audubon Society, and the Everglades Transway Service has a concession to conduct short boat trips from bases within the park. The Audubon tours are arranged by Charles M. Brookfield, south Florida representative of the Society and an outstanding naturalist. One tour leaves from the Society's downtown Miami office and after a station wagon trip along the southeast coast where a number of land birds can be seen it enters the park, stops to take in "The Anhinga Trail," and then goes to Flamingo for a boat cruise through Florida Bay. It is not unusual on such a trip for the visitor to check off a hundred species of birds on the list the Society furnishes him.

The other Audubon tour is a two-day affair, starting from Tavernier on the Florida Keys and going down the Keys to the Great White Heron Wild Life Refuge and the Big Pine Key where there is a possibility of seeing the rare tiny Key deer. This is just outside the park area but the second day's tour by boat from Tavernier embraces a number of islands in Florida Bay, including the one where the rare spoonbills, sometimes called "flame birds," have re-established a nesting colony after an absence of thirty years.

The Anhinga Trial, just inside the Homestead entrance to the park, is one feature easily reached without a guide and which is always rewarding. It is no more than a high wooden boardwalk built out into a marshy pool screened by reeds and willows where there is a concentration of wildlife. The walk is high enough above the water to be safe from the alligators and assortment of snakes below. Here one may see at close range a great variety of egrets, herons, waterfowl, a population that is constantly changing with the season.

Construction of the trail was begun in September of 1949, and completed that December. It winds in and out along the edge of the slough terminating at a large raised platform. Maintenance men and Rangers who participated in the construction worked with an am-

(*National Park Service*)
A great white heron photographed from the Anhinga Trail

phibious Navy "Alligator" for pile driving and hauling lumber. During the work real alligators watched from the slough.

Daniel B. Beard, superintendent of the Everglades National Park, says: "We did not know, at the time, whether the alligators, birds and other creatures would resent the intrusion of the boardwalk and leave for areas of greater privacy. We could only hope for the best. Of particular concern was the winter roosting area of several thousand herons and ibis located at the end of the trail. Fortunately, the wild creatures did not seem to object to the intrusion. Each year a new bird or animal, before shy and difficult to locate, assumes the park visitor is a part of the natural environment, and in turn, becomes easily approachable. The alligators and purple gallinules were the

first. Now, during the winter season, a visitor can also observe white
ibis, limpkins, glossy ibis, sora rails, coots, turtles, fish, snakes and
seven kinds of herons at close range. In the summer most of the birds
scatter throughout the Everglades."

But for the untiring industry of what was at first a small group
of devoted men and women, all these wild creatures would either be
extinct or driven from south Florida years ago. The battle was not
won until at least two lives had been sacrificed and even today constant vigilance is required for their protection. Long before the establishment of a national park in this region was considered there
was a fifteen-year war fought on several fronts to save the birds,
particularly the American and snowy egrets, from utter extinction
and without the blood of martyrs it might never have been won.

There is an old song about "The Pretty Little Bird on Nellie's
Hat." During the latter part of the nineteenth century Nellie and
all her girl friends wore hats gaily decked with plumes, wings,
breasts and even the whole plumage of wild birds as standard head-
gear. But the most sought-for trophies and the highest priced were
the sprays of white egret plumes, called "aigrettes" by French milli-
ners, which came principally from the great rookeries in the Everglades. What made this traffic so devastating was that the plumes
were at their peak of perfection during the nesting season and the
practice of the plume hunters was to go into a large rookery with
shotguns, kill every adult bird, and leave the young to starve in the
nests. It was dirty business but there were plenty of "crackers" in
south Florida and Key West willing to work at it, for the rewards
were considerable. The plumage of the roseate spoonbills was often
a lucrative side line.

By 1900 the white birds were almost extinct in Florida, which put
the price of their plumes up still higher. Many attempts had been
made to control the slaughter without avail, but in 1901 William
T. Dutcher, later president of the National Association of Audubon
Societies, succeeded in getting a bird protection law through the
Florida legislature. No funds were appropriated for wardens, and

though much less powerful than it is today the Audubon organization raised enough money to employ four wardens to patrol the Everglades rookeries, one being Guy M. Bradley who lived with his wife and parents in what is now the south area of the park. Bradley was relentless in his pursuit of the plume hunters and more than once was fired on from ambush. On July 8, 1905, Bradley met up with Walter Smith of Key West and his two sons near the Cuthbert rookery. Smith had been arrested before for game law violations. Later Smith was to say that Bradley had been killed in self-defense, but the fact remains that Bradley was found dead in his boat the next day. Smith was jailed but for want of evidence a grand jury failed to indict him. Guy Bradley was buried near where he was killed and his lonely grave on the shore of Cape Sable is reverently pointed out by Audubon guides.

Although it aroused a lot of bitter comment this martyrdom failed to halt the plume raiders. Another warden, Columbus G. McLeod,

Charles M. Brookfield of the National Audubon Society and R. H. Fitzpatrick pay homage at the grave of Guy Bradley on Cape Sable

(Oliver Griswold)

was killed by them in the Charlotte Harbor area in 1908. But the persistence of the Audubon organization began to tell. With typical Southern *laissez faire* the Florida state government sat on its hands, but in 1910 Governor Charles Evans Hughes, of New York, signed a bill that at last brought real protection to the white birds of the Everglades. It was a bill that outlawed traffic in the plumage of wild birds in New York. As New York City was the great wholesale millinery market the law was effective but still left a few loopholes.

The measure did not pass the New York legislature without a bitter fight. Assemblyman Alfred E. Smith (no relation to the Smith involved in the Bradley killing!), later governor of the state, headed the opposition in the lower house. Judge Julius Meyer appeared for the Eastern Millinery Association and Benjamin Feiner for the Feather Importers Association. Nonetheless the bill passed and Governor Hughes signed it. With the supply cut off, egret plumes in Paris became worth twice their weight in gold. There were surreptitious killings in the Everglades and the plumes were smuggled out through Havana and entered New York as "imported." One more step remained. The embattled champions of the birds succeeded in having a Federal law passed forbidding the importation of the plumes and making it an offense to have them in one's possession.

With the double protection of the Federal law and the National Park sanctuary the egrets again make beautiful the water fastness where they had flourished for so long. Roseate spoonbills are coming back to Florida in increased numbers, and in 1954 two wild flamingos, the first to be seen in Florida in half a century, were spotted in the southern area of the park.

The first move toward making a national park of the south Florida wilderness was made by the late Ernest F. Coe, a landscape architect of Miami, who in 1928 organized the Everglades National Park Association and continued to write and talk about the idea for two decades. The next year the Florida legislature created an Everglades National Park Commission with Coe as chairman, but later governors failed to continue the appointments and the commission was not revived until 1946. Early road maps marked the Everglades area as "proposed national park," but for fifteen years the plan was kicked around while the spoliation of the region continued in spite of what the Audubon wardens could do under their limited authority. After World War II interest in the project revived. Daniel B. Beard, one of the ablest men in the National Park Service, took over an area of 865,000 acres with wardens deputized by the state, and the Secretary of the Interior agreed to accept it as a park if Florida would appropriate two million dollars for the purchase of additional lands. Such an act was passed in spite of injunction proceedings brought by the state attorney general. At last all the difficulties were overcome, the necessary moneys and signatures obtained, and on December 6, 1947, President Truman formally dedicated the new national park at an elaborate ceremony in Everglades city.

The Seven Mile Bridge between Vacca and Bahia Honda Keys

XVII. *The Florida Keys*

THERE is but one road from Miami to the Florida Keys at present and that is U.S. No. 1 through Homestead and Florida City, but by the end of the present decade there will probably be another. Leaving Florida City Route No. 1 runs twenty miles through the Everglades and then crosses a drawbridge over a narrow neck of water called Jewfish Creek. The south end of the bridge is on Key Largo, longest of the Keys. The Overseas Highway bends southwest at this point and continues to Key West, 110 miles distant. But a newly paved road leads in the opposite direction to the north end of Key Largo and from there several smaller Keys point toward Key Biscayne which is opposite Miami. The water between these islands and the mainland is Biscayne Bay. Agitation has begun for a new "Overseas Highway" from Key Biscayne, already accessible by bridge, across the intervening Keys to Key Largo where it would join the present route, bypassing a number of small towns between Miami and Florida City. No appropriations have been made and no engineering plans approved but the growing interest in this region as a winter resort and fishing paradise make it "a natural."

Looking at the map of southern Florida one who has never seen the Keys will get the impression that the highway is always right at the water's edge. On the contrary, after reaching Key Largo the motorist will travel more than a dozen miles before getting other than a passing glimpse of Florida Bay (an arm of the Gulf of Mexico) on one side and the Atlantic Ocean on the other. This is because the Keys are completely covered with a tropical jungle high enough to shut off the view, except where bulldozers have recently been at work clearing the way for buildings. So thick is the tangle of mangrove, gumbo limbo, ficus, wild coffee and similar growths, all tied together with vines, that it forms a solid wall. Fourteen miles from Jewfish Creek is the town of Tavernier and the first of forty bridges that tie the Keys together. Key Largo is followed by Plantation Key, Upper Matecumbe, Indian Key, Lower Matecumbe and other such as Grassy, Crawl, Key Vaca, Ramrod, Bahia Honda, Big Pine, Saddle Bunch—there is a hint of legend even in their names.

In all there are more than seven hundred islands, large and small, that hang like a necklace of green beads around the southern point of Florida. The number is constantly changing as the gaps between some fill with sand and vegetation and make one island out of two, or when the floating seeds of the red mangrove anchor in a shallow marl bank, take hold, and catching the drifting soil and debris in their roots build up another islet. Not more than fifty of the Keys are reached by the Overseas Highway and its side roads. Some of the others are too small and low to be of consequence, and the larger isolated islands are occupied by private owners or the proprietors of fishing camps.

Just as there is no place in the world quite like Florida's Everglades, so there is nothing comparable to the Florida Keys. They were among the very first features of the Western Hemisphere to be mapped by the early Spanish explorers, and their sunlit beaches have seen much of man's inhumanity to man. Ponce de Leon may or may not have been the first European to see the Keys but he was the first to give them a name. Sailing around the Florida peninsula in 1513 after having explored part of the Atlantic Coast the adventurous Spaniard coasted along these scattered islands and gave them the name, "Los Martires" (The Martyrs), because their twisted outlines resembled men in the throes of being tortured. There was something prophetic in the term.

When the Spaniards sailed past they were watched with hostile eyes by the Calusa Indians that lived along the islands. Already word had filtered across the neighboring waters that the coming of the strange men in great ships meant death and slavery for the Indians. When the more docile tribes of the Caribbean died under the lash or because of the pure misery of slavery attempts were made to replace them with Indians from the mainland. The Calusas, however, were too warlike and too independent for such submission, an attitude they maintained until they were eventually exterminated.

Time and the vagaries of Caribbean weather were to give the Indians of the Keys a bitter revenge in the two centuries that followed. When the gold and silver, the emeralds and pearls, reached the seaports after being looted from temple and palace, the ships that carried this treasure to Spain were compelled by the Gulf Stream to pass through the Straits of Florida that lie between the island of Cuba and the Keys. Spanish admirals had no knowledge of the hurricane season from August to November when violent storms sweep across this region, and were too stubborn to learn. On his fourth and last voyage Columbus, discredited at home and scorned by those who had followed his early voyages, asked permission of the Spanish governor of Santo Domingo (now Ciudad Trujillo) to put into that port to repair a damaged ship and escape the storm he knew from past experience was imminent. The permission was refused. Columbus rode out the hurricane in another bay, but the greatest convoy that at that time had ever sailed from the New World put out from Santo Domingo in spite of Columbus' warnings and only one ship survived. The lesson went unheeded and time and again treasure-laden caravels started out in late summer from their rendezvous at Havana to be blown on the reefs and lost.

The Indians learned to watch for these disasters. There would be bales of strange fabrics, foods, tools, weapons, gold in bars and golden ornaments that glittered in the sun. Sometimes, too, there would be survivors clinging to the wreckage to be picked up by the Indians in their canoes. Many of these would soon regret that they had not perished with their shipmates. A dark-eyed Latin girl might be given a place in the household of a chieftain, and now and then a young, quick-witted youth like Escalante de Fontaneda would be kept as a slave, but most of the rescued were sacrificed on a flaming altar to the Sun God.

Along with the treasure and the sacrificial victims the Indians picked up from the white man his diseases, particularly smallpox. Lacking the immunity which the Europeans had in part acquired by exposure to disease, time came when the Indians began to fall like wheat before the scythe. Added to this was the pressure of the Creek Indians from the north, traditional enemies of the Calusas, and under these disasters their numbers declined.

As the Indians began to disappear from the Keys their place was taken by men no less cruel and even more avaricious. The British, the French, privateers and plain old-fashioned pirates began to prey on the increasing Spanish commerce, some with the excuse of war for their legalized plunder and some with no other credentials than the "Jolly Roger." Many of the latter established themselves in the maze of islands from which their small swift vessels would strike, loot and return through devious channels where their pursuers could not follow. As the cities along the Gulf Coast grew, the shipping grew and the number of wrecks along the Keys increased. Between the pirates and the hurricanes it became a dreaded passage and one reason the United States was anxious to acquire Florida from Spain was to police these waters so important to the commerce of Galveston, New Orleans, Mobile, Pensacola, Tampa and other ports along its southern shores.

With such a background it was inevitable that there should spring up innumerable legends of lost treasure ships and buried pirate gold. The tales are many and enough of them have proved true to keep treasure hunters alert. With electronic metal detectors they sweep the depths beside the coral reefs searching for the sepulchers of lost ships. Sometimes the find is only a few old cannon encrusted with barnacles and seaweed, and sometimes ingots of silver. Perhaps the total amount spent on such expeditions approximates the value of the lost treasure.

Soon after the United States took possession of Florida in 1821, Commander David Porter was ordered to the Caribbean area to clean out the pirates. He established headquarters on Key West which then had no permanent buildings and began his task with characteristic energy. Many of the Spanish officials in the West Indies were secretly sharing the profits of the buccaneers and regarded Porter with hostility. When one of his lieutenants sailed into Fajardo, Puerto Rico, to investigate a suspected freebooter, he was imprisoned by the Spanish. Learning of this the commodore entered the harbor, got the lieutenant released, and demanded and received an apology from the authorities. The high brass in Washington held this to be in excess of his authority and ordered him court-martialed. He was suspended from the service for six months and the following year resigned his commission to accept command of the newly organized Mexican Navy. Later he served in the diplomatic service under President Jackson until his death in 1843. (*Note*: David Porter was the father of David Dixon Porter who served under

Admiral Farragut in the attacks on New Orleans and Vicksburg during the Civil War.)

Porter was succeeded as pirate-chaser by the doughty Lieutenant Lawrence Kearny in the *Enterprise*, who destroyed four pirate schooners in as many weeks. He was later joined by Captain Biddle and a fleet of small war vessels, and when the British began to clean up the waters around Jamaica the sun of the pirates had set.

Wrecks continued to pile up along the Keys but the salvage was conducted according to law, and the rescue of crews and passengers took precedence over salvaging cargoes. The goods taken from the wrecks and transported to the Federal court at Key West no longer consisted of loot from Aztec and Inca, but the merchandise of international trade, such as cotton, textiles, foodstuffs and manufactured articles. The big business of salvage was carried on by private vessels, some manned by New England sailors and some from the Bahamas. Except for a beacon at Key West there was no light for 120 miles along the Keys. In 1824 the salvage at Key West was valued at $293,000 on which the government collected $100,000 in import duties. More than five hundred wrecks broke up along the Keys in the ten years following 1850 but that was the high point. As steam replaced sail the ships became more maneuverable and warning beacons were placed along the more dangerous reefs. Now when the watcher on the Keys looks to the south he sees the misty outlines of the steel-hulled vessels moving along in perfect safety, and if a hurricane is blowing up somewhere in the Caribbean the captain knows its force and course in ample time to find a haven.

William Wordsworth wrote of Peter Bell:

> A primrose by a river's brim
> A yellow primrose was to him,
> And it was nothing more.

It is doubtful that Peter Bell would have enjoyed the drive along the Keys from Tavernier to Key West, but for those with an eye for

changing color and islands against a background of blues and greens
it has a fascination. The shallow waters reflect in soft pastels the
hues of marl and sand, coral and seaweed. A cloud passing over the
sun will give every color a new value, and the lights at midday are
different from those of morning or late afternoon. Every road is two
roads, for the returning traveler will notice things he did not see
on his first trip. More than six hundred varieties of fish are found
in these waters, some like tarpon, sailfish, bonefish, pompano and
snapper, much sought by anglers, and some such as parrot fish and
angel fish remarkable for their exquisite coloring. Whatever the
species they all have an iridescence when first taken from the water
that suggests the colorings of the sea in which they lived.

Some of the forty bridges that span the channels between the Keys
are only a few yards long, some are hundreds of yards, and the
longest, Knight Key Bridge, is seven miles from end to end. The
total length of the bridges is 17.7 miles and the bridge approaches
add up to seven miles of causeway. At most bridgeheads there are
parking spaces and several are provided with picnic tables and
facilities for overnight camping. The parking places are for fishermen who find the bridges ideal spots to try their luck, and if it
proves to be poor—well, it is not far to another bridge.

For ninety years after their acquisition by the United States the
only way to reach the Keys and Key West was by boat but in 1910
Henry M. Flagler, builder of the Florida East Coast Railroad, concluded that Key West was the logical place for a great seaport. Flagler had become one of the richest men in the United States through
his investments in the Standard Oil Company and as early as 1885
had recognized the possibilities of Florida's Atlantic Coast. He built
the sumptuous Ponce de Leon Hotel at St. Augustine and then
pushed his railroad on down the shore to Daytona Beach and Palm
Beach, where he constructed the Royal Ponciana Hotel. Still his
railroad was not carrying enough freight to break even and by 1896
he had extended its tracks to Miami, hoping to develop a seaport
there. He did not envision it as the winter playground it has since

become. When Miami's port facilities proved very limited he decided Key West, only ninety miles from Havana and with a fine deep-water harbor, was the logical terminus of the Florida East Coast. Construction across the Everglades south of Homestead began in 1904. Only a Flagler would have dared to push a rail line across that 130 miles of swamp, sand and water. Already he had passed the age at which most men retire but his purse and his purpose never faltered, even when a severe storm in 1909 swept away much of the embankment and made it necessary to change the route as originally planned.

With great acclaim the first train rolled across the Keys in 1912. It was literally a "seagoing railroad" and a marvelous feat of engineering. As the great Florida boom began to get under way following World War I and the automobile became a universal mode of transportation there developed a demand for a highway to Key West. Monroe County, in which the Keys lie, issued bonds for that purpose and by 1926 the road was complete except for two gaps of fourteen miles each which were crossed by ferries. This was good but not good enough. It was impossible to get to Key West from the mainland and back the same day, so in 1933 the state legislature created the Overseas Road and Toll District which issued bonds for the construction of bridges across the gaps.

Before the work got under way several things happened. The national depression which began with the stock market break in 1929 was getting deeper all the time, banks were closed throughout the country, and the United States went off the gold standard. In the midst of this dark national picture a devastating hurricane struck the Keys on Labor Day, 1935, killed a number of persons, damaged property to the extent of several millions, and so badly wrecked Flagler's seagoing railroad that its reconstruction was out of the question. Building of the highway went on nonetheless. The District acquired the right-of-way of the railroad and the bridges started creeping across the waters from Key to Key. All are of concrete arch or girder span type, the railings are of welded railroad steel encased in concrete, except on the long Knight's Key Bridge where the steel is protected by aluminum paint. A number of hurricanes have thrown their force against these structures but they are as firm as the rocks in which their foundations are imbedded.

The new Overseas Highway was opened as a toll road in 1938. The charge was one dollar for car and driver and twenty-five cents for each passenger. So heavy was the traffic that the rate of income exceeded all estimates and in 1954 the bonds had all been retired, tolls were abolished, and the road turned over to the State Highway Department. But the project that had started under difficulties was to wind up the same way. Charges were brought that there had been collusion between the Toll District authorities and certain contractors, and that considerable sums of money had gotten into the wrong pockets. There were indictments and trials and the state filed a civil action to recover $200,000 in alleged overpayments. In the meantime the cars and busses roll merrily over one of the finest highways in the United States.

With the opening of the highway, business and real estate values along the Keys began to soar, but it was not until the end of World War II that development really got into high gear. There is no wild speculation about this, no turnover of the same piece of property two or three times a week as was common in the Florida boom of the 1920's, but only such risks as invested capital always takes. Bulldozers tear into the jungle growth and level the ground to the water's edge; giant draglines scoop out channels so the cottager can tie his cabin cruiser alongside his house; where the beach is too low dredges pump out sand and marl and deposit it behind retaining walls; a causeway is built to a near-by Key which is soon cleared off and divided into building lots, glaring white under the tropic sun. Such operations require the expenditure of a million or two dollars before there is any return. Sometimes it is the capital of a wealthy individualist whose winter home is part of the development; and sometimes the money is put up by a syndicate that clears the land, puts up the cottages and offers them for sale. No property

along the Keys is cheap but there is variety in what is offered—
motels, hotels, two-bedroom houses on small lots and higher-priced
homes for those who have a long purse and want neighbors in the
same category. Buyers often follow close on the heels of the builders,
and the six hundred varieties of fish in the adjoining waters are in
for a tough time.

Along with this burgeoning growth come the restaurants, tea-
rooms, taverns, filling stations, souvenir sellers and fishing guides
with charter boats. The gastronomic specialties all along the Keys
are "turtle steak and Key lime pie." Which is not to say those deli-
cacies cannot be abused. In some places the servings are mediocre
and in others they have inspired poets.

The real charm of the Keys begins at Tavernier, which is the
starting point for Audubon Wildlife tours which run from. late
November until the first of May and are becoming increasingly
popular. Eight miles below Tavernier is the village of Islamorada
("IS-la-mo-RAD-a"), one of the older settlements on the Keys. Here
a tall shaft of coral rock, bearing in bold relief coconut trees in the
agony of a hurricane, memorializes one of the most tragic events of
these sometime-happy isles. The inscription reads: "Dedicated to
the memory of the civilians and war veterans whose lives were lost
in the hurricane of September second, 1935." Like the explosion in
Texas City in 1947 it is a tragedy that might have been in part
avoided.

The unemployed veterans of World War I had made their "Bonus
March" on Washington and had become both a political and an
economic problem. The new administration had organized the
Florida Employment Relief Administration in 1934 and as a part of
that program had set up three camps on Upper Matecumbe Key
where the veterans could be employed in building the Overseas
Highway. All admissions to the camps had to be cleared through
Washington but by midsummer of 1935 there were more than seven
hundred enrolled. They were victims both of the war and the unemployment crisis and some should have been in a psychiatric hospital,

a form of veteran care that was to come later. The men were well fed and had plenty of time for fishing and recreation. They did not have to work very hard and they received thirty dollars a month in addition to their sustenance.

When the camps were established the question was immediately raised: "What if there is a hurricane?" The authorities answered glibly that arrangements had been made with the Florida East Coast Railroad to send a special train for the men as soon as hurricane warnings were received, and they would be evacuated to the mainland.

Saturday, August 31, 1935, a hurricane was spotted north of the island of Haiti and the Coast Guard hoisted warnings along the Florida coast. Before daylight Monday morning (Labor Day) Grady Norton, leading authority on the vagaries of hurricanes and head of the Miami Weather Station, called the officer in charge of veteran camps, who was stationed at Jacksonville, and told him the hurricane would probably strike lower Florida and advised precautions. The Jacksonville official called the officer in command on the Keys and told him to order the train to evacuate the men when he thought it necessary. There followed calls to the Miami Weather Bureau for more information about the storm, and finally, shortly after noon, the railroad was ordered to send the train which was supposed to be ready to move from Homestead, fifty miles north. But the train was not at Homestead and it was not ready. Between government officialdom and railroad officialdom it was almost half-past four in the afternoon before the train left Miami for the FERA camps eighty miles away.

The relief train that had been promised so glibly the year before reached the camp at Islamorada shortly after 8:00 P.M. just in time to meet the hurricane in a head-on collision, and the train lost. A great wave, estimated by a lighthouse keeper to be ninety feet high, tumbled the train over like it was a toy under a Christmas tree, ripped up the track, and twisted steel rails as though they were wires. Fortunately many of the veterans and administration per-

Hurricane Monument at Islamorada

sonnel had gone to Miami to see a Labor Day baseball game, for most of those who remained in camp were to perish. As was the case in the Galveston storm of 1900, the violent waters piled up by the force of the hurricane did more damage than the wind. Buildings were tumbled about and their occupants crushed or drowned. Captain John Russell had seventy-nine relatives living along the middle Keys, of whom only eleven survived. The veterans never had a chance.

There was, and still is, bitter criticism for what followed, directed principally against Miami where the hurricane had done little damage. More than four hundred bodies were caught in the mangrove thickets, lying half-buried in the sand, or floating in the swells of the shallow bay. For the next ten years bleached skeletons would be discovered in the near-by jungles. A few volunteers came from the mainland the day after the storm, but there was little drinking water, few supplies and no organization. Somehow the indestructible mosquitoes had survived and they were everywhere. By Wednesday the first dazed and injured survivors reached the small town of Homestead, where the citizens did all they could for their relief. From Miami a crew of Negroes was sent to the Keys to help retrieve bodies from the swamp, and these were augmented later by boys from a near-by CCC Camp and a company of the state's National Guard.

The wreck of the rescue train that was engulfed by the hurricane
(Miami *Daily News*)

Still there were not enough to bury the dead nor aid the living. Bodies were swelling in the hot sun and on Friday orders came from somewhere to cremate them. One resident had managed to get metal caskets for the bodies of his wife and child, and while he and a fishing captain commanding one of the crews recovering corpses were putting them in, a National Guard officer appeared and demanded the woman and child be cremated. The captain pointed a pistol at the guardsman and swore to shoot him if he caused further trouble.

"And I'm not going to report it to anybody," he added. "I'm burning eighty-two bodies at Islamorada this morning, and if I throw you in there nobody will know the difference."

This incident was typical of the confusion that followed the hurricane until the survivors gradually picked up the broken threads of their lives. Harry Hopkins, head of the Relief Administration in Washington, sent an official investigator down who interviewed survivors and finally issued a report that held no one responsible for anything. It must be written off as another chapter in the tragedies of the Keys.

Between Upper Matecumbe and Lower Matecumbe Keys is an islet called Indian Key. To the south, half a mile out in the Gulf, is another Key, much larger and covered with a mantle of ever-green jungle. Its only settlement is a fishing camp at one corner and there is no scheduled connection with the mainland. Yet this larger island is the Indian Key of history, and an unhappy history it is. A century and a quarter ago it was a thriving village and a headquarters for salvage vessels, but even then it had a past. In the sixteenth century a number of shipwrecked Frenchmen had taken refuge there, only to be attacked and massacred by the Calusa Indians. Later it was a haven for piratical cutthroats until Lieutenant Kearny put them out of business.

Captain Jacob Houseman began a questionable career early in life when he stole one of his father's schooners in New York and headed for the Caribbean Sea, reaching Key West about the time the United States took it over from Spain. Quick to see the fortune to be made by a clever salvager he got into the business and soon was taking short cuts to riches that made him wealthy but frequently brought him in conflict with the law. Eventually his license as a salvager was revoked. Houseman came to Indian Key in 1825, built houses and wharves, opened a store and beautified the place with palms and shrubs. The government opened an Indian Key post office and installed a deputy customs inspector. There was still a threat of Indians so Houseman fortified the island, mounted cannon on a breastworks, and organized a militia from the residents. He then submitted a proposition to kill off all the Indians in south Florida for a bounty of two hundred dollars per head. The territorial legislature in Tallahassee endorsed the idea and forwarded it to Washington where it received no attention. But the Indians learned of it and their bitter resentment was to have serious consequences.

More closely linked with the story of Indian Key is the name of Dr. Henry E. Perrine, a man as different from Houseman as noonday is from midnight. Dr. Perrine, who was born in 1797, was a young New York physician when his health failed. Seeking a warmer climate he obtained an appointment as U.S. Consul at Campeche, Yucatan. Here he became fascinated with the study of tropical botany, in which few American citizens had any interest, and when Richard Rush, Secretary of the Treasury (there was no Department of Agriculture at that time), sent a memorandum to all consuls asking them to send home seeds and cuttings that might grow in the United States Dr. Perrine responded with enthusiasm. No money was allowed the consuls for this work but the doctor met the expenses of collecting out of his meager salary and began a correspondence with interested persons in southern Florida and Washton. Charles Howe, postmaster at Indian Key, shared this enthusiasm and to him Dr. Perrine sent many seeds and cuttings, some of which like the Key lime and the century plant still flourish in the region.

When Dr. Perrine evolved the idea of establishing an arboretum and propagation garden somewhere in the southern part of the United States for the culture and study of tropical plants the idea met with instant approval, due to the interest of Secretary Rush and leading botanists with whom Dr. Perrine had corresponded. The state of Louisiana offered him one of its coastal islands for the purpose but the doctor-botanist believed the southern tip of Florida around Cape Sable was a more desirable location. He went to New York and Washington in pursuance of this idea and in 1838 the Congress voted him and his associates a township of land, almost 24,000 acres, to be selected by him and surveyed. This was not prompted entirely by an interest in botany or science. The land was a refuge for marauding Indians and had no economic value, and a large installation, such as Dr. Perrine proposed, might help pacify the region. Elated with his success Dr. Perrine with his wife and three children landed at Indian Key on Christmas Day, 1838, to begin his great work.

There had been a few years of uneasy peace in the Everglades, but the whites in northern Florida and Georgia still cried out for complete extermination of the Indians, the government at Washington temporized and changed its policy, and the patience of the Indians who still refused to be transported to Arkansas wore thin and broke. Late in 1839 a detachment of soldiers under Colonel William S. Harney was attacked near Fort Myers, a number were killed, and the colonel escaped in his underwear. He would live to hang many an Indian from a cypress tree. The war was on again and a boat was sent to warn the inhabitants of the Keys.

When Dr. Perrine heard the news he was not greatly disturbed. For almost two years he had been exploring the area around Cape Sable and had decided on the place he wanted to establish his tropical plantings. He knew a number of the Indians in the region and their relations had always been friendly. Furthermore, the Secretary of War, Joel R. Poinsett, had promised him to protect the colony from the Indians. But Houseman had always been contemptuous of the red men, had treated them brutally on occasion, and they remembered his offer to kill them off for two hundred dollars per head. Even when two obviously spying Indians had been captured on Lower Matecumbe Key and later escaped there was no apprehension.

The night of August 4, 1840, Chief Chekika with seventeen war canoes slipped quietly into the shadows of Indian Key. There were thirty-five white persons and ten slaves sleeping in the cottages. Before they had formed for the attack the Indians were spied by two men who had risen early to go hunting, shots were fired and the fight was on. The Indians made first for Houseman's home but aroused by the shots he and his wife slipped out a rear door and hid among the rocks with the water up to their necks. The attackers looted the house and then the store. They took some of Houseman's small boats and loaded them with food and merchandise of all sorts.

Dr. Perrine and his family were living in a house built partly over the water at the foot of a small wharf. Beneath it was a "turtle crawl," a few square feet of water enclosed by pilings a few inches apart where sea turtles were held after being captured until they could be sent to market. When Dr. Perrine heard the shooting he led his family to this shelter and then went back upstairs. He knew the Indians held him in some awe as a physician, so he stepped out on his porch and told them in Spanish, which they understood, that if they would go away he would give them some medicine later. They seemed satisfied and left after telling him they only wanted Houseman. The doctor went to the second floor to get some papers but before he joined his family another group appeared, wildly drunk on the liquor they had discovered in the Houseman home and enraged because they could not find Houseman himself. With drunken savagery they battered down the door, dragged the doctor from his hiding place in a closet, and clubbed him to death while his family listened in silent horror below. Then they looted the building and set fire to it.

As the heat began to torture the refugees they crouched as low as possible in the water and covered their heads with wet marl. Finally young Henry squeezed out between the pilings and when he found no Indians watching he was joined by his mother and sisters. They got unnoticed into a boat the Indians had partly loaded with loot and with great difficulty made their way to a small schooner anchored in the open sea. It was one owned by Captain Houseman and he and his wife and other refugees were already on board. Two nights later, still in their nightclothes and wrapped in Navy blankets they were taken aboard the Navy vessel, *Flirt*, by Captain McLoughlin and taken to a settlement on Cape Florida, near Miami. Captain McLoughlin returned to Indian Key where he rescued a few persons who had managed to hide from the Indians. Dr. Perrine's partly consumed body was found in the ashes of his home and with a number of other dead was buried on Lower Matecumbe Key. Dr. Perrine's grave was in the little nursery he loved so well and which he had visited with his small daughter, Hester, only a few hours before the attack. Years later his son returned to remove the father's remains but storms had swept the nursery away and changed the contour of the beach so much that the grave could not be found.

Thus ended the great dream of a great man, which, if fulfilled, would have meant much to southern Florida and benefited the whole country. More than a century later the dream would be realized by the U.S. Plant Introduction Garden and the Fairchild Tropical Garden, both a short distance south of Miami. No monument of stone rises above the bones of Dr. Perrine, but along the Keys where tiny, fragrant blossoms turn into golden limes and the century plant blooms on a giant stalk and then dies the Great Mother Nature still remembers him. A town, Perrine, in the heart of the Redlands, has been named in his honor.

It was one of Fate's ironies that Houseman, whose capture by the Indians probably would have saved Dr. Perrine, got away with a whole skin. But he lost most of his fortune, which he estimated at $200,000. When he was accidentally crushed between two ships a year later his widow buried him on Indian Key beneath a heavy slab of marble on which is the epitaph: "To his friends he was sincere, to his enemies kind, and to all men faithful." Ah, well! *De mortuis nil nisi bonum.*" There was a further wry tragedy in the Houseman saga when his widow was barred from inheriting his property on the grounds she had never been married to him.

Four months after the Indian Key attack Colonel Harney with ninety men, dressed like Indians and traveling in Indian canoes, made an incredible march from the headwaters of the Miami River across the Everglades, hanging all the Indian warriors they could catch. Crawling all night through a rain the soldiers attacked a small encampment on a hammock at dawn. A huge Indian was slipping into a tangle of shrubbery when a soldier shot him dead and immediately scalped him. It was Chekika, who had led the sortie against Indian Key. Harney left the chief's body hanging from a tall tree between those of two of his braves and pushed on across the 'Glades to a small river which he followed to the Gulf. You can find the stream today on a map of Everglades National Park. It is called Harney's River.

Long Key, Conch Key, Grassy Key, Vaca Key, Knight Key— sometimes they run together where it has been cheaper to fill the gap between them than to bridge it, but there is a break at the west end of Knight Key for that is the bridgehead of the seven-mile bridge. Here is the town of Marathon, largest of the settlements between Homestead and Key West. In 1938 J. J. Hall bought two large lots on this site from W. A. Parrish for three hundred dollars. Hall put up a store and several cottages along the bay shore, the first in the area. He is still in business there as is Parrish, who is still selling real estate, and the lots are worth twelve or fifteen times their price in '38. There is a big wholesale fish house on the ocean side and a large fleet of charter boats and "U-Drive-It" craft. Marathon is the center of the big construction program that is making the Keys over into a town a hundred miles long with only one street.

Two miles from Knight Key the Overseas Highway crosses Pigeon Key without coming to the ground. The roadway is carried

The highest bridge on the Florida Keys, west of Bahia Honda

on a trestle over this islet which covers a scant two acres. It is termed
"the smallest inhabited island in the world" and a ramp from the
bridge leads down to a little park with picnic tables and a seldom-
used swimming pool. The several buildings on it were occupied by
the late Overseas Road and Toll District officials but until the controversy over that body's actions is settled the status of the tiny Key
will be in doubt.

The west end of the long bridge is anchored on Bahia Honda Key,
one of the most picturesque of the island chain, and beyond that is
the Bahia Honda Bridge, the only high bridge along the Keys. At
the top of its high arch one can get a magnificent view of the Keys

in either direction, but unfortunately the signs say: "No stopping on the bridge," so the glimpse is a fleeting one. At the bridgehead on Bahia Honda Key is a well-furnished park with picnic tables, water, toilets and a safe wading beach.

From Key Largo to Bahia Honda the Keys are generally long and narrow but from here on to Key West they are an archipelago of irregularly shaped land surfaces with innumerable small bays and coves. The first and largest is Big Pine Key which extends several miles north of the main highway and is traversed by several side roads. It is famous among wildlife enthusiasts and biologists as the home of the Key deer, smallest of the deer family and standing a scant two feet high. Once fairly plentiful on the lower Keys they were almost exterminated by local hunters who sometimes set fire to the dry grass to drive the deer into the open where they could be shot. Recently the surviving herds have been put under the protection of the state and Federal governments and it is hoped they can be saved.

Torch Key, Ramrod Key, Cudjoe Key, Saddle Bunch Keys, Boca Chica. Here, nine miles from Key West, is the last of the Naval Air Stations that dot the Gulf Coast all the way around from Corpus Christi, Texas. It is "Brown Shoe Navy" and on the other side of Key West is "Black Shoe Navy," the boys who travel on the surface of the sea and beneath it. Between them they are responsible for most of Key West. The Navy established an air base here in 1918, four years after the first such installation in Pensacola. It was not on Boca Chica Key but nearer town and housed only a few light aircraft that were used for patrol and training purposes. Even these activities were discontinued at the end of World War I, but with another war coming over the horizon in 1939 the base was reopened. There was a small private air field on Boca Chica and in 1943 the Navy took it over and began to build what is today one of the country's best equipped Naval Air Stations. Near the air base and facing the ocean is the U.S. Naval Hospital, established in 1942 after the Navy had struggled along with a makeshift hospital in an old

The southern terminus of U.S. 1

school building during the First World War. There are twenty buildings on the sixteen acres of attractively landscaped grounds.

Across Boca Chica Key and Stock Island, then over the last of the forty bridges, and U.S. Highway 1 enters Key West over Roosevelt Boulevard that runs along the water's edge on the north shore of the Key. As it approaches the business district Roosevelt Boulevard becomes Truman Avenue. Continuing one block past Duval Street, the main business thoroughfare, there is a highway marker pointing to the right down Whitehead Street. Follow this for seven blocks and you come to wrought-iron gates between two stone pillars. Flanked by two spread-eagles is a bronze sign: "U.S. Naval Station, 1906." This is the southern terminus of U.S. Route No. 1 that begins at Fort Kent on the Canadian border and winds for more than 2,350 miles through fourteen states along the Atlantic seaboard, touching all of the original thirteen except Delaware. Maine and Florida came into the Union later. At one end are the dark pine forests of New Brunswick made dazzling white by winter's snow, and at the other are coconut and royal poinciana trees that have never known frost.

The island of Key West is four miles long and less than half as wide, with an elevation ten feet above sea level. Its name does not derive from the fact that it is the most western of the Keys, but is a corruption of "Cayo Hueso" (Bone Key) because early settlers found the small island all but covered with Indian skeletons. Whether they had died in battle or succumbed to some ravaging disease is a matter of conjecture, but it is generally believed that they were the victims of an epidemic, such as smallpox or yellow fever, contracted from shipwrecked prisoners. The Key has gone by various names and as late as 1822 it was called Thompson's Island, after the Secretary of the Navy, Seth Thompson, in President Monroe's cabinet.

Key West is 157 miles from Miami but only 90 miles from Havana. Since the toll was taken off the Overseas Highway it has become increasingly popular to drive to Key West, park the car at the local airport, and go by plane to Havana, which is only forty-five minutes away by air. Usually such tourists arrange for a two- or three-day "package tour," and during the winter season there is a plane leaving for Havana every hour during the day. The U.S. and Cuban governments get a nice cut out of this business, as there is a $2.00 per person "transportation tax" in Key West and a $3.50 per person "landing tax" in Havana. For many years the "Casa Cayo Hueso," an imposing brick residence at the end of Whitehead Street, was famous as the most southern residence in the United States. Recently another building was put up in the same block which some say now holds that distinction. But the difference in their latitude is only a few feet at best and the souvenir postcards still picture Casa Cayo. At 205 Whitehead Street is the Geiger home where James J.

Audubon stayed in 1832 while studying and painting the birds of the Keys. From here he went to Indian Key and the Cape Sable area. His first volume of bird paintings had already been published in England and this was one of his last expeditions into the unspoiled wilderness.

Next to taking care of the several Navy installations the principal business in Key West is shrimping, an industry that took a big jump in 1950 when a new fishing ground, seventy miles long and twenty miles wide, was discovered in the region of the Dry Tortugas, west of the Keys. Now there are four hundred shrimp trawlers bringing their catches to Key West where their cargoes sell for five million dollars annually and give employment to fifteen hundred persons. Shrimp is the one factor that is found everywhere along the Gulf Coast. From Port Brownsville by the Rio Grande to this tip of the Keys there is hardly a tidewater city or village that does not have a shrimp fleet cruising the prolific waters of the warm sea. A popular point for tourists is the "turtle crawl" at the foot of Margaret Street where the big green sea turtles are impounded after being netted in the western Caribbean. The word "crawl" as here used comes from "kraal" as does "corral," meaning an enclosure to hold animals. Green sea turtles weigh from 200 to 350 pounds and are kept alive in these pens made of concrete pilings driven into the water a few inches apart. Some are eaten locally and some are shipped alive to the North, but most of them eventually wind up in cans as turtle soup or chowder.

For more than a century after it became a permanent settlement Key West had no drinking water except what it caught in cisterns. When the Navy moved in this was not enough, so it pioneered an eighteen-inch water main from wells near Homestead, 130 miles away and made an agreement with the Florida Keys Aqueduct Commission to supply fresh water to Key West and other communities along the Keys. Along most of the Overseas Highway the big pipe line lies uncovered beside the road.

Though Key West (the island) appears on the earliest maps of the New World it had little history before Florida was acquired by the United States in 1821. Protected by shallow reefs, inhabited by unfriendly Indians, and obviously without gold or other precious treasure, it was left alone to become a rendezvous for freebooters, escaped prisoners and unsavory gentry of every type. It belonged to the Spanish Crown and in 1815 (Cuba was then a Spanish colony) it was granted to one Juan Pablo Salas for his services to that country. Seven years later Juan sold the island to John W. Simonton, of Mobile, Alabama, for two thousand dollars which is less than a a waterfront lot sells for today. That same year Lieutenant Matthew C. Perry took possession of the place in the name of the United States. This was the same officer who in 1853 as Commander Perry sailed into the waters of Japan, supposed to be closed to all foreign vessels, left a letter from President Fillmore to the Emperor, and returned the following year to sign the first treaty which allied Japan with Western civilization. The first U.S. Marines arrived in Key West in 1824 and they are still here.

After the lawless squatters had been chased out Key West began to grow and for a time the handling of cargoes salvaged from wrecks was the principal business. It was incorporated as a town in 1828 and Congress established a superior court here, the principal litigation involving title to salvaged property. It was Judge Webb of this court who revoked the wrecking license of Captain Jacob Houseman. There were a number of Southern sympathizers in Key West when the Civil War broken out but Fort Zachary Taylor on the western end of the island was manned by Union troops, the U.S. Navy patrolled the Gulf, and the Stars and Stripes continued to fly over the little city.

There had been Cubans among the earliest settlers of the place but the real migration began in 1869 when Señor V. Martinez Ybor transferred his big cigar factory here because of revolutionary distractions in Havana. He was followed by others and soon Spanish was heard on the streets with greater frequency than English. Earlier immigrants had come from the Bahamas and because of their fondness for the meat of a type of large mollusks they were called "Conchs" (Konks). The name persisted and today Key Westers are frequently referred to as "Conchs," a term they accept with good humor. Labor troubles continued to disturb the cigar-making industry and in 1886 many of the big factories moved to Ybor City, now a part of Tampa. But cigars are still made in Key West and Spanish is heard everywhere.

Key West broke into headlines all over the country when the battleship *Maine* blew up in Havana Harbor, February 15, 1898, and the dead and wounded were brought here. There was no hospital and the Catholic convent was quickly converted into one under the direction of Major W. R. Hall of the Army Medical Corps. Many of the 268 who perished in the disaster are buried in a special plot in the old cemetery, enclosed by a wrought-iron fence. In the center is a modest pedestal on which a bronze sailor stands in perpetual salute. The Spanish-American War brought Key West into prominence as a supply depot but it was handicapped because it could only be reached by boat.

There was literally dancing in the streets on January 22, 1912, when the first Florida East Coast train rolled into the city, bringing Henry M. Flagler in his private car. He had celebrated his eighty-second birthday on January 2 and the work had been speeded up that he might be certain to see it completed. Key West gave itself up to a three-day celebration in his honor. Sixteen months later ne died at his home in Palm Beach, and so did not live to learn that his last great enterprise was to fail. Yet it failed only in part, for the Overseas Highway is built largely on the foundation of his "seagoing railroad." Like the residents of the little town of Panama City on the west Florida coast, Flagler and the citizens of Key West believed the opening of the Panama Canal in 1914 would bring a great increase in business. But when the big freighters came through the new route they continued on to the already established ports and the boom never developed. The Overseas Highway with two gaps to be crossed by ferry brought the first motorists to the city in 1926,

Memorial to the victims of the *Maine* explosion

but the railroad was operating then and there was not much vehicular traffic.

When the "depression" of 1933 hit Key West the town really collapsed. There was no employment, no food, no money. So in 1934 the new administration in Washington set up the Florida Emergency Relief Administration and the community was helped to its feet. It was under the auspices of this body that the veteran camps were established at Islamorada with such unfortunately tragic results. Completion of the continuous Overseas Highway in 1938 and the establishment of a fresh water supply three years later brought Key West a new era of prosperity that was still further enhanced in 1946 when President Harry S. Truman, after his first visit, unofficially established the "Little White House" in a cottage at the Naval Base. This publicity immediately brought an increase in the winter tourist trade, and motels, hotels and motor courts sprang up along the beaches at the south side of the island. Between 1940 and 1950 the population jumped from thirteen thousand to twice that number and is still growing.

The town responded to President Truman's endorsement by rechristening the western end of miles-long (Franklin Delano) Roosevelt Boulevard as Truman Avenue, and so established a precedent it is pledged to respect as long as presidents go there for a winter rest. This called for some hectic action when President Eisenhower on the advice of his physicians decided on short notice to relax in the midwinter sunshine of the Keys. Mayor C. B. Harvey learned from a radio newscast the evening of December 27, 1955, that the President was emplaning at once for Key West. He immediately drafted an ordinance changing the name of North Bay Road to Eisenhower Road, called the several members of the city council by telephone, and obtained their "vote" for the measure. By that time it was late but the mayor routed the official sign painter out of bed, and by eleven o'clock the next morning the new signs were all in place to greet President Eisenhower on his arrival two hours later.

Coming to the almost empty island of Key West in 1822 to establish a base for putting the pirates out of business, Commodore David Porter called it "The Gibraltar of the Gulf." With the establishment of the U.S. Naval Base here the commodore's statement has been justified. The components of the base today are: a Naval Station and Annex, Naval Air Station, Naval Hospital, Fleet Sonar School, Naval Advanced Underseas Weapons School (submarines), Naval Ordnance Unit, Marine Barracks, Naval Magazine and Naval Communication Station.

The first permanent construction at the base was a depot for supplies in 1856, but the appropriation ran out and it was left without a roof until the Civil War brought a hurried development in 1861. During hostilities Key West was the base of the Eastern Gulf Blockading Squadron, which captured 299 blockade runners from points as far away as London and Honduras, and the docks were often piled high with contraband. In the summer of 1864 yellow fever broke out among the Navy personnel and every ship in the squadron had patients in its sick bay. Civilians were dying at the rate of fifteen a day and the Navy removed the squadron temporarily to Tampa. For more than thirty years after that the base was almost dormant with only one or two ships in the harbor most of the time. Activity flared again with the Spanish-American War when the fleet sailed from here to blockade Cuban ports held by the Spanish. World War I brought another period of activity and a number of new piers were constructed, but in 1932 as a gesture of disarmament, the government deactivated the station and combined it with the Sixth Naval District at Charleston, South Carolina. For seven years the only Navy personnel at the Key West station was a detail of less than twenty radio operators. WPA workers kept the place cleaned up and the buildings in repair. Part of the property was opened to the public as a bathing beach and yacht basin. When President Franklin D. Roosevelt declared a state of emergency to exist, September 8, 1939, the civilians were barred, the base was reopened, and a busy program of renovation and reconstruction started. Four city blocks were

Fort Jefferson on Garden Key, the Dry Tortugas

purchased and added to the area and by the end of World War II more than fourteen thousand ships of all types had put into Key West for maintenance and repairs.

As part of the perimeter of defense of the Panama Canal it is doubtful that the Key West base will ever again be allowed to fall into a state of disrepair. Today the big warcraft and the little destroyers move in and out of the harbor on their various missions, the submarines slip from their moorings to follow the hidden lanes along the ocean floor, and weird antennas rotate endlessly to find what may be approaching from distances beyond the power of vision. This is indeed a second Gibraltar, looking to the south and west and guarding the entrance to the Gulf of Mexico.

While Key West is the official southern terminus of the Gulf Coast

Gun rooms or "casemates" that were never used

no book on the curving shore would be complete without mention of the Dry Tortugas, an almost inaccessible cluster of coral islands sixty-eight miles west of Key West, first seen by Ponce de Leon in 1513. Lying athwart the Gulf Stream they were in a position to control the greater part of the Gulf of Mexico in the days of sailing ships and smooth-bore cannon. In the early 1840's the United States decided to build there one of the strongest coast defenses of the world, and accordingly on sixteen-acre Garden Key they began construction of the great brick-walled Fort Jefferson. It was to mount 450 guns inside a six-sided bastion surrounded by a twenty-five-foot moat. Only one "sally port" behind a drawbridge gave entrance to the seven-acre parade ground inside the walls. There being no fresh water supply (hence the "dry" in Dry Tortugas) 109 cisterns were built with a capacity of a million and a half gallons of rain water. But before it was quite finished the development of rifled cannon made it completely obsolete.

Today the brick ramparts stare out across the vacant seas, fish swim in the clear waters of the moat, and tourists sometimes sleep in the dark chamber where Dr. Samuel A. Mudd was imprisoned because he set John Wilkes Booth's broken leg. Bush Key and Long Key, only a rifle shot away, are renowned as nesting places for sooty terns, noddy terns and roseate terns—more than a hundred thousand were counted there last year—and a company of man-o'-war birds are usually hanging motionless in the updrafts over the fort awaiting opportunity to rob them of their catch as they return from the sea. All the early explorers commented on the bird life of these islands. John J. Audubon visited them in 1832 and Louis Agassiz in

Beyond the parade ground and walls of Fort Jefferson stretches the empty sea

1858. Only two other locations in North America, Bonaventure Island in the Gulf of St. Lawrence and the Aleutian Islands off the coast of Alaska, have so great a concentration of sea fowl.

In 1935 the islands were declared a national monument and are now under the jurisdiction of Everglades National Park, with a staff of three men in charge. They live with their familes in a portion of the officers' quarters that have been modernized and get their water from rebuilt cisterns.

There is no regular transportation to the islands and no accommodations for overnight. It is a seven-hour boat trip each way from Key West, but a group of bird lovers or historians with the price of a charter and the hardihood for camping out in the gunrooms of the old fort will find a trip to this romantic spot well worth while, a fitting climax to exploring the tip of the curving shore.

Appendix

A Few Tips for the Tourist

IN preparation of this work the author and his wife drove more than eight thousand miles along the Gulf Coast, following the main highways where they were near the beaches and taking the little side roads to tidewater where the principal routes were inland, as in Louisiana. While no attempt was made to compile a complete guidebook for the coastal region, a few comments on towns, roads, accommodations and food may be of some value to visitors to the same areas.

The motel, or overnight cabin, has become the universal stopping place for motorists. Hotels are to be found in all cities of any size but they shelter only a small percentage of the pleasure-seeking tourists. There is an increasing demand for "efficiency" or housekeeping motels and they can often be had without extra expense.

Usually we found such places well supplied with cooking utensils and dining table ware. There is a wide variety in the character of motels and management. A few are ill-kept and obviously run-down, others are swank to the point of snobbishness. Usually guests get about what they pay for, but we always made it a point to look at the accommodations before we registered.

Nearly all the motels we saw were air conditioned, but we made little use of this feature, even in midsummer. Having lived on this coast I knew that there is always a breeze from the Gulf at night.

Good plain food is not often a problem. One of the first questions an experienced tourist asks when he prepares to stop is: "Where is a good restaurant?" Motel operators know that if they do not have an answer they will get little business, and that point governs their location. Many of the large motels operate their own restaurant. There is, however, a "sameness" about the food of the great majority of American restaurants. We are not a nation of epicures and whether it is Texas, Alabama, Florida, Kansas, Illinois or Connecticut the meals taste very much alike. This may have something to do with the growing popularity of housekeeping quarters. Gourmets looking for unusual dishes, superservice or five-dollar steaks will do well to stick to the big cities and their environs.

TEXAS

Brownsville is the largest municipality of the lower Rio Grande Valley but neighboring communities are of the same character. As this region is on the edge of a semidesert the sun is hot at midday but the nights are pleasant. All of the motels are air conditioned and it is usually pleasant to sit in the shade of a mesquite tree in the patio during the afternoon. The town is separated from the Gulf by twenty miles of desert but this is traversed by good concrete roads, one leading to Boca Chica Beach and the other to Isla Blanca Park at the south end of Padre Island where there is excellent surf fishing and bathing. The tourist in the Valley will have a wide choice of first-class motels except at fiesta time when most of them hang out the "No Vacancy" sign.

Between Brownsville and Galveston, a highway distance of 384 miles, there is no highway within sight of tidewater. The two main roads to the north are U.S. 281 to San Antonio, and U.S. 77, nearer the coast, which runs through the mesquite and prickly pear of the cattle country for almost a hundred miles before it reaches Kingsville. There are two or three excellent motels just north of the town, and usually the management can arrange a visit to the famous King Ranch, or one may inquire at the ranch offices which occupy the second floor over the bank in the center of the town.

From Kingsville to Corpus Christi is forty miles but the motorist in a hurry to get to Houston or points east will stay on Route 77 which bypasses the town. Corpus Christi is a booming, blooming metropolis with several good restaurants, and the Driscoll Hotel is outstanding. A toll causeway leads to Padre Island where there are excellent fishing and bathing facilities, not to be duplicated up the coast short of Galveston. Just north of town and centering around Aransas Pass is some of the best fishing on the Texas coast, and there is duck hunting in the marshes in the fall.

State Route 35 keeps nearest the coastline between Corpus Christi and Houston and while it is a good road it is not the shortest. It is not so heavily traveled as Route 77 and offers a greater variety to those interested in the flora and fauna of the coast. This area is rapidly developing as an industrial region but the greater part of it is still unspoiled. Freeport at the mouth of the Brazos River and fifty-three miles south of Houston is dominated by the Dow Chemical plant and those of allied industries.

Houston, being a convention city, has plenty of all types of accommodations for visitors. There are several smart and expensive restaurants, and the larger hotels will compare in accommodations and cuisine with any in the country. Galveston is famous for its beautiful beach and there are ample hotel and motel facilities within a block or two of the surf. State Route 87 is the best and most inter-

esting road for the eastbound motorist leaving Galveston. A free
ferry runs between Galveston and Point Bolivar, and from there it
is ninety-nine miles to Port Arthur, with the highway only a few
yards from the beach most of the way. This is the shortest way to
the east out of Galveston but because of the ferry it is not very
heavily traveled.

Although there is a strong Mexican influence along the south
Texas coast it seems to have small influence on the restaurant menus,
only a few of which feature south-of-the-border dishes. We had a
good Mexican dinner in Brownsville, but it was a "TV" dinner in an
aluminum foil pan which we bought in a chain grocery and cooked
in our motel. It included tortillas, frijoles and tamales. A restaurant
proprietor in the same town said it was difficult for him to get the
best shrimp although one of the greatest shrimp ports in the United
States was at Port Brownsville only a few miles away. There the
big catches are processed by the ton to be sent to the markets in the
large inland cities, and no one wants to bother with the comparatively small orders of the local trade. Food prices are much the
same along the Gulf Coast as they are farther north, the size of the
check depending on the size of the order and the character of the
restaurant.

LOUISIANA

U.S. 90 is the southernmost highway across Louisiana, but because of the salt marshes it is twenty to twenty-five miles north of
tidewater most of the way. It runs through the heart of the rice and
sugar cane, or "Evangeline" country. There are adequate motels
around most of the towns but it is well not to put off finding a place
to spend the night. The only adequate motel we found near Lake
Charles was four miles west of the town.

There is a novelty and charm about the so-called "Cajun" (Aca-
dian) region with its French-speaking population, its slow-flowing

bayous and lush fields of cane that somehow suggest Southern
Europe. New Iberia is the trade center of this area and St. Martinville, site of the "Evangeline Oak," Longfellow-Evangeline Memorial State Park, the Evangeline Church and the quaint shop with the
sign "Evangeline Enshrined," is but seven miles north. The Bayou
Teche which winds through the area is an ever changing variation
of dimpling waters reflecting green trees and blue skies. Those with
an interest in natural history should not fail to visit the bird sanctuary and jungle gardens on Avery Island, a few miles southwest of
New Iberia. The entrance fee is one dollar but there are seven miles
of roadway along which may be seen everything from snowy egrets
to alligators. Here, too, is the place where peppers are grown and
processed to make the world-famous Tabasco sauce.

Highway 90 enters New Orleans by way of the Huey Long Bridge
over the Mississippi but there are not many accommodations for
travelers in the west end of the city. East of the town where the
route becomes Chef Menteur Highway there are plenty of motels,
some very well appointed and some mediocre.

Books have been written about the charm of New Orleans and
its famous eating—and drinking—places. Out of considerable experience we would make these suggestions to the visitor arriving
there for the first time. Take one of the several guided tours, which
can be arranged by any hotel or motel office. The prices are reasonable, the guides know the interesting places and how to describe
them. Then if you have time, as you should have, go back on
your own and stop for a closer look at those places in the French
Quarter that appealed to you. You can stop at the little shops where
they sell antiques, books, paintings, jewelry and such without being
importuned to buy. When you are too tired to walk farther take
a trip on the big sight-seeing steamer that leaves from the foot of
Canal Street and get a ride on Old Mississip' at one of the few
places it flows due north.

Some of the more famous restaurants have been mentioned in the chapter on New Orleans, but there are others worth investigating if you have time. This is not a city to be covered in a few hours, and three days will barely suffice to see it properly.

In the unlikely event that the traveler wants to avoid New Orleans and save considerable mileage between southern Texas and southern Mississippi he can drive twenty miles north from Lake Charles to U.S. 190 which crosses the Mississippi at Baton Rouge and connects with Route 90 just west of the Louisiana-Mississippi line. This is an excellent road and there are ample accommodations around Baton Rouge, but the route is not so interesting as the one farther south.

MISSISSIPPI AND ALABAMA

From the Pearl River that marks the eastern boundary of Louisiana to the Perdido that is the western boundary of Florida is not more than 150 miles by highway, yet this stretch is one of the most enjoyable along the entire Gulf Coast. Most of this was vacation country before the days of the automobile, when only the well-to-do could relax by the seaside, but it has kept pace with progress and the traveler can find meals and lodgings fitted to his purse. For much of the distance the highway is within sight of the beach. Where there are side roads, such as that to Dauphin Island and Fort Gaines south of Mobile or down to old Fort Morgan on the east side of Mobile Bay, they are well worth the casual traveler's time. The principal motels around Mobile are to the west of the city. Not all are on Route 90, and we found a very satisfactory place on "Old 90" just south of the new highway.

FLORIDA

Accustomed to regard Florida beaches as "winter playgrounds" the stranger from the North is surprised to learn that the busy tourist season around Pensacola, Fort Walton Beach, Panama City and

Apalachicola is midsummer. In this region U.S. Route 98, "The Scenic Route," runs within sight of the Gulf for almost two hundred miles. It is a comparatively new highway and most of the motels and restaurants outside of the larger towns are of recent construction. In several places building is still going on at a rapid pace and there is no dearth of accommodations for a night, a week or the season. Tourists entering the state by way of Route 90, seventeen miles northwest of Pensacola, are directed to a handsome building maintained by the State Road Department of Florida where they can find clean rest rooms, free maps of the state, information as to highways and tourist accommodations, and be given a refreshing drink of fresh orange juice.

After crossing the St. Marks River and starting down the long peninsula the traveler finds overnight accommodations scarcer. There are several motels at Perry and a number, some quite pretentious, where the route crosses the Suwannee River. Strangely, although this is a popular stopping point, there are no public facilities here for a boat ride on the beautiful and historic stream. South of the Suwannee the motels become more numerous as Tampa and St. Petersburg are neared. Those on the waterfronts are usually more expensive but are not always the best.

Crossing Tampa Bay over the bridge from St. Petersburg or going around it by way of Tampa one comes to Bradenton, which is essentially a "trailer town" but which also has several good motels, some of them near the center of town. This is "winter vacation" country and although there are thousands of stopping places along the coast it will pay the visitor in January, February or March to get under a roof before sundown. Otherwise he may have to sleep in his car. This is country to travel through leisurely, stopping to fish a bit (any time of the year), pick up a few shells along the famous beaches, and explore the minor highways and waterways. Unfortunately many motorists seeing the fine straight roadway point the car toward Miami and push the accelerator to the floorboard.

At Naples the route across the Everglades begins. Those interested in the wildlife of the region will do well to stop at the town of Everglades, forty miles southeast of Naples, and take a boat trip through the "water gateway" of Everglades National Park. The old Rod and Gun Club is now a hotel serving excellent food, but there are no overnight accommodations of consequence between this point and the outskirts of Miami, seventy-five miles east. If the traveler bypasses Miami and heads for the Florida Keys he will not find a motel until he reaches Homestead, nine miles from the main entrance to the National Park. There are no overnight accommodations in the park.

Automobiles may enter the park over a new highway that leads down to the small settlement at Flamingo on the very tip of the Florida peninsula, some thirty miles from the entrance. Here is a "marina" where boat trips may be arranged for fishing or sight-seeing. There is a camping area near by, but no motels or other arrangements for overnight guests are nearer than Homestead. As this is written the National Park Service in Washington has forbidden the construction of overnight accommodations in the park but that has aroused so much criticism because of the hardship on park visitors that the ban may be lifted.

Just inside the park entrance a spur road to the left leads to the Anhinga Trail area, easily the most popular attraction of the park and one that has been repeatedly described in nature periodicals. An elevated boardwalk a few hundred feet long leads to a sequestered pond where the bird and reptile wildlife of the Everglades is concentrated and pursues its natural course unmindful of the watchers above it. This should not be missed.

Along the Keys one is seldom out of sight of motels, completed or under construction, while taverns and restaurants are going up almost as fast. In the city of Key West there are some very smart motels along the south side of the island, and here were the only first-class restaurants that we found in the area. All this development in the Keys has many of the old-timers in southern Florida shaking their heads. "They're from up North and haven't any notion what a hurricane is like," is the comment. "Let another blow like that of 1935 hit the Keys and it will be the worst disaster this state ever saw."

Cassandras? Well, maybe.

Index

Set in Linotype Caledonia
Format by Marguerite Swanton
Manufactured by The Haddon Craftsmen, Inc.
Published by HARPER & BROTHERS, *New York*